More Praise for Dr. Langs and

Rating Your Psychotherapist

"This book will step on a lot of toes. Many therapists who have shielded their practices from outside scrutiny won't like *Rating Your Psychotherapist*, but, as Freud said, 'You can't make an omelette without cracking the eggs.' Suffice to say that Langs has written a gem. For those readers interested in entering therapy, or for those who are already involved, he has offered a first-rate work shedding much new light on a complex and controversial subject."

Irving Weisberg, Ph.D.
Adelphi University

"For once, here is a book with profound insight for anyone concerned with psychotherapy—patients and therapists alike. Langs shows that if we can only listen to our own unconscious wisdom, it is we—not he—who have set the universal standards by which to judge how therapists work. Anyone currently in or contemplating beginning psychotherapy is well advised to read this fascinating book. It is certain to change your view of therapy, if not your life itself."

Brian Quinn, M.S.W.
Executive Director
Rapport Counseling Clinic

"Langs lucidly outlines the functions of the conscious and subconscious mind and describes briefly the ground rules of psychotherapy. He then presents a sound method for evaluating the therapist's approach to crucial stages of the process. . . . For anyone considering psychoanalytic therapy, and for those currently in therapy, this book is an important, useful adjunct."

Library Journal

Also by Robert Langs
Published by Ballantine Books

Decoding Your Dreams

ROBERT LANGS, M.D.

• • •

Rating Your Psychotherapist

Ballantine Books ◆ New York

This edition published by arrangement with Henry Holt and Company, New York.
Library of Congress Catalog Card Number: 90-93219

ISBN: 0-345-36986-6

Cover design by Sheryl Kagan

Manufactured in the United States of America

First Ballantine Books Edition: August 1991

10 9 8 7 6 5 4 3 2 1

In memory of
Harold Langs, M.D.

Contents

Acknowledgments

I am the fortunate beneficiary of an established backup team. Though I take responsibility for the final word, I owe much to: Lenore Thomson, for her wisdom and deft touch in reworking this manuscript; Channa Taub, for her artful editing and guidance— and support; and Kate Josephson, for her skills in getting the manuscript onto the page. My deepest gratitude to all.

PART I

• • •

Understanding Psychotherapy— and the Human Mind

·1·

The Power of Psychotherapy

Although most of us take psychotherapy seriously, few appreciate the power, intensity, and duration of its influence on a patient. Whatever the outcome—failed or successful—a therapeutic experience is not usually examined deeply in retrospect. Some people are haunted by a therapy interlude, but seldom do they have enough knowledge to determine what happened or judge its ultimate worth. Others end up with a rather casual dismissal: "Oh well, I guess it was OK; it was interesting anyhow, though it's hard to say if it helped or not. How can you really tell?" All too often, we fail to appreciate that therapy has had very specific effects—effects that last well beyond our memory of the therapeutic process.

In fact, psychotherapy is in no way a benign experience. Usually, a person goes to a therapist to get relief from an emotional problem. The way that therapy works best, however, is not by providing immediate relief, but by probing the source of the problem. As a result, from the very outset of a decision to enter therapy, the patient's immediate wish is usually in conflict with the process of cure. Many of us are content to have satisfied our immediate goal of obtaining relief from emotional distress; we perceive the therapy as having been successful, though we have not actually faced the unconscious truths at the source of our problems. Practically speaking, this means that we have exchanged our current set of defenses, which no longer work well enough to keep the truth at bay, for a set of defenses that will. But every set of defenses has its price. And some prices are extraordinarily high. Therapy patients pay this price day in and day out without consciously realizing that their "cure" helped to create a whole new series of problems. To protect ourselves from conscious pain, we simply dismiss evident signs that something is amiss—while we're seeing a therapist and after it's over.

Much of the influence that a therapist exerts is unwitting, and it goes unnoticed—at least by the patient's conscious mind. Patients naturally focus their attention on the symptom or problem for which they sought therapy; they have no logical reason to connect their other life experiences to the therapist's way of conducting treatment. For example, I interviewed a woman who had seen a therapist because of anxiety attacks.* Within a few months of sessions, this symptom had notably diminished, and she described her therapy as successful. As the interview proceeded, however, it became clear that several casual comments made by her psychotherapist about his pending divorce were a major, entirely unconscious factor in the patient's sudden dissatisfaction with her marriage—and in her precipitous separation from her husband. Neither patient nor therapist connected her therapist's remarks with her newfound preoccupation with divorce. If anything, the patient, like most patients who experience some relief in a therapeutic encounter, overidealized her therapist and simply denied that there were any detrimental consequences to the interlude.

It is true, of course, that psychotherapy may turn out favorably in every sense for a particular patient. Not only may symptom reduction occur, but one's life may take a genuine turn for the better. However, my thirty years of supervising the work of hundreds of psychotherapists, and my other efforts at clinical re-

*This was part of an intensive study of twenty former patients who had run the gamut of psychotherapists, as described in my book *Madness and Cure* (Newconcept Press, 1985). The clinical vignettes in *Rating Your Psychotherapist* are based on that research and on actual therapy experiences drawn from my years of work supervising and teaching other therapists how to conduct psychotherapy. Names and identifying data have been changed, but the vignettes are faithful to reality.

search, have forced me to confront the frequency with which, on balance, a seemingly positive therapy outcome is accompanied by unnoticed negative consequences.

The psychotherapy consultation room is an enormously charged space. The conscious mind, however, is occupied almost entirely by strategic maneuvers directed toward immediate goals. Powerful emotions and forces are screened out by the conscious mind as potential irritants. Outside of awareness, however—*unconsciously*, if you will—emotionally charged information and meaning have an intense impact, whether or not it is recognized and dealt with by patient, therapist, or both. The mystics tell us that the conscious mind is asleep and that only the truth will wake us up. Psychotherapy bears out the accuracy of this characterization. A therapy patient is not unlike a surgical patient under anesthesia, merely trusting the therapist/surgeon to intervene and make things better.

This medical model of therapy is dangerous and antiquated. Therapy, as currently practiced, is neither a science nor subject to exact standards. Yet the interventions of a therapist have consequences every bit as enduring as those of a surgeon.

In the United States alone, some fifteen and a half million people are in some form of psychotherapy each year. Given the power of psychotherapy, its influence for better or worse—not only on emotionally founded symptoms, but on how people live their lives—it is astonishing how much faith we put in the claim of an individual to be a good therapist. Psychotherapy is a service, a business, an industry, yet the mystique of psychotherapy endures beyond all reason. The history and formal assumptions of psychotherapy have clearly been influenced by the economics of psychotherapeutic practice. As a profit-making service industry, psychotherapy warrants an informed consumer.

We tend to confer on the therapist the mantle of a magician, as though lay status as a patient precludes any possible assessment and evaluation of the ritual kit bag of therapeutic ministrations. This is the Tinkerbell approach to therapy: If you don't believe hard enough, it won't work. In a very negative and destructive sense, this is true. Achieving a cure without insight requires naïveté and ignorance.

There are clear and good reasons to rate a psychotherapist, before you start treatment, during a course of treatment, and even after all has been said and done. And there is a way to do this that is sound, fair, and within the competence of any patient or potential patient. Unquestionably, a therapist has training and knowledge beyond your immediate capacity to judge. But that's true of anyone who offers a service for profit. Say you want a decent stereo system. You don't walk into the first store you see and take the salesman's advice on the advertised specials. If you want a used car, you don't buy one on blind faith because some friend got a good deal at the same lot. You first assess your needs and then learn something about the kinds of purchases available to you. This doesn't mean that you have to go to auto-repair school before you visit your local car dealership. But it may mean, for example, that you bring a mechanic with you, who will give the car a trial run, look under the hood, and perform a series of tests to check out its overall viability.

In the matter of psychotherapy, think of me as the mechanic who will look under the hood with you and give you a sense of what you're getting and paying for.

Still, for the moment, you may feel skeptical. You may be thinking something like this: "Yes, I'd like to judge the worth and competence of my psychotherapist, but you're talking apples and oranges here. Shopping for stereo equipment or a car, even shopping for a good surgeon, is not at all the same as trying to find a good therapist. Turntables and car engines have a standard set of components; so do bodies. What's inside a mind is unique to each person. My therapy is unique. How can you possibly help me rate my therapist? I'm not qualified to do it, and you don't know enough about my individual situation to help me do it."

I certainly realize that in a very significant way every psychotherapeutic experience is unique. Moreover, as a belief system, psychotherapy has undergone schism and reformation; psychotherapeutic techniques exist presently under the auspices of some 325 therapeutic denominations, many with dozens of variations and offshoots. Therapy is conducted not only with individuals, but with couples, families, and groups of all sorts.

Different therapists engage in very different kinds of practices. The strict psychoanalyst argues for what is called psychodynamic, insight-oriented psychotherapy. This kind of therapist uses techniques designed to help the patient realize consciously the unconscious basis for emotional problems. The behavioral therapist eschews the quest for such insight as spurious and unnecessary, recommending instead that a patient be confronted with his or her problematic behavior and retrained consciously to behave differently. The cognitive therapist concentrates on the habitual thought patterns held to create negative behavior. The encounter-group therapist emphasizes dramatic interaction and even physical contact between patient and therapist. And even within particular schools of thought, psychotherapists generally behave in terms of their own priorities and experiences. How is it possible to establish a single set of standards with which to rate such diverse practices?

I will define as a *therapist intervention* any behavior of a therapist within (or outside of) the therapeutic space. What we are talking about here is a system that will allow one to rate individual therapeutic interventions. And such a system does exist. It will explain, for example, how to rate a therapist who forces a male patient to wrestle with him physically in front of ten other members of his encounter group. Or a woman therapist who injures her back and continues to see her patients from her home bedroom—there are many possibilities.

You may ask: Doesn't the general worth of an intervention depend on the context in which it occurs? What about a therapist who accepts referrals from his or her other patients? Can you really rate a therapist's request for more money per hour? What if a therapist lends a patient a book he has written? What if a therapist hardly says anything more than "Uh-huh" and "Go on"? How can a patient possibly assess these behaviors?

This attitude is not unlike the idea that was once commonplace about the interaction between husband and wife in their home; the assumption was that the privacy of a household was sacrosanct and the behaviors within it determined by the complexity and needs of the relationship—even when those behaviors were abusive or seemed harmful to an outsider. Today that assumption about the home is breaking down, but books on the subject of psychotherapy perpetuate comparable stereotypes and clichés: Choose a therapist who is warm and empathic, someone you can talk to, someone who is "there for you." The implication is that therapy is the sort of listening and counseling that a sympathetic neighbor could supply over coffee and danish. But doing therapy is a skill; how it is done has real and lasting psychological effects. Does anyone wise select a surgeon on the basis of personality alone? Say you were looking for a minor face-lift; would you disregard matters of experience and expertise or the surgical conditions under which the operation would take place?

Yes, it is difficult for a nonexpert to evaluate the services of a purported expert in any field. If you have acute abdominal pain and a surgeon removes an inflamed appendix, in time you will probably feel well enough to know that you have received effective care. But what if you don't? How can you be sure that residual symptoms could have been prevented by some other physician— or whether your own behavior and physical state are the limiting factors?

Given all of these uncertainties, it is natural to wonder: Isn't psychotherapy even more difficult to evaluate? After all, if the vicissitudes of life and other seeming intangibles outside the operating room can influence the course of a physical illness, this is far more true of emotional symptoms outside the treatment space. Moreover, psychotherapy patients frequently respond paradoxically to blatantly destructive interventions from their therapists. I interviewed a male patient whose therapist actually screamed at him for not heeding her advice to leave his present girlfriend. His response was to feel that his therapist's anger was justified and to follow her directives belatedly. Neither took notice of subsequent problems at work, where the patient became increasingly embroiled in angry exchanges with his colleagues.

Oddly enough, however, rating a psychotherapist is far easier and more precise than rating a physician's medical expertise. The patient I just mentioned need not have complicated his life with a new set of problems had he known how to properly assess his therapist's interventions. Assessment of psychotherapy seems so difficult because we think of evaluation and rating as a purely conscious process of judgment made in terms of directly known criteria. But the human mind actually has two ways to evaluate emotionally charged information. One way is the conscious process that we are familiar with. The other way is unconscious. Popular wisdom contends that unconscious thinking is irrational and colored by emotional needs and wishes, and that conscious thinking is rational, logical, and objective. In a sense, the truth is quite nearly the reverse of this assumption. Conscious judgment is often superficial, inconsistent, and driven by immediate goals, whereas unconscious judgment is incisive, consistent, thoughtful, and highly reliable.

We will be talking about the difference between the conscious and deep unconscious systems of the mind throughout this book, but for the moment, consider the following: The conscious system is constructed for the purpose of survival. Its role is to adapt the organism to its environment and to exploit that environment to meet the organism's needs. The conscious system is particularly adept at screening out the complex and the unfamiliar in favor of information that elicits direct adaptive responses. The conscious system, therefore, also discriminates among possible options and stresses the differences among objects. However, its overall objective is to resolve conflict by coordinating all its efforts in one direction. Ambiguity, emotional complexity, and information that threatens familiar assumptions are avoided if at all possible. And all of this defensiveness is actually essential for smooth conscious functioning.

The deep unconscious system is constructed differently. It, too, is an adaptive mechanism, but one of its purposes is to work over the very information that the conscious system has screened out. This is the task of a part of the unconscious mind that I will call *the deep unconscious information-processing system* (or *deep unconscious wisdom system*, for short). But the deep unconscious mind contains more than this particular system. It also contains a *deep unconscious memory system*, which has been created over a lifetime. The deep unconscious memory system has registered all of our subliminal (unconscious) perceptions of terrifying and painful experiences—both inner experiences and experiences with others: parents, siblings, friends, teachers, etc. It continues to experience emotionally charged perceptions in terms of these fears and hurts. This deep unconscious memory system—this collection of disturbing *introjects*, as they are called—often has the ear of the conscious system, though we are not aware of it. That is, this memory system of fear and pain deeply influences our conscious thinking and direct behavior without our knowing it.

The unconscious mind, therefore, is inevitably divided and in conflict. One part of it—the deep unconscious wisdom system—prefers understanding over ignorance, and self-cure over self-harm. The other part—the deep unconscious memory system—advocates behaviors that will satisfy unconscious needs and terrors. Since the conscious system would just as soon not know about these unconscious needs and terrors, it will strike bargains with the deep unconscious memory system. The conscious system, as it were, will engage in behavior that partially satisfies deep unconscious wishes or guilt in exchange for continued ignorance of their very existence.

In summary, the deep unconscious system is perceiving *at every moment*—accurately, though subliminally—information that the conscious system is denying or ignoring. What's more, this information is of a kind that the conscious system could use to make more informed decisions about emotionally difficult situations. One of the extraordinary potentials of therapy is to make available to us information that has been perceived unconsciously. But getting at that cogent knowledge requires a little work. The deep unconscious system does not communicate its contents to the conscious system directly. The conscious system couldn't tolerate it. After all, this information entered the deep unconscious system in the first place because the conscious system could not endure direct awareness.

Unconscious knowledge is always expressed indirectly; that is, when the unconscious part of the mind communicates, it uses a conscious piece of information as a disguise for its meaning. Although we are saying one thing consciously, another meaning is being expressed unconsciously by way of the same images. In other words, when a patient in therapy tells a story or a dream, there are two levels of meaning in the images being expressed. One level is the conscious level. A story refers directly to the people and events being talked about. But a story may also contain unconscious information—that is, the details and images may pertain indirectly and unconsciously to what has taken place in the treatment experience itself.

These displaced and disguised stories, when properly decoded, generate a set of remarkably sound ratings of any type of psychotherapy whatsoever. They can provide us with a reliable guide as to what should be rated in the work of a psychotherapist as well as to what, in general, the rating itself should be. In my work with the deep unconscious wisdom of literally thousands of patients, I have found that certain kinds of interventions have a consistent and apparently universal unconscious effect on patients, no matter who they are or what the context of the therapist's behaviors. Each patient, to be sure, reacts in terms of his or her own particular unconscious memory system; but the kinds of reactions that patients have to certain kinds of interventions are consistent to the point of predictability. These reactions constitute the backbone of this book—they reflect a set of reliable unconscious standards for good therapy and a healthy cure.

Let us take a look at some of the more compelling reasons for rating a psychotherapist:

1. You need to rate a psychotherapist in order to force yourself to *think about* what your therapist is actually doing. As I've suggested, many patients are remarkably complacent about the comments and behaviors of their therapists, just as though the therapist's claimed authority required that the patient suspend the use of common sense. In extreme cases, patients will create what may be called a folie à deux with their therapists, a kind of shared madness. How else can one explain situations in which both patient and therapist become convinced that someone outside of therapy is totally responsible for the patient's own emotional symptoms? Or situations in which patient and therapist become sexually involved so that the patient will feel "acceptable"? It has become a cliché that patients "discover" themselves in therapy and immediately initiate an ill-fated affair or a divorce. These various possibilities are so commonplace that they are the stuff of movies and novels.

I interviewed a patient whose therapist gave her an abominable ultimatum: Either terminate an out-of-wedlock pregnancy or leave therapy. The patient was understandably enraged, and she quit treatment, only to suffer a miscarriage. She subsequently became depressed and, reasoning that her former therapist at least knew her history and had some sense of her problems, returned to the same therapist for "help"!

If little thought is given to the kinds of comments a therapist makes, even less thought is given to the way in which a therapist creates and manages the conditions of treatment. Whether we pay attention or not, the physical setting and the ground rules (frequency, fees, etc.) that define the therapeutic relationship and the circumstances under which the treatment will unfold are part of the therapy. They are part of the environment to which both parties must adapt. No matter what we believe or ignore or deny, adaptation is taking place both consciously and unconsciously all the time. If you see your therapist in a home-office, where you are aware of the spouse and overhear arguments or interactions with the children, that environment is unavoidably part of the therapeutic experience. Inconsistent fee arrangements, the tendency of a therapist to stroke the patient's hand when the patient is upset or to hug the patient good-bye before a vacation—these are rarely understood as interventions, but they have major unconscious implications.

The deep unconscious system sees and rates the therapist in terms of these implications. And these ratings are expressed indirectly—in the subsequent stories and dreams that the patient communicates.

When you are able to decode these encoded ratings from your deep unconscious system, you will begin to recognize how pervasively your therapist's behaviors are affecting the course of your therapy and the way in which you're conducting your life. This book will help you to make a more definitive assessment of your therapist that can lead to an informed decision: Is this person likely to be a competent and helpful therapist or not? Am I likely to get the help I need if I enter or continue this treatment experience? Will I get this help at little cost to my emotional life and balance? And just what are the ramifications of what he or she is doing?

2. You need to rate a psychotherapist in order to counteract inevitable needs in yourself as a patient to find a poor or hurtful therapist. This is an extremely powerful and generally unrecognized reason to rate your psychotherapist. I mentioned at the beginning of this chapter the fact that a patient's desire for immediate relief from emotional symptoms is in direct conflict with the purpose of insightful therapy, which is to expose and to resolve the source of the symptoms. That is, we develop emotional symptoms as a way to stay unaware of an underlying emotional disturbance. More than anything else, we would like to get rid of the symptoms without having to make any difficult changes in our accustomed behaviors. Therefore, despite the conscious belief to the contrary, there is a strong need in every patient to engage a psychotherapist who in some significant way is *unlikely* to be helpful.

On the surface, patients consistently believe that they are trying to find the most effective therapist available to them. Nevertheless, a careful decoding of the displaced and disguised messages from their own deep unconscious system reveals another picture. With a remarkable degree of consistency, therapy patients have pervasive self-defeating unconscious needs. These pressures arise from the fearful deep unconscious memory system and, as I said, they have a strong, though silent, influence on what we do and on who we choose as our therapist. The results may range from unwittingly seeking out a therapist who will not be helpful at all, to finding one who is likely to be actively destructive in order to relieve the pressures of guilt and conscience without actually solving the problems. In other words, the defensive wish to *not* know often outweighs the wish to know.

Unconsciously, patients often hope to find relief from their emotional symptoms by gaining permission from the therapist to act against and exploit others rather than by confronting their inner selves as a means of promoting change. The point I am making, of course, is that patients are unconsciously motivated to seek out a poor therapist, all the while rationalizing their choices with defensive conscious reasons. This is what I mean by the fact that the conscious system makes judgments under pressure from unconscious fears and according to the need to keep dreaded unconscious secrets at bay. The irony is that poor therapy can indeed provide symptom relief. But the price is too high.

Rating your therapist is just about the only means by which the tendency to obtain poor services can be countered. For this reason alone, the need to rate a psychotherapist becomes an absolute necessity.

3. You need to rate a psychotherapist in order to combat your fear of revealing the secrets you must expose for insightful cure. Virtually every individual seeking psychotherapy has a number of guilty secrets, conscious and unconscious. I have already suggested that patients will unconsciously seek out therapists whose punishing behavior will relieve their sense of guilt without requiring

the revelation of their secrets. But patients also attempt to deal with these secrets by unconsciously finding a therapist who will in some way share in their guilt. Certain kinds of interventions, particularly the way in which the therapist manages the ground rules of therapy, have implications that suggest the therapist's own possession of guilty secrets (see chapters 9 and 10). The patient is able to obtain unconscious relief from his or her sense of guilt simply by realizing that the therapist has similar problems. But such relief cannot lead to constructive change and growth and, in the long run, it will in some way perpetuate the patient's emotional difficulties.

Let me give you an example. I interviewed a woman who felt conscious guilt and shame over secret homosexual encounters she was having sporadically with women she met at a local lesbian bar. As it turned out, the unconscious secret she was keeping at bay involved latent (unconscious) homosexual stimulation by her mother's extensive physical contact with her. Although her conscious desire was to come to terms with her need for promiscuous lesbian encounters, this woman unconsciously selected a psychotherapist whose interventions had strong homosexual implications and who had a tendency to make direct physical contact with her patients. Although the patient told the therapist nothing about her lesbian encounters, she gradually felt less anxious about the conflicts that had brought her to therapy. But her anxiety was decreasing on the basis of unconsciously perceived homosexual tendencies on the part of her therapist, and she soon became involved in an overt homosexual affair that was quite destructive. She also quit the therapy rather than tell her therapist about any of this.

If this woman had rated her psychotherapist according to the standards described in this book, she would have been confronted with the realization that she was becoming involved in a highly questionable therapeutic experience. She might then have gone further in her assessment and begun to recognize consciously some of the unconscious needs involved in the choice she was making.

In general, rating your psychotherapist is almost the only means by which a potential or actual patient can get a sense of unconscious wishes for a guilt-sharing and/or punitive and ultimately hurtful psychotherapist.

4. You need to rate a psychotherapist in order to avoid blind overidealization of your therapist. This is a tendency shared by almost all patients. Idealization has two aspects—one is to overlook, deny, and avoid the negative; the other is to overstate the positive.

Remarkably few patients have clear and well-founded complaints about their psychotherapists, and even fewer hold their therapists notably accountable for a failed therapeutic outcome. Indeed, for both patients and therapists alike, the poor therapeutic result is either ignored entirely or viewed as the consequence of the patient's intractable emotional disturbance. Virtually the only way to stand against such defensive needs to protect and idealize a therapist is to rate him or her and to recognize what is revealed by these ratings.

On the other side of the coin, patients have virtually no standards and means through which they can identify a psychotherapist who is likely to engage in essentially constructive therapeutic practices and to facilitate both symptom alleviation and constructive life consequences. Rating your psychotherapist is again virtually the only means through which such a therapist can be discovered. And indeed, therapists with high ratings tend to be legitimately helpful—that is, they promote symptom relief without extracting a price of havoc and disillusion in another domain of life.

5. You need to rate a psychotherapist in order to help you choose the best therapist available to you at the moment. In most situations, a patient has a choice among available psychotherapists. Rating your psychotherapist provides a sound method for making a comparison and effecting a solid choice. This is especially valuable before actually calling a psychotherapist for a first appointment.

You may wonder how one can rate a therapist before one has even contacted him or her, but an important dimension of assessing a therapist is the means through which his or her name was obtained. Beyond that, if you choose to consult with two or more therapists before deciding on whom you will see (a practice with some problems in itself), rating your psychotherapist should be a vital part of your ultimate decision.

6. You need to rate a psychotherapist in order to be an informed consumer, and to avoid therapists who are likely to be more destructive than helpful. Most danger signs are, or should be, obvious—for example, sexual or aggressive physical contact between patient and therapist or violent verbal attacks of a patient by a therapist; but others fly in the face of common practice—such as referral by another patient, or by a friend or relative of the therapist (see chapter 5). Rating your psychotherapist compels you to face these unsound or even dangerous situations and, once you understand their implications, to confront your own tendency to accept such practices without serious questions and concern. Rating your psychotherapist is, then, a means both of obtaining the individual most likely to offer the best possible cure and of avoiding the therapist most likely to cause personal damage.

You may be asking at this point why psychotherapy is so uncertain an art, and particularly, why the very field that presumes to understand unconscious functioning fosters practices that have far-reaching and destructive unconscious effects. This is a hard question to answer, but I would quote the old Sufi maxim—that counterfeit gold exists because there is such a thing as real gold. In other words, genuine encounter with the deep unconscious system is valuable and enriching, but rare; and, as I've suggested, the vast majority of patients prefer the counterfeit: symptom relief without insight. I say this with no judgment intended. Unconscious secrets are frightening; they have their source in the naked sense of our own vulnerability and mortality, our capacity for doing harm. Therapists are human, too, and a genuine encounter with the unconscious terrors and agonies of a patient's psyche inevitably brings to light the therapist's own unresolved anxieties and emotional difficulties. If nothing else, many therapists have an unconscious need to provide the kind of therapy their patients unwittingly seek out. Certainly, the great majority of us become therapists because we are genuinely interested in and care about people, and it is difficult to forfeit the inclination to build a community of two by sharing guilt and locking out our common terrors. Around such needs grow myths and delusions that are shared by many practitioners as to what is supposedly helpful for patients.

Of course, certain practices are simply departures from the ideal standards offered in the various psychotherapy training programs—lapses that occur in the privacy of the office of a particular therapist, or at moments of stress. Such departures reflect, too, the many conflicting factors that influence the treatment experience. Just as patients will seek out poor therapists because of unconscious defensive needs, some therapists are defensively invested in practices that meet their own sick needs, and are blinded to the detrimental consequences of their efforts.

Therapy lacks a scientific foundation, at least for now; and there are no clear standards of practice to serve as a constant reference point for all practitioners. There is certainly no agreement on how a therapist should manage the ground rules, setting, and framework of therapy, yet these aspects of therapy have implications that become part of the therapeutic exchange. Even when a therapist accepts the idea of latent (unconscious) meaning in a patient's material at all, he or she is likely to believe that this meaning pertains only to past events and relationships that are being "replayed" in the therapy. Once a therapist recognizes that a patient's material contains unconscious perceptions of the therapist in light of the implications of his or her own interventions, it becomes quite clear that the therapeutic environment is emotionally charged for the patient and is constantly being worked over outside of awareness. By heeding a patient's unconscious intelligence, the therapist can construct an optimally helpful therapeutic experience for each individual—in terms of what that individual needs.

However, the neglect of the unconscious resource that so incisively informs psychotherapeutic practice has left the field in a state of disarray. The only way for a patient to come to terms with this situation is to learn to decode his or her own unconscious communications.

I realize that this is a strong and candid statement of my sense of psychotherapeutic practice today. Perhaps it should be noted that the field of psychotherapy is merely one hundred years old, having had its origin in the 1880s with Josef Breuer, Sigmund Freud, and hosts of other physicians who began experimenting with psychotherapeutic methods, some of which were crudely adumbrated in prior years. Given the complexity of the undertaking, the multiple dimensions of emotional dysfunctions, and the powerful need for self-protection and defense in all concerned, it is small wonder that it has taken us so long to begin to unravel the intricacies and fallacies of the psychotherapeutic endeavor.

Still, this book is dedicated to this very unraveling, and to the clarity that can then follow. Many of the ratings to be described here, because they stem from the heretofore untapped strength of the deep unconscious system, will be somewhat disturbing to patients and therapists alike. Yet this book is by no means a work of despair. Instead, it is truly a book of hope, and a book of promise as well. Recognizing that problems exist is the first step toward their rectification. You can, for example, explore with your therapist the nature of an intervention that this book has flagged as dangerous; or you can find a therapist whose ratings are high; or you can work out a way to generate a positive outcome to your therapy, whatever its overall rating may be, because you are no longer reacting blindly to your therapist's interventions.

You may well be feeling protective of your therapist right now as I say this, as though I were inviting you to do something behind his or her back, or to subvert your therapy. This is exactly the kind of defensiveness that perpetuates the problem. This is *your* therapy, and you have a right to know what's going on in it. Not knowing is a bargain struck between the deep unconscious memory system and the conscious system; it is a symptom that needs to be resolved in a constructive way.

On this note of hope, promise, and interest in the truth, let us begin to develop the means by which we can effectively rate any psychotherapist practicing in the field today.

·2·

Deep Unconscious Wisdom

Many people select a therapist almost blindly—by asking friends about their therapists, picking a name out of the Yellow Pages, or calling someone who once lectured on the subject. And very often, a patient will see a therapist for years, or try many therapists, having no idea at all whether he or she is being helped.

The irony, as I've said, is that there are very specific criteria for judging a psychotherapist and the treatment he or she provides. You may have been surprised to learn in the first chapter that the source of this information is your own unconscious mind. In fact, before you go any further, you should forget everything you've read or been told about "the unconscious."

Popular psychology says that therapy is designed to resolve unconscious conflict. The logical conclusion of this view, of course, is that the unconscious mind is a problem because it has a negative influence on our feelings and behavior. As I pointed out in chapter 1, this is only partly true. The deep unconscious memory system does have a negative influence on our conscious feelings and behavior. But the fact is that your unconscious mind—the part that I am calling the deep unconscious wisdom system—is also your best ally in a search for a good psychotherapist. Paradoxically, then, the deep unconscious system is both a source of suffering and the best available resource for resolving that suffering. You simply need to learn how to understand what it says.

The conscious and deep unconscious systems work together. I

said in chapter 1 that the conscious system is designed essentially for survival needs and will screen out complicated emotional considerations. Roughly speaking, the conscious system takes care of the practical details of life, while the deep unconscious system takes note of the emotional considerations. This division of labor ensures our ability to react quickly and pragmatically when we need to.

Certain decisions are almost purely conscious-system decisions. They depend for the most part on direct information and common sense. For example, if you want the news delivered to your home on Sunday mornings, your course of action is straightforwardly goal-oriented: You look up a home delivery service in your phone book, call them, and find out how much they charge. If other delivery services are available to you, you compare prices.

The conscious system takes note of sensible and concrete details, envisions a goal, compares and contrasts real possibilities, and is designed, for the most part, to ensure your safety, survival, and pleasure.

Other kinds of decisions may involve practical considerations but also have an emotional basis. Choosing a marital partner, for example, is not a cool or rational decision, no matter how seemingly logical your surface approach. In fact, no choice that involves a relationship with another person is purely a conscious-system decision. Choosing a psychotherapist is a good case in point. The process may seem like a matter of pragmatics and luck—you explore the possibilities, get advice, and make an appointment; but all the while, deep unconscious factors are silently influencing your approach and your impressions—even before you've met the therapist for the first time.

These deep unconscious factors may well be in conflict with the way you feel consciously, *because your deep unconscious system knows more about the emotional stakes of a situation than your conscious system does*. While your conscious system is juggling clear-cut facts and figures, your deep unconscious system is taking account of your wishes and needs, your subliminal perceptions, your fantasies, your nonverbal memories—all manner of experiences that your conscious system would just as soon ignore.

My investigation of the human mind has shown that the conscious system is a grosser instrument than the deep unconscious system; it's structured for nuts-and-bolts thinking and experience. Embroilment in the emotional considerations of an issue would stop the conscious system in its tracks and keep it from going about the business of everyday living. For this reason, the deep unconscious system stays out of the conscious system's way; it takes care of the emotional issues silently, outside of conscious awareness. And it operates without awareness for another and perhaps more compelling reason: Our unconscious (subliminal) perceptions—the "information" the deep unconscious system works over—are, as a rule, very disturbing. The conscious system relegates such perceptions to the deep unconscious system precisely because they *are* emotionally charged, and we experience these perceptions in terms of the fear and pain contained in the deep unconscious memory system. None of this can enter awareness directly. At best, such impressions and processing must be disguised or encoded; at worst, they find no communicative expression at all.

One of the major differences between the two systems of the deep unconscious mind lies in the way each contends with emotionally charged perceptions. The deep unconscious memory system, which contains all the accumulated fear and anger and pain of a lifetime, sees each new emotionally charged situation in terms of the painful moments it has handled before. It mobilizes accustomed defenses and methods of getting relief, and presses for immediate action. In contrast, the deep unconscious wisdom system, which is processing the perceived information for meaning and import, presses for delay, insight, and awareness.

The conscious system, of course, wants immediate action that is oriented to a specific result—without having to contend with painful memories or complex emotions. Thus, in an emotionally charged situation, the conscious system's first instinct is blindly to implement the deep unconscious memory system's familiar defenses and methods of getting relief. This means that the conscious system may be engaging in behavior that is familiar, but inappropriate or destructive—without even knowing the factors involved or the price being exacted! The only way to short-circuit this collusion between the conscious system and the deep unconscious memory system is to listen to the counsel of the deep unconscious wisdom system. The deep unconscious wisdom system is more interested in the emotional truth of a situation than it is in the outcome. Obviously, the conscious system would be better off if it had direct access to this deep unconscious viewpoint.

Unfortunately, no such thing exists. Because the information has been screened from consciousness, it does not yet have conscious form, and the conscious system would just as soon keep things that way. So the deep unconscious wisdom system communicates its information indirectly—by using the conscious system's communications as a disguise. When the deep unconscious wisdom system wishes to convey a message, it silently directs the conscious system to tell a story or remember a dream that contains that message in some encoded or camouflaged form. The surface story, then, carries an obvious and direct meaning, but it also serves as a vehicle for a second story embedded in its images. This second story is not obvious. It is indirect, or latent (present, but hidden), and must be winnowed from the surface story by means of decoding. This book will show you how to decode your own encoded unconscious messages so they can be used by the conscious system. By decoding your unconscious messages, you can rely on your deep unconscious system as a wise, perceptive, and even witty guide to decision making.

We are concerned here, of course, about rating your psychotherapist—either before you commit to therapy or while you are undergoing treatment. I have spent thirty years as an analyst, twenty of them decoding unconscious messages from my own patients and from the patients of the therapists who worked under my supervision. This work has given me an extraordinary amount of information about how the deep unconscious system thinks and sees the world. Because of the immediate concerns of the patients involved, much of the unconscious communication that I have decoded has been about choosing and rating therapists. I have learned that there is a great difference between conscious choice and unconscious choice. I have also learned, to my surprise, that the unconscious choice is almost invariably the wiser.

Let's look at a few brief examples of unconscious communication outside of psychotherapy, just to illustrate the point.

Consider Helen, who had been dating Mark exclusively, but without an expressed commitment, for the better part of a year. In an attempt to push Mark, Helen asked him whether he would feel upset if she dated someone else from time to time. Mark reacted in a characteristically rational manner. He said he thought that if Helen felt interested in someone else, she had an obligation both to herself and to him to satisfy her curiosity. "For example," he said, "when I was away on a business trip last month, I wouldn't have been upset to find that you'd gone out to dinner or to a movie with someone else, if that's what you wanted to do. I think our relationship is strong enough to survive a dinner out with other people once in a while." Helen felt irritated by Mark's answer; it was objective enough to indicate a kind of indifference, and it made her wonder whether he, in fact, was seeing other women. She dropped the subject, however, and they began to talk about Mark's new job situation. He said, "One of the things that drove me nuts about my last job was the fact that I just didn't feel like I was taken seriously. I mean, I'd go away on a trip and come back to find someone else in my office, or some piece of my job parceled out to someone else. I really hated that."

Helen knew enough about unconscious experience to recognize that even though the subject of their conversation had changed, Mark was still reacting to Helen's original question about her seeing other men. Mark's conscious image of himself as both tolerant and sure of the relationship was at variance with his deep unconscious fear of not being appreciated and of being replaced. He was suggesting, without consciously realizing it, that Helen not take the advice he'd just given her. The following week, Mark readily accepted a dinner invitation from a couple who knew that Mark was seeing Helen, but invited only Mark, intending to introduce him to a single female friend of theirs. This was Mark's classic way of handling both his fear of commitment and fear of being replaced—by increasing his options at the expense of an ongoing relationship.

This story may seem nearly inconsequential. But it is important to recognize that the attempt to protect one's sense of equilibrium and stability occurs at many levels. We have here an example of the two deep unconscious systems at work in an emotionally charged situation. Helen's question was a form of emotional blackmail that is common enough in everyday social interaction. Another man might well have appreciated Helen's motivations consciously and responded to them directly. But for Mark, being rejected, humiliated, and displaced were long-standing concerns represented in his deep unconscious memory system by terrifying childhood memories and impressions of abandonment. He therefore screened out the implied threat in Helen's words, along with her veiled request for a declared commitment, and responded only to her surface question. Mark's rational answer, however, was immediately followed by a disguised communication from his deep unconscious wisdom system, which had registered the perceptions screened out by his conscious system. Mark's conscious statements about his former job served as a vehicle for his deep unconscious perceptions: Indirectly, he was telling Helen that a lack of security in their relationship would prompt him to look for another girlfriend. In fact, Mark had taken that former job as a kind of interim position while he was looking for "the real thing." Unconsciously, he was telling Helen exactly where she stood in his affections—a revelation that Helen managed to screen out.

Notice, however, that Mark was also pressed by his deep unconscious memory system for relief. Ultimately, he responded to Helen's request/threat by putting *her* in the position of feeling displaced and by letting her know that he was "still looking." Again, I'm including this example because it is the sort of thing that occurs all the time—the conscious system rationalizing to keep from acknowledging a perceived threat to its well-being, expressing that perceived threat unconsciously, and then responding to it behaviorally—all without specific awareness of the factors involved or the price to be paid.

Take a look at another kind of example. Mrs. Acker was feeling a vague sense of discontent in her marriage. She knew that she was being abrupt with her husband, but she didn't know why; she told herself that she was "out of sorts." One night she had a brief dream: A man who resembled her father was coming on to her daughter, Lisa. When she thought about the dream, Mrs. Acker immediately recalled the time when she, as an adolescent, discovered that her father was cheating on her mother. She was distressed by this memory, and couldn't link it up to the dream in any way that made sense. Her father's mistress was nothing like Lisa. Then she remembered that Lisa was also the name of her husband's production assistant. He had mentioned this assistant a number of times recently. "This is stupid," Mrs. Acker decided, and dismissed the dream as unpleasant and not worth thinking about.

Consciously, then, Mrs. Acker was feeling discontent, but her grasp of the situation was vague. Had she been able to decode her dream, she would have discovered that her deep unconscious system had a very specific view of the situation and, unfortunately, a very accurate one: Her husband was having an affair with his production assistant. Unconsciously—subliminally, if you will—Mrs. Acker had perceived clues that were minimal and subtle, but were present nonetheless. Mr. Acker had seemed distracted of late, and although his references to his assistant were casual enough, he seemed to be quoting her opinions frequently. He also seemed to be unusually aware of and interested in other people in the office who were involved in illicit relationships.

For the conscious system, these various comments were random and had no meaning. For the deep unconscious system, however,

they were a telling confession. Still, to maintain her mental equilibrium—at least for the time being—Mrs. Acker did not recognize
the problem directly, even though her deep unconscious system
knew full well what was going on. The price for this conscious
ignorance or denial was the restlessness she felt and the unnamed
sense of unhappiness. As vulnerable human beings, we are all
willing to pay a price for momentary subjective peace—often a
higher price than the absence of knowledge is worth. Accordingly,
most patients in psychotherapy are willing to pay the price for
defensive conscious views of their therapists, while remaining entirely ignorant of a vastly different set of ratings made by their far
more incisive and reliable deep unconscious systems.

Let's look at one more example of this discrepancy between the
two systems of the mind—this one drawn from psychotherapy.
Mr. Dillon's therapist—a man—inadvertently overcharged him on
his monthly bill. The patient's conscious response was considerate
and forgiving—keep the money as credit toward next month's bill.
Yet the patient went on to tell a story of a garage mechanic who
overcharged him for repairs. "The man's not only greedy," said
Mr. Dillon, "he's an idiot; he didn't even fix the problem!" This
sentiment was, of course, a displaced and thinly disguised perception of the therapist's error, and this angry response was virtually
the polar opposite of the patient's conscious reaction.

The problem is that the wisdom of the deep unconscious system
is accompanied by the ignorance of the conscious mind. We know
unconsciously only because we are unwilling to know consciously.
This makes for self-deception at both poles of any decision-making
process that involves the emotions. The conscious system, at one
pole, will always opt for coping with emotional problems, however
poorly, rather than resolving them. At the other pole, the deep
unconscious memory system will press for relief without awareness, while the deep unconscious wisdom system will opt for emotional truth, regardless of the outcome. The only way to resolve
emotional problems in a healthy way, then, is to enlist the aid of

the deep unconscious wisdom system, and combine that knowledge with the desire of the conscious system for goal-oriented action.

When it comes to choosing a therapist, remember that the conscious system, above all, is interested in self-preservation. This is a healthy motivation, but it necessarily directs our conscious behavior toward maintaining the status quo, even when we have convinced ourselves that we want to change. Thus the conscious system, which is all we have going for us directly, is all too likely to make choices that are expedient, defensive, and protective rather than insightful.

In fact, as I have already suggested, you may well select a therapist who will offer you no more than a better defense against your emotional symptoms; or you may rationalize a damaging and destructive therapist because the interchange supports a manner of coping that is familiar to the deep unconscious memory system. You may even opt for a therapy that will increase your suffering. The conscious system is a fine instrument, but it is an unreliable guide to just about anything that is emotionally charged. For this reason, I have not assembled a book of practical "commonsense" suggestions on which the conscious system can rely for protection and rationalization. This book relies instead on the tendency of the deep unconscious wisdom system to take a long-range view of emotional circumstances, to prefer insight to ill-gotten defenses, and to genuinely wish for the best possible cure.

The deep unconscious wisdom system sends disguised and encoded messages by way of the conscious system; once decoded, these messages can tell you a great deal about your emotional response to a therapist and the kind of therapy being conducted. It should be noted, however, that the deep unconscious system has its own way of working over emotional issues. Because we are so used to conscious-system thinking, and so unfamiliar with our own deep unconscious viewpoint, many of the ratings that we will be carrying out will seem strange and unexpected, and even disturbing. But in time, as you come to know how the deep unconscious system thinks and works, and how much you can rely on its viewpoint when it comes to any emotionally charged situation, the entire rating system will not only make sense, but will also hold up very well in its practical applications.

In the main body of this book, you will have a chance to rate an actual or potential psychotherapist on just about every conceivable—and in some sense, inconceivable—dimension of today's psychotherapeutic experience. But before we begin this somewhat formal activity, it will be helpful to have a framework for this information. This framework is necessarily different from others that you may be familiar with. For one thing, I don't overclassify emotional dysfunctions. All forms of emotionally founded problems in human adaptation—whether psychological, psychosomatic, interpersonal, or whatever—have their source in attempts to cope with emotional issues unbearable to the conscious system.

I believe it is essential to realize right off that all emotionally founded problems have a deep and extensive subterranean base that is frightening and disorienting. This situation is part of the human condition. I do not mean by this that we are all fundamentally "crazy"; I mean only that all emotional disturbance issues from an inevitable core of terrors and contradictions and pain that is inherent in being human and having conscious awareness. Some people cope with these issues better than others.

There are many classification systems, many ways of defining the problems brought into therapy. But all these problems are essentially unsuccessful attempts to cope with the emotional issues of life. Particularly unsuccessful attempts to cope are experienced as symptoms of emotional disorder; we tend to seek help when the price of coping becomes so high that it interferes with our everyday functioning.

In this respect, then, we are not talking about an unconscious conflict that is disturbing to the conscious system. We are talking about an unconscious attempt to cope with a problem that the conscious system doesn't want to know about. The conscious system experiences the unconscious coping strategy as an emotional symptom. But the real issue is beyond awareness, based on clues perceived unconsciously (so-called subliminal perception) and worked over, entirely without conscious knowledge. This is why emotional symptoms seem so puzzling or irrational; the conscious system has no access to the emotional basis of the symptoms with which it is struggling.

When an unsuccessful coping strategy begins to interfere with your life, your conscious system will generally focus on the immediate symptom and prompt you to do something about it. More often than not, you'll try to change something in your life that seems to be related to the problem—a relationship, your job, your appearance. If that fails to bring some relief—and that is often the case—you might turn inward and try to figure out what's going on psychologically. But the path to relief is simply beyond your conscious vision; it is laid out in the unconscious part of your mind, and therefore not there for you to see. So your conscious system remains ignorant of what is really involved.

Perhaps at this point—either for reasons of your own or because other people advise you to get help—you decide to talk to a psychotherapist. This is an emotionally charged decision for many reasons, not the least of which is that it seems like an admission of failure. Even though you consciously reassure yourself that thousands, even millions, of people are presently in or have been in psychotherapy, you may feel embarrassed or even afraid that you're losing control. You think that you should be able to handle the problem yourself.

But even these fears and ideas are based on unconscious perceptions of yourself and your inner state, which you simply cannot bring to consciousness and alter. In this sense, having a perception, image, fantasy, or whatever that remains within the deep unconscious system means you are being influenced by something very difficult to change. Unless you learn the proper way to reach into the deep unconscious system, get to know what it's about, and find the means of changing its position—the goals of insight-oriented therapy—your options are limited.

I will grant you that emotional suffering can be alleviated in other ways—altering life circumstances, developing new defenses, sharing your dilemma with others in a comparable situation—but all of these methods are limited and extract a price. As I have suggested, the conscious system will often choose to pay that price in exchange for continued ignorance of unconscious knowledge. Emotional truth is submerged in the first place because it is unbearably painful and potentially disorienting to the conscious system. Activated emotional knowledge—the sense of loving someone and also wanting to hurt them, the sense of being both loved and hated by the same person, perverse desire, sadistic pleasure, the anticipation of death—is frightening in its naked state. Psychic organization depends on keeping some kinds of emotional truth at bay.

Recall the vignette involving Helen and Mark: Mark's encoded response to Helen clearly indicates a contradiction that his conscious system is unable to resolve—the fear of commitment vying with the fear of displacement. This contradiction is an inherent part of being human—the hunger for both freedom and security—but Mark's childhood has left him with a backlog of unconscious fear and anger around that issue. Mark has been able to maintain his psychic equilibrium by screening from awareness any emotionally charged perceptions involving that contradiction, but the price for this defensiveness is becoming very high: He is unable to sustain a long-term relationship with anyone. He is driven to establishing emotional triangles. Although this pattern is interfering with his life, the relief he is provided by this behavior has kept him from changing, along with his disinclination to face the truth.

You can see, then, that the possibility of coming to terms with real emotional truths in therapy will generate conflict in and of itself. Every patient is mind-divided. Part of you wants the best possible therapy and a chance at the least costly solutions to your emotional woes. But another part of you is perfectly willing to accept compromised and even damaging forms of psychotherapy, as long as the truth need not be known.

For most of us, the truth-seeking part of our deep unconscious system is no match for the part that will bargain with the conscious system regardless of the ultimate cost. This is true of life in general: The truth often seems cold and discomfiting, even disturbing, whereas lies have an infinitely wide domain in which to operate. They are attractive and persuasive—because we want to believe them, especially if every lie we accept helps us to lie to ourselves about our fallibility and our mortality.

Most of the time, when you are trying to decide whether to see a therapist, you look at the obvious: Do I like this person? Do I like what he or she said to me during the hour? Did I feel all right after the session? Did he or she "feel" like a therapist? Even so, you're likely to feel that ultimately you're playing a hunch—going with your gut feeling, as they say.

Sad to say, none of this has much to do with your actual final decision. The bargain-basement part of the deep unconscious system will make the choice in collusion with conscious-system defenses. Years of experience have shown me that, with few exceptions, the potential psychotherapy patient will hire a therapist who can help him or her to *avoid*, rather than deal with, the truth. Often, instead of seeking help, the person seeks to trade one questionable solution for another that is easier to tolerate.

With this kind of collusion going on, the yardstick by which you rate your psychotherapist is going to be terribly bent out of shape. Instead of accumulating a set of ratings that give you the best possible shot, you accumulate a favorable impression of a therapist who, *unconsciously*, you know quite well is potentially damaging.

Needless to say, the guidelines offered in this book are as free of mad and defensive needs as is humanly possible. They are practical guidelines based on unconscious communications from hundreds and hundreds of patients. They are constructive guidelines based on observing the outcome of many psychotherapeutic experiences. They are solid guidelines intended to direct you away from potentially destructive psychotherapeutic interactions and to-ward something constructive and healthy. And they are tough guidelines, in that they often run counter to self-deceiving "com-monsense" ideas and what is done in general practice. And they run counter, as well, to many of your own conscious wishes and rationalizations.

Indeed, it can be safely said that among the millions of people in some form of psychotherapy throughout the world today, only a remarkably small handful are receiving treatment that would meet the highest standards of the ratings we will be using. Rare indeed is a therapist who really understands and is willing to deal with the deep unconscious system. Even more rare is the therapist who shows full and deep respect for the ground rules and bound-aries of the therapeutic relationship, or, more practically speaking, for the deepest needs of his or her patient. By learning how to properly rate your psychotherapist, then, you not only have a chance to optimize your own psychotherapy, but also to have an effect on a field too long without viable standards by requiring that it be accountable within the limits of human knowledge.

·3·

The Two Great Systems
of the Mind

I have a friend I'll call Herbie. Herbie is single, in his mid-thirties, and I've known him for many years. About two months before I began writing this book, he telephoned me.

"Look, Bob," he said, "I've got a problem. I thought you might be able to help me. I really don't know where else to turn. I know I should have asked for your advice before I got involved, but I was feeling self-conscious and just didn't feel like talking to you about it. Anyhow, I've gotten into psychotherapy, and I don't know if I'm coming or going. What I mean is, I don't know if I should stay with this guy or leave him. It's all turned into a real mess."

Rating your psychotherapist usually begins before you actually meet him or her. It may sound odd, but how you hear about a therapist is very much related to the kind of therapy you are likely to receive. We'll explore that issue at length later on, but for now we can see how it plays a role in Herbie's case. As I said, I've known Herbie for a long time; Herbie is familiar with my work, and he knows that I would refer him to a good therapist if he asked. The fact that he didn't ask—and felt that he should have—is a good indication of the conscious system's uneasiness with the emotional realm. If the conscious mind operated according to clear logic and common sense in the emotional domain, Herbie would have called me when he first decided to seek treatment.

Instead, Herbie asked his girlfriend, Viola, about the therapist she was seeing. On the face of it, you might assume that Herbie felt embarrassed about approaching me in my professional capacity and was more comfortable asking the advice of someone in therapy herself. It's very possible that he didn't want to complicate our friendship with the inequality of our positions as therapist and potential patient.

But as I suggested in the first chapter, choosing a psychotherapist is not a purely conscious-system decision. There is no particular logic in asking one's girlfriend if her therapist is any good. One has to suspect immediately that the deep unconscious memory system has made a deal with the conscious system's unwillingness to deal with the real issues. Okay, says the deep unconscious memory system; I'll trade you the emotional symptoms you can't tolerate for another stopgap solution to the real problem you don't want to face. In fact, I'll wrap this whole thing up in a bit of fail-safe logic: Viola is obviously a woman of good taste; she chose *you*, didn't she? Her therapist seems to be helping her. Why not ask her advice about finding a therapist of your own?

This may sound facetious, but take a look at what actually happened. Viola, not surprisingly, recommended her therapist highly and suggested that Herbie begin to see him. She said that she liked him because he was an "eclectic psychologist," and therefore wasn't rigidly tied to any one school of thought. (Another way to look at this, however, is to understand the word "eclectic" as a wastebasket term for a therapist who does pretty much what he or she pleases without adhering to the constraints developed by any particular school of psychotherapy.)

Viola had been seeing Dr. Rumford once a week for seven years, and she felt that he was "pretty sharp." She was also impressed with his apartment, where he maintained his office, on the Upper West Side of Manhattan. Herbie suggested that Viola ask Dr. Rumford whether he had room in his schedule to see another patient. Viola liked that idea; she felt that she was doing both men a favor—drumming up business for one, and easing the way for the other. At her next session, Viola told Dr. Rumford that Herbie was looking for a good therapist and wondered if he had time to see him. She also told Dr. Rumford that Herbie had been having problems recently with impotency, and she felt that this was why he wanted to be in therapy. Dr. Rumford was sympathetic and interested and immediately offered to see Herbie in consultation. He told Viola that he had had great success in treating problems of impotency in the past.

By the time he called me, Herbie had seen Dr. Rumford four times. At Dr. Rumford's suggestion, Viola went with him to his first session and stayed for part of the hour. Herbie saw right away why Viola was so taken with him. He *was* sharp. He made interesting comments about Herbie's incestuous conflicts with his mother and sister, his fears of being castrated by his father, and his whole "oedipal mess," as Rumford had put it.

On the other hand, Herbie wasn't much of a believer in psychoanalytic concepts, and it was hard for him to identify with the fears and desires that Dr. Rumford was ascribing to him. But on one occasion after the second session, he found himself able to make love to Viola, and he figured, hey, whatever is going on, it seems to be working, so why jinx it with a lot of questions?

And yet he wasn't comfortable. He found himself wondering about the woman he caught glimpses of in the other rooms of Dr. Rumford's apartment; was she a wife? A mistress? Another patient? And he was embarrassed by the screaming fights he heard between Dr. Rumford and the patient who had the hour before his. Sometimes the smell of cooking from the kitchen permeated the office and nauseated him.

Worse, he was beginning to find Dr. Rumford irritating—he had a way of pulling at his lower lip when he was about to say something clever, and he was an inveterate chain smoker. When he brought up these quirks to Viola, she said that Herbie was resisting; after all, there were signs of progress, weren't there? Maybe he couldn't tolerate success.

By the fourth session, Dr. Rumford wanted Herbie to talk about his relationship with Viola, but Herbie felt reluctant. He couldn't get past the fact that Dr. Rumford had been seeing Viola for the past seven years. He just didn't feel right telling him the intimate details of his sexual relationship with her. In fact, Dr. Rumford's interest struck him as less therapeutic than prurient.

Dr. Rumford told him that his reluctance was actually part of his problem, and he attempted to encourage Herbie by pointing out Viola's physical appeal. What had attracted him to her in the first place? What did he like best about her body? How did he go about arousing her? What was she like in bed?

Dr. Rumford seemed inclined, in fact, to give Herbie detailed advice on technique, counseling him that a better method of arousing Viola would be exciting for him as well. Herbie found himself wondering whether the point of this wasn't actually Dr. Rumford's arousal at his expense.

When Herbie talked this over with Viola, he found out that Dr. Rumford had been telling Viola a good deal of what was taking place in Herbie's sessions. Viola seemed to know more about Herbie's hours than he could remember himself. When Herbie suggested to her that Dr. Rumford was perhaps attracted to her physically, Viola admitted that he had already made that clear to her. On several occasions he had told her that he couldn't understand a man's not being excited by her, and suggested that Herbie's impotency might be the result of her own lack of sexual technique—perhaps he could help her to improve her skills. Viola had told him that she wasn't interested in a sexual surrogacy relationship with him, and that, she said, was that. If he was attracted to her, well, maybe that was part of the response she engendered in people. So what? Why shouldn't that response be part of the therapeutic exchange?

Ultimately, we will be rating Dr. Rumford on everything from the kind of referral he accepted, to the structure of his office, to the kinds of comments he made to Herbie and Viola. But for the moment, suffice it to say that many people would have questions about Dr. Rumford's manner of practicing therapy. Others, however, might say that none of this is especially important, particularly in light of Herbie's recent ability to make love again. What matters is whether the therapy works or not. After all, a sex therapist would go much further, showing Viola and Herbie quite concretely what to do to arouse Herbie and sustain his excitement to orgasm.

Again, all of this activity is aimed at treating an emotional symptom from the point of view of the conscious system. The conscious system doesn't care about motivation; it wants lights, camera, action: immediate relief, pragmatic advice, and protection from the real issues at the base of the problem.

Herbie and I spoke on the phone for nearly two hours, during which time he went back and forth in his impressions of Dr. Rumford. Maybe he was being too critical; maybe he just didn't understand Dr. Rumford's game plan. And the next therapist could be even worse, right? How was he supposed to know, anyhow? Why should a therapist be obligated to meet his expectations? Maybe his expectations were the problem.

Until this point, I didn't have much to say to Herbie. Why pit my own conscious impressions against his? But then Herbie happened to mention something that proved to be decisive. In fact, Herbie mentioned it just as he was winding down and had talked himself into sticking with the therapy for a while. Then he said, "You know, I almost never dream. But last night I really had a weird one. I'm standing in the water—the ocean—with Viola. Suddenly I realize there's a shark coming at us. I realize he's going to rip us to shreds. I yell to Viola to get the hell out of the water. And the two of us turn toward shore, running for our lives. I woke up in a sweat."

Now, I'm not one to play psychotherapist for my friends. And, as I've said, up to this point in our conversation, I pretty much let Herbie go on by himself, grunting an "Uh-huh" here and there to let him know I was listening and to encourage him to go on. And even though the encoded or disguised meaning of Herbie's dream seemed clear, given the context of his telling me about it, I decided to get out of his way and let him go where he was going. Human beings are inherently self-healing when both systems of the mind are brought into play. Conscious reasoning, quite predictably, had led Herbie to opt for the line of least resistance. Now his unconscious system had expressed itself. A comment from me would have disrupted Herbie's process of making that encoded message conscious.

"Now why in hell would I have a dream like that?" Herbie asked me, more rhetorically than directly. "You know, it's odd, but Rumford told me last session that he has a house on the ocean, right on the beach. (He should have, with the fees he's charging me.) He even suggested that Viola and I use the house some weekend this spring. He said it was an infallible cure for impotency."

Herbie was in the process of free-associating to his dream—allowing his mind to wander here and there, into this or that, guided only by the fleeting images of the manifest or surface dream experience. And right off, Herbie had associated the dream to Dr. Rumford—specifically to one of the suggestions he had made to Herbie. At the time, Herbie had questioned Dr. Rumford's offer, but he finally accepted it as a grand and generous gesture of support.

Herbie next remembered a joke about a minister and an attorney adrift in a rowboat surrounded by sharks in sight of a tropical island. The minister volunteers to swim to shore, but the attorney quickly stops him and jumps in himself. The minister is astonished to see that the sharks are neatly moving aside and clearing a path for the attorney's swim to shore. Several hours later, when the minister is rescued and brought to the island, he asks the attorney why the sharks did that, and the attorney says, "Oh, that. Professional courtesy."

Herbie saw almost immediately that the dream had labeled Dr. Rumford a professional shark. He realized, in fact, that Rumford probably saw himself in the role of the attorney—a man willing to jump in and negotiate dangerous waters, a rescuer, a therapist capable of bending the rules to get the job done. The dream challenged Rumford's self-image, however; it said that he was actually one of the sharks, and that Herbie and Viola had jumped into the waters of therapy naïvely—that is, without obligating Rumford to extend them professional courtesy. Far from rescuing them or helping them, he was doing violence to them.

The dream presented this unconscious view in no uncertain terms. It said: Run like hell, Herbie, and take Viola with you before you're both torn to pieces. The man's a predator, and his offer is dangerous.

The end of the story is a happy one: Herbie and Viola both left therapy with Dr. Rumford and I referred each of them to different therapists. When I talked to Herbie again, he was making genuine progress, and the questions he had about his present therapist were far less disturbing than the ones that had come up with Dr. Rumford. My advice to Herbie was to bring these questions up with his therapist and to continue decoding his dreams—with his new therapist if possible, but, if his therapist had no ear for encoded messages, on his own. By properly decoding his dreams, he would have a sound and reliable sense of what was actually going on—not only on the surface, but in the depths as well.

In a sense, then, Herbie rated his psychotherapist with both systems of his mind. Let's take a closer look at that. Herbie's *conscious-system* ratings were reflected in his debate with himself on the phone with me—his discussion of the pros and cons of being in therapy with Dr. Rumford. On the other hand, the ratings generated by Herbie's *deep unconscious wisdom system* were reflected in his dream. It is the reactions of the deep unconscious wisdom system that I will be stressing in this book. In fact, from this point on, when I use the term *deep unconscious system*, I mean the wisdom system.

You may wonder why I have used the term *deep* unconscious system. My reason is that the conscious system has its own unconscious component. That is, the conscious system consists of immediate awareness, but it also maintains a superficial unconscious "storage bin" for all sorts of practical information that we are not currently using. For example, you know your own telephone number, how to get to the nearest supermarket, and what you have in the refrigerator, but you don't spend every waking moment thinking about calling home, shopping, and cooking left-overs. Information that has already been conscious, but is not immediately useful, must be set aside somewhere until it is required again. This is what the *superficial unconscious* part of the conscious system is for.

Herbie's deliberations on the phone with me are entirely consistent with conscious-system operations. The information he was working over was clear and straightforward, entirely without disguise. And his manner of working with his problem reflects the great strengths of the conscious system—its ability to reason, to sort things out, to learn, to store information, to retrieve it, to envision a goal, and to define a process of action on its behalf. These strengths derive from the overall purpose of strategic conscious thinking: the maintenance of both immediate and long-term survival. This purpose is primarily served by ensuring an individual self-protection, shelter, food and energy, supplies of information, companionship, and the opportunity for procreation. To this end, the conscious system operates quickly, with Aristotelian logic: the commonsense logic of everyday connections among objects.

As a survival mechanism, the conscious system is closely allied to our physical senses—to our eyes, ears, skin, and so forth. By and large, it will prompt us to react directly to incoming sensory information with behaviors appropriate to the stimulus. If you've stepped into the path of an oncoming car, it is the conscious system that will react with alacrity and alarm and prompt you to jump out of the way. This is a mark of the great efficiency of the conscious system when self-preservation is at stake. Even in that brief second between alarm and response, you will have directly calculated the consequences of impact, given the fact of a large moving object swiftly and progressively occluding your vision, and you will have reacted accordingly long before your sense of the situation could be mediated by language.

Recall that Herbie took in information about Dr. Rumford in a variety of ways—he observed him, listened to him, experienced his surroundings. He took in a wide range of *manifest* or directly conscious impressions and worked them over in his conscious system. Then he responded according to his conscious evaluation of the incoming information: Yes, I'm uncomfortable, but maybe I should wait and see.

Herbie also extracted *implications* from the surface events that he observed and experienced. For example, Dr. Rumford often introduced sexual topics in Herbie's sessions, even when Herbie was talking about other kinds of concerns. Consciously, Herbie tried to puzzle that out. Was Dr. Rumford overly preoccupied with sex? Or was he perceiving Herbie's efforts to talk about other things as a way to avoid talking about his impotence?

In other words, Herbie was asking whether Dr. Rumford's remarks *implied* an overconcern with sexuality, or whether they simply reflected the work of a sensitive Freudian psychotherapist who believes that sexual conflicts underlie most emotional symptoms. Maybe Dr. Rumford was just trying to do his job as well as he knew how. Implications are typically varied and often uncertain and confusing.

The conscious system works very well in a world of concrete objects and information, particularly when the emotions involved are confined to experiences of wanting something, feeling deprived, and feeling gratified, which are part and parcel of survival in the real world. But as emotional issues become more complex and ambiguous, the conscious system fares less well. One very practical reason for this is the fact that we can be aware of about six bits of information at a time. Even memories that have been conscious but involve complex emotional issues are retrieved with some difficulty.

The conscious system just isn't designed for matters of that sort. Emotional issues tend to get in the way when we are trying to work, obtain food and shelter, and negotiate safe passage. We need to stay cool in these situations or we get into trouble. The same mental system simply cannot do both jobs—guarantee survival and deal with extended emotional problems. The deep unconscious system is designed to take the pressure off the conscious system, and it works over not only complex and highly charged problems, but also implications whose meanings are too painful for direct conscious awareness.

We can see from Herbie's deliberations the limitations of the conscious system in a situation of emotional conflict. Herbie really didn't have the wherewithal to evaluate the problem. He shifted about in his feelings and impressions, leaning one way and then another, and finally decided to let things be until he had more information. This is typical of conscious-system resolutions: a series of pros and cons and contradictory possible implications, leading ultimately to a stalemate. One might say that Herbie's decision to stick with Dr. Rumford was not a conclusion of any sort, but a desperate attempt to close off the conscious conflict at a point where it had become unbearable.

Remember, the conscious mind is also undergoing pressures from the deep unconscious memory system, which contains the disturbing residuals of our life traumas—especially those experienced early in life with the nuclear family. These residuals are shaped by our actual experiences as well as our selective way of taking them in and processing them. The contents of this memory system constitute a powerful unconscious force, which may press for self-punishment and self-destructive behaviors. Each of us has internalized the value system of the culture at large (parental strictures, social ethics, religious morality, etc.), much of it centering on feelings of being "bad" or guilty. As a result, one of the ways the conscious system can stay ignorant of deep unconscious issues is to opt for psychic equilibrium by way of self-damage—entering into abusive relationships, setting oneself up for failure, and so forth.

That is to say, the conscious system, rather than deal with the pain of awareness, may unwittingly satisfy an unconscious need for punishment and remain ignorant of the issues being dealt with in this manner. Self-punitive decisions are usually rationalized and excused, and we deceive ourselves into thinking that we are taking the sensible course of action.

The deep unconscious system, however, does not deceive itself; the underlying motives for self-destructive behavior are encoded and communicated in disguise. Take another look at Herbie's dream. The dream images tell us that Herbie had unconsciously perceived Dr. Rumford as a man-eating shark. Yet, before he recalled his dream, Herbie had made a conscious-system decision to stay with Dr. Rumford. What are we to make of this? We can only speculate that Herbie's unconscious memory system had marked out a need to be devoured or destroyed. Entirely unaware of that self-punitive inclination, Herbie found any number of reasons to stay with Dr. Rumford, despite his questions and his doubts. His conscious system became the tool of an unconscious need he didn't realize was his. Indeed, if Herbie had consciously recognized that need, he probably would have rebelled against fulfilling it. But as long as the need remained unconscious, Herbie's ratings of his psychotherapist were based not on logic but, among other things, on a hidden need to suffer.

Clearly, we need the input of both systems of the mind—the unconscious search for emotional truth despite the cost, and the conscious priorities of survival and gratification. This places a great burden on the conscious system, which would just as soon strike deals with the deep unconscious memory system—bargaining for its continued ignorance by fulfilling a self-destructive unconscious need. It is imperative to understand that although the deep unconscious wisdom system tells the truth and is an ally, its truth is not necessarily beneficial in its unrealized state. Unconscious needs that remain unconscious come under the influence of the unconscious memory system, which will prompt the conscious mind to blind action if it can. Indeed, conscious ratings of your psychotherapist are almost entirely unreliable because the conscious system is so likely to be at the mercy of self-destructive needs beyond its awareness.

This may sound extreme, but I would go so far as to say that a therapist who obtains a high conscious-system rating based on likability, charm, warmth, cleverness, and so forth, is quite likely to be more damaging than helpful—more suited to self-defeating unconscious needs than to conscious wishes to get well. Unfortunately, human beings tend to react quite paradoxically to painful and destructive interventions by their therapists—for example, with conscious praise rather than horror or disappointment, so this particular state of affairs is difficult to change.

Let's turn now to the deep unconscious system. This system also receives sensory information—with the eyes, ears, skin, and so forth, but it obtains a rather different reading of reality from the one obtained by the conscious system. It is as though the senses were like radios, operating on both AM and FM frequencies. Two different sets of information are being picked up and processed. One set of information is being picked up consciously and directly; the other is unconscious and will generate unwitting behavioral responses and/or can be conveyed indirectly and in disguise.

The deep unconscious system immediately senses implications, encoded meanings, and other impressions that we dare not experience consciously—indeed, the system is designed for this activity. But the deep unconscious system is more than a submerged conscious system for underground meaning; it has its own set of premises and its own kind of logic. Where the conscious system is constantly breaking down objects into their constituent components and defining each element separately, the deep unconscious system is looking for relationships among elements and for unnoticed similarities between seemingly different objects and events.

One might say that the deep unconscious system experiences life holographically: Each constituent part of an object contains the meaning and potential of the whole. A person's hand is equivalent to the total person; a person's glasses or shoes or favorite chair are equivalent to that person. In the same way, symbols are experienced as concrete reality. In the deep unconscious system, *to mean* and *to possess* is *to be equal to*. Along with this manner of perceiving the world, the deep unconscious system maintains a premise not unlike the classic version of Murphy's law: What *can* happen *will* happen; what happened before will happen again. Thus, when the deep unconscious memory system registers a perception that can be related to a frightening or painful memory or fantasy, the perception is experienced as equivalent to that very memory or fantasy, and old responses are called immediately into play.

The deep unconscious system also experiences reality quite viscerally, so that even its indirect expressions often represent emotional trauma in raw physical terms. For example, when Dr. Rumford pressed Herbie about his sexual relationship with Viola, Herbie's conscious system experienced him as intrusive; but then again, Herbie thought, perhaps the questions were appropriate. This is the typical conscious system pro/con gambit. But if we look at Herbie's dream, these same pressured interventions were *unconsciously* perceived in terms of pursuit by a man-eating shark. Typically, the conscious system is either blind (using denial) or defensive (toning down manifest meanings and implications), whereas the deep unconscious system processes incoming information without modifying the power of the experience.

Although each view of the world, conscious and deep unconscious, has some legitimacy, it is important to realize that the conscious view of the world does not *explain* emotional symptoms, nor does it explain people's choice of a psychotherapist. Conscious logic does not bear up well in the face of a careful assessment of how we rate our psychotherapists, nor does it help to predict the therapeutic experience and its outcome. Consciously, patients are often terribly surprised when a therapy turns sour; in their deep unconscious system, however, this is exactly what was expected. These latter expectations are revealed in our encoded dream narratives and stories (and we become aware of them only if we properly decode the images involved). It is the impressions of the deep unconscious system, founded on raw and unencumbered perceptions, that most boldly and accurately portray the hidden intentions and meanings of others. This system both predicts and rates our experience with a psychotherapist with compelling incisiveness.

You may well ask at this point why anyone would interfere in the division of labor that nature set up. Clearly, the deep unconscious system processes everything that is terrifying to our conscious minds. Of necessity, we are unaware of this information, lest it disturb our immediate equilibrium, or engender a form of psychopathology that we can't control. On the other hand, the great resources of this system in the emotional realm ultimately can be used by the conscious system to positive ends. Encoding is a form of communication—the deep unconscious system does not send any messages that are too unbearable to be received. But, as we have seen, these messages don't yet have a conscious form. They are still unconscious. The reason the unconscious system has the information in the first place is that the conscious system is defended against the perceptions involved.

Therefore, communications from the deep unconscious system are like personae non gratae; the only way they can gain entrance into the conscious system is by riding piggyback, as it were, on bits of information that are already conscious. It was Freud who first showed, in *The Interpretation of Dreams* (1900), that communications from the deep unconscious system are *displaced* from their immediate and raw emotional context in reality, to some other, conscious, less disturbing context that is in some way analogous to the original. The original perceptions have also been symbolized or disguised, so that the conscious message that serves to carry information from the deep unconscious system seems to be about something else entirely.

Before we look at Herbie's dream for ample illustration, let's look at this process still another way—in terms of its natural history.* The situation is somewhat confused by the fact that we begin our search for understanding at the end of a process. We first learn about what we are working over from a disguised message—a

*For more details, see my book *Decoding Your Dreams* (New York: Henry Holt, 1988).

communication that is actually the end of a journey, rather than the beginning. It is something like finding yourself on the top of a mountain without any idea as to how you got there, or who pushed you in that direction in the first place. A dream or any other message that carries deep unconscious meaning is the product of extended unconscious processing, even though it is the first indication we have that we are worried about something—much as Herbie's nightmare was the first sign that something was terrifying him.

To begin, then, at the beginning, first we merely register emotionally charged perceptions. On the surface, what we have perceived may seem ordinary and without exceptional meaning—a passerby, an offhand comment, someone jostling you on the subway. Freud called such events, when they turned up in dreams, "day residues." Often a dreamer will say, "Yes, that happened yesterday, but it wasn't important; why would I dream about it?" I think of such events as *trigger* situations: For whatever reason, they trigger unconscious information processing. The point is not whether a trigger situation has been perceived consciously; often it has been, sometimes it hasn't. The point is that a trigger situation activates the deep unconscious system, which perceives any number of ramifications that the conscious system is ignoring. These ramifications are processed silently and worked over. If the unconscious system expresses the conclusions it has reached, it does so by creating a dream or selecting a conscious vehicle to carry its messages in disguise. This vehicle will have something in common with the actual trigger situation, but will not be as anxiety-provoking to the conscious mind. As a rule, a *theme* that characterizes the original hurtful trigger experience is simply lifted from this original situation and placed into another context—the context that appears in the remembered dream or story.

Using Herbie's dream as an example again, the emotionally charged trigger situation was Herbie's experience of Dr. Rumford, who had been pressuring him for details of his sexual relationship with Viola. The ramifications of that trigger were perceived unconsciously and worked over in the deep unconscious system. The conclusions reached by the deep unconscious system were expressed in disguise by way of a conscious vehicle—Herbie's dream report. If Herbie hadn't recognized that the dream was about his therapist, he wouldn't have been in a position to undo the dream disguise and arrive directly at the dream's unconscious meanings and wisdom.

Again, the trigger for this dream was certainly conscious for Herbie. Dr. Rumford had been intrusive with him, seductive with Viola, and had not kept Herbie's sessions confidential. Although Herbie had questions about these behaviors, he was able to rationalize most of them away with his conscious-system thinking. His deep unconscious response was far different. In Herbie's dream, Dr. Rumford's behaviors are collectively characterized and symbolized—encoded—as those of a *shark*. Herbie saw this by thinking about the dream's images and allowing his thoughts and feelings to wander about freely, unencumbered—the process of free association. The themes and images—memories, other stories, and so forth—that come to mind when associating can be taken as part of the dream—as further reflections of the thinking of the deep unconscious system. The wider the range of associations, the broader the perceptions portrayed. In fact, the greater the number of images generated, the more complete the "ratings."

When associating to the shark image, Herbie not only thought about the old joke about professional courtesy, and the idea of being eaten alive; he also thought about loan sharks—men who take advantage of other people's needs and exploit and hurt them while appearing to provide a useful service.

Notice that this deeper, silent response to Dr. Rumford became clear when we recognized the trigger for Herbie's dream. The trigger is the key to decoding unconscious messages. We didn't have to "reach" for our reading of the dream. The first association that Herbie had was to be reminded by the dream's setting that Dr. Rumford had offered him his beach house for a romantic encounter with Viola. This is the immediate trigger for his dream; in fact, it makes sense of the joke's reference to professional courtesy. Herbie had thought at the time that Dr. Rumford's offer seemed like the sort of favor one would do for a colleague—an equal. Now he realized that *unconsciously* he saw the offer as the kind of loan that an unscrupulous person would make to a victim.

Decoding a dream or any story usually begins with recognizing the trigger situation. In all of the narratives considered in this book, the triggers will involve psychotherapists and their interventions. All we need to do is substitute the therapist for other people in the dream, and the dreamer's unconscious view of the therapist is revealed. To put this another way, we take the surface *themes* in a dream or story and transpose them to the therapist. These themes describe the dreamer's unconscious perceptions of the therapist in question and provide an especially useful and valid view usually quite inaccessible in any other way.

In Herbie's deep unconscious system, then, Dr. Rumford was perceived as devouring, dangerous, exploitative, and out to prey on people. Although Herbie's conscious system was unable to develop a clear picture of these traits, his deep unconscious system did so incisively. One might say that the deep unconscious system created a dream to let Herbie know what he was experiencing. The dream displaced and disguised the perceptions of Dr. Rumford so that the unconscious perceptions could enter the conscious system. The dream, then, is a disguised or encoded version of Herbie's raw perceptions of his therapist. Its images both reveal and conceal his true concerns.

If Herbie had ignored the dream, or had ignored the encoded nature of the images, he would have developed no awareness of his unconscious perceptions of his therapist. In fact, there are many ways to work with the dream images symbolically, without recognizing them as displaced from a specific context. A psychoanalytically oriented therapist might have suggested, for example, that Herbie was experiencing *Viola* as devouring and demanding, perhaps as the result of unconscious fears concerning his mother. Had he told the dream to Dr. Rumford, one might predict an interpretation involving castration anxieties—the perfect pseudo-explanation for Herbie's sexual problems. The grain of truth lurking in such an interpretation would hardly serve as a vehicle for insight; in fact, it would serve as a means of avoiding a deeper and more compelling truth—about Dr. Rumford himself—accessible only through trigger decoding.

The point is that no amount of direct study of Herbie's manifest dream and its evident implications could connect this dream to Dr. Rumford. The only means by which Herbie could understand the most active and important meaning of his dream would be to recognize that the dream had been triggered by a series of incidents with his psychotherapist. He could then readily see that this connection to Dr. Rumford was thinly disguised in his manifest dream experience. The clearest clue to this is the fact that Dr. Rumford had offered Herbie and Viola the use of his oceanfront house. It is this kind of *bridging image* that helped Herbie connect his dream about sharks and the ocean with his therapeutic experience. With this connection established and firmly supported, it was easy to decode the remaining unconscious messages (perceptions) contained in Herbie's nightmare.

The bottom line, of course, is a simple directive from the deep unconscious system: Get out of therapy before you are destroyed. Without trigger decoding, Herbie would have no idea of this message—this sensible piece of advice contained within his own mind. Yet through the use of trigger decoding, the message is so clear as to be inescapable.

Much the same applies to rating your psychotherapist. If you rely on conscious impressions, you will seldom really know where you stand. If you allow your dreams and the other stories you tell yourself to go unanalyzed, undecoded, and untapped, you will remain ignorant of your deepest feelings. Dreams are not the only source of encoded messages; *any* type of narrative and image can serve as a good vehicle for disguised unconscious perceptions and reactions. You need to be alert, however, to their existence.

Without decoding your dreams and stories, you will be subjected to powerful unconscious influences without conscious choice. You will very likely assess your psychotherapist self-defensively.

On the other hand, if you properly identify the trigger for your dream or narrative and allow yourself to free-associate, you can develop a series of ratings that are likely to be quite reliable. As a backup to this process, here we will also be rating therapists on many dimensions of the therapeutic experience. These ratings are derived from the unconscious comments of patients whose dreams and stories I had the good fortune to study in the course of my teaching and supervisory efforts. Assessments made by the deep unconscious system are not only incisive, they are remarkably consistent from one person to another. Despite the anxiety surrounding deep unconscious perceptions, they are far more consistent and easy to comprehend—that is, logical, once all is known—than the highly rationalized and defensive things we tell ourselves consciously. In rating psychotherapists, we will make good use of the wisdom of the deep unconscious system.

·4·

The Ground Rules
of Therapy

Psychotherapy is a peculiarly intimate, personal experience. The patient essentially entrusts his or her most deeply felt secrets to a stranger, who in turn commits his or her own interest and concern—and expertise—to another's experience of pain and confusion. The relationship exists only within one particular context, and within that context it is intense and even frightening for both parties. This relationship exists, moreover, in a world of commerce, where psychotherapy is a service for which the client is charged a fee. This may at first glance seem like a strange mixture of elements.

Given the realities of our culture, it is the very nature of its existence as a commodity that limits psychotherapy and sets it apart from a friendship or from the sharing of problems with a neighbor. In fact, one might say that the therapeutic interchange exists *only* by virtue of its structure as a service. The therapeutic relationship brackets off a time and place for activities removed from the linear effort of everyday survival issues. The static nature of this structure and the concrete impersonality of its elements— however human its creation and management—permits an immediacy of participation within its confines. Two people commit themselves to a relationship defined by this structure and agree to work in terms of it toward one participant's greater self-awareness and maturity. (The gains for the therapist should be coincidental, though in a sound therapy they are inevitable.)

I am making this point to indicate the great importance of the specific elements that constitute the structure of psychotherapy. We tend to take the respective "frames" of our various relationships for granted, but, as any physicist will tell you, the boundary conditions are *part* of the system they define. Meaning depends on boundaries. Even something as simple as a drum depends for its sound and resonance on the materials used in its construction, and on how those materials have been put together. Think about a game of tennis. What happens in a competition depends for its meaning on the maintenance of rules and proper playing conditions. If the structure is forfeited, you may have fun and get some exercise hitting the ball back and forth, but you won't have a tennis match.

In every formal structure, fixed rules and a common sense of purpose permit us to assess and to recognize meaning. Without fixed reference points, we have no vantage point on what is happening.

As I tried to make clear in the previous chapter, the deep unconscious system is exquisitely sensitive to issues of structure and meaning. The point of psychotherapy is the establishment of conditions under which deep unconscious material can be expressed and worked over consciously. In every interaction that is set apart from conscious survival questions, the deep unconscious system comes into its own. One might say that in situations of this kind, the conscious system is dislodged from its accustomed position of privilege. Psychotherapy is designed to accomplish precisely this kind of displacement.

The conscious system is naturally uncomfortable with the structured frame of psychotherapy; although stable conditions are experienced as secure, they are also registered as entrapping, and they liberate fears of death and dissolution. The deep unconscious memory system plays a role in these anxieties; a secure frame engenders fears of being harmed by someone who appears trustworthy—all of us have childhood memories, fantasies, and terrors of that sort. Because the conscious system finds these fears intolerable, they are immediately relegated to the deep unconscious system. Thus, in a therapeutic relationship, the deep unconscious system struggles with two conflicting points of view: The deep unconscious wisdom system appreciates the sound frame as a clear reference point and strong support for therapeutic work, but the deep unconscious memory system experiences fears of being trapped and annihilated. These deep unconscious memory system fears are constantly mobilizing old defenses and pressing the conscious system to break the frame in the seeming interest of survival.

Psychotherapy, therefore, presents every opportunity for the two systems of the mind to collude in defensive operations. The conscious system will continually strive to break down the formal structure of therapy in order to avoid its implications of vulnerability and mortality. The unconscious system will express itself through encoded messages that support the maintenance of the "secure frame"; but it will also register the anxiety and even terror of being "held" or constrained by that frame. This paradox—the desire for security contending with the fear of annihilation—is at the heart of every committed relationship, of every relationship that requires self-sacrifice to a larger structure. It is a paradox that cannot ultimately be resolved as long as we are alive and know that we must die. But the psychopathology that it generates *can* be resolved.

I am saying this because the ratings that you will be doing as this book progresses are based on the fact that a good therapy brings this fundamental paradox into play one way or another. Because this paradox is an issue for all of us, therapists as well as patients feel the same kinds of pressures to defend against awareness. The easiest defense open to either party is to undermine the frame of therapy.

I have said that the therapeutic interchange exists only by virtue of its structure as a service. By this I mean that the therapeutic relationship is constituted by the very conditions of its operation: Two people agree to meet at a certain time, in a certain place, for a certain amount of money. Other conditions to the relationship are also set—what kinds of communication are permitted to each or required of each? Is anyone else privy to that communication? What is the physical proximity of patient to therapist?

These conditions may not seem terribly important to you—certainly not as important as warmth, tolerance, and empathy in the therapist, but this is because the conscious system has only minimal interest in ground rules, and quite a bit of interest in feeling immediately comfortable. (Indeed, studies of assessments made by psychotherapists of their own therapists indicate that they themselves are concerned mainly about warmth, tolerance, and empathy.) The conscious system pays little attention to the office setting, absence and vacation policies, and other issues that might collectively be termed the therapist's management of the psychophysical boundary conditions of treatment. Yet it can be readily shown that *unconsciously* these very issues are at the crux of psychotherapy—and of optimal cure.

The unconscious system not only recognizes a sound framework as crucial to the therapeutic relationship, but actively seeks the establishment of certain ground rules as preconditions for resolving emotional symptoms. This is an interesting phenomenon, because the unconscious system, by way of encoded messages, will actually attempt to rectify mismanaged conditions toward an "ideal frame" therapy. The unconscious sense of what constitutes an ideal frame is so consistent that I am tempted to regard it as universal.

In brief, the unconscious view of ideal frame conditions is as follows:

1. A single, set fee
2. A single, set location
3. A set time for and length of sessions
4. A soundproof office
5. The rule of free association (the patient says everything that comes to mind)
6. The therapist limited to *neutral* interventions, i.e., those that do not stem from the personal needs of the therapist (no advice

giving or directions, only decoding of unconscious communication, silence, or ground-rule management)

7. The relative anonymity of the therapist (no self-revelations or opinions; work limited to the material from the patient)
8. Total privacy
9. Total confidentiality

I fully realize that this list may sound arbitrary to the conscious mind; it is nonetheless a set of guidelines for which the deep unconscious wisdom system speaks most forcefully. In fact, therapists from many schools of clinical practice would, at least nominally, accept or advocate most of them. The point here hinges on the word "nominally." For many therapists, these unconsciously sought-for conditions to therapy are honored in principle far more than in practice.

This is not a question, however, of preferring the work of certain kinds of therapists over the work of others. I believe that the workings of psychotherapy stand beyond any particular school of treatment. My appreciation for these ground rules is derived entirely from decoding unconscious communications in therapy, as both an analyst and supervisor. I have been surprised myself to discover that the deep unconscious system in each of us is so consistent and uncompromising in its preferences for very specific conditions of therapy. These preferences exist and are expressed in disguised form, *regardless of the actual treatment being used by a particular therapist*. It is clear that the deep unconscious system is advocating certain conditions because of their *meaning*: They imply security and a quest for truth.

Some therapists would object to one or another of these principles. For example, those who give advice, training, use deconditioning, and the like would question the idea of neutral interventions. Others might recommend personal self-revelation by the therapist, or dispense with the rule of free association. In fact, all the rules that I listed have been objected to at one time or another for a host of *conscious* reasons. And, as I said, breaches are far more common than adherence, even where the ground rules are accepted in principle. But, as I will show repeatedly, the deep unconscious wisdom system pays attention to the management of these rules, and reflects a price paid for every departure from them—a price that usually goes unnoticed consciously or appears to have no connection to the ground-rule infraction. Sometimes compromise is all that is available—but you should know that you are compromising, and that the relief obtained by way of compromise may not be worth it in the long run.

In addition to these fundamental ground rules for therapy, there are a host of supplementary conditions to treatment that are consistently supported by the deep unconscious wisdom system. Some, such as the absence of physical contact between patient and therapist, are accepted in general by the conscious system as well. Others, such as the use of the couch, are a bit more puzzling to the conscious mind. Many therapists prefer face-to-face therapy with their patients, and a therapist's decision to conduct therapy in that way is probably the least hurtful departure from the ideal conditions of therapy. If the objection to using the couch comes from the patient, however—that is, if the couch is offered and refused—the departure could be quite significant. One female patient who made such a refusal immediately went on to speak of her fear of a pending medical examination—X rays, blood work, and such. "I know the tests need to be done if the doctor is to find out what's wrong with me. But I'm thinking of canceling out entirely, I'm so afraid of what he'll find." In the deep unconscious system, avoidance of the couch is not only a wish to avoid unconscious (hidden) meanings, but is tantamount to quitting (meaningful) therapy entirely.

To speak more generally, when a therapist departs from the ideal ground rules, the patient may have no particular conscious reaction, but will tell stories or dreams whose themes and images clearly encode an unconscious objection to that departure. If the therapist attends to the patient's encoded objection and rectifies the frame, the patient may actually object consciously, but will tell stories or dreams whose themes and images involve positive and helpful figures. If the therapist ignores the encoded objection, the patient will tell stories or dreams whose themes and images involve damage, or the failure to hear, or instability and madness.

The idea that ground rules and boundary conditions play a crucial role in psychotherapy is surprising not only to patients but to many therapists as well. As I have suggested, however, rules, regulations, and boundaries are fundamental to our lives in every context. Many boundary conditions crucial to our understanding of who we are and what is expected of us are so much a part of our vantage point that we take them for granted until someone renders them explicit. Every relationship operates in terms of ground rules and boundaries that define permitted behaviors, expected behaviors, and even the satisfactions and frustrations possible in each interaction.

Rules or laws not only set limits and involve restrictions; they also provide a sense of safety, definition, and certainty to relationships. When the ground rules change, we feel disrupted; we have to think about what we've been taking for granted and adjust our behaviors accordingly. An example of this at the social level would be questions of civil rights, where traditional boundaries are declared unjust and exclusionary. An alteration in the ground rules, even where positive and necessary, disrupts behavior, undoes old rationalizations for bias, and changes the nature of relationships. At the level of the individual psyche, rule breaking of any sort tends to provide the rule breaker with momentary feelings of power, omnipotence, and immortality.

From birth onward we are sensitive to interpersonal boundaries—the degrees of closeness permitted among family members and with outsiders, the extent of physical contact and intimacy—and their fluctuations. We are responsive as well to the ground rules, explicitly stated and implied, that prevail within a family structure—the rules of the household, so to speak. Much of what we absorb we absorb unconsciously; the information is subliminal. Thus in the deep unconscious system all of us come to appreciate the value and importance of frame considerations. It is the conscious system that varies. Some of us consciously value and adhere to the prevailing rules of family, social, and societal behaviors. Others tend to prefer altering or circumventing these rules, insisting on being the exception.

Again, the conscious system is concerned with self-preservation—in a sense, with triumph of the will over all boundaries, even ultimate boundaries, such as the limits of time, space, and physical existence. The conscious system enjoys the idea that transcending illness, weakness, and death is possible. We may well require such illusions for the maintenance of psychic health. But sometimes illusions come at too great a price, and they can lull a person into unconscious feelings of entitlement and grandiosity, where the sense of being special, invulnerable, and privileged to exploit others is preserved at great cost.

To illustrate briefly what I mean by the cost of illusion: Mr. Zerbe had only admiration for his male therapist, Dr. Shannon. Dr. Shannon had saved Mr. Zerbe's job by calling his boss and reassuring him that his employee was making excellent progress in his therapy. Mr. Zerbe felt strong; he and his therapist had put the boss in his place. However, soon after the telephone call, Mr. Zerbe began to moonlight behind his boss's back. This was strictly forbidden by the patient's contract. Again, though, he felt powerful and invincible. Yet the cost now was being dishonest, breaking a contract, and living in bad faith. Associations in his session with Dr. Shannon showed that this choice of the role of a rule breaker and exception was modeled unconsciously on the rules broken by Dr. Shannon in his call to Mr. Zerbe's boss (modifications in neutrality, privacy, and confidentiality). No matter how well-meaning the intention, the illusion of being the exception—in both patient and therapist—proved to be costly for both. (Mr. Zerbe left therapy abruptly several sessions after the therapist had made the call.)

I would go so far as to say that ground-rule issues are an element of every emotional symptom and problem. Poor frames—in any context—invite the emotional disturbances of childhood and adulthood to "fill in the blanks." A sound frame is the best context within which to correct such ills. Poor frames invite corruption and dysfunction in many ways. The example we just looked at with Mr. Zerbe is a case in point: The frame violations by his therapist unconsciously promoted a symptomatic action—that of gross dishonesty and exploitation—in the patient. Throughout this book we will find that one element contributing to every expression of emotional disorder—in patient or therapist—is that of an alteration in the ideal frame, either in life or in therapy.

I am aware that most therapies are not conducted with an eye toward the conditions required by the deep unconscious system. It is possible, however, to receive decent therapy in a framework that is less than ideal—if the therapist is consistent about maintaining the frame that exists and pays attention to the encoded level of meaning in the patient's communications. As I said, inconsistency in frame management is the easiest defense in therapy against dealing with fundamental issues. And the biggest problem with this kind of defensive strategy is that it feels good. It threatens neither patient nor therapist with the human fears and frailties that come to light in secure-frame therapy.

On the other hand, a frame break or a frame that deviates from the unconscious ideal is experienced unconsciously as seductive or attacking. This unconscious experience and reactions to it are often disguised and enacted elsewhere—that is, when the basic therapeutic hold required by the unconscious system is impaired, the unconscious system reacts by feeling persecuted and will be unable to trust the therapist. But because deviation is also gratifying, the patient will feel magically better and may even feel downright infatuated with the therapist.

The unconscious feelings of persecution that persist nonetheless are played out instead with people outside of therapy. The connection between the conditions of therapy and difficulties in relationships outside of therapy is virtually never recognized. In fact, the patient generally believes that he or she is becoming more aware and assertive in extratherapeutic relationships—recognizing the burden of others' expectations, realizing the injustice of social constraint, and so forth.

Unquestionably, self-revelation and insight are time-consuming and difficult. It is far easier to stabilize the psyche quickly by interacting with a therapist who is unconsciously experienced as fundamentally unstable. This is what happens when a therapist mismanages the frame. The deep unconscious system registers the therapist's behavior as undisciplined and weak, and the conscious system actually begins to feel better. I generally think of this as "cure by nefarious comparison." This all-too-human defense resembles the everyday strategy of making friends with people of lesser potential or intellect or position than oneself in order to feel comfortable with one's own failings.

Frame alterations also involve action—doing something; because of this, they tend to sanction and to promote the action-oriented, relief-seeking aims of the deep unconscious memory system, which are often hurtful to oneself and to others. As we have seen, this is a quick route to feeling better. But the lesson learned in a therapy without frame-management standards is that such defenses are *needed* in order to feel good. The patient remains action-prone, with no insight into the real problems brought to therapy. Such a patient is very likely to adopt a pattern of exploiting others outside of therapy—asking for special considerations or seeking out mutually exploitative relationships.

Therapy should be doing something more constructive than providing an opportunity for unconscious collusion with the conscious need to feel better right away, preferably without insight. This sort of collusion inevitably makes for dependence on the therapist, and will lend itself to the most appalling rationalizations in order to maintain the relationship. The most common, of course, is "I feel better; so therapy must be working."

This is not to say that the ultimate goal of therapy is something other than "feeling better." My point is that uninsightful relief and defensive stabilization are psychopathology just as surely as the emotional symptoms that seem to have disappeared. This kind of relief is not only costly, but actually damaging. In essence, a therapist who allies himself or herself with a patient's need for stabilization without insight is teaching the patient another way to defend against deep unconscious perceptions. Once therapy is over, the patient will necessarily try to maintain his or her stabilization by seeking other relationships that will permit the kinds of defenses learned in the therapeutic interchange—or by cutting off relationships that don't permit those new defenses to operate.

Trade-offs, such as exchanging a severe depression for repeated affairs or giving up a masochistic relationship for one in which your own sadism prevails, are too often taken by patient and therapist alike as signs of a successful therapy. Of course, within the therapeutic context, the new behaviors are not experienced as defenses in their own right. A person who has struggled with depression and is now experiencing a renewal of interest in social and sexual contact will naturally affirm therapy as having been helpful. A person who has endured a series of abusive and damaging relationships may well experience a newfound need and ability to control and hurt others as a justifiable and welcome sign of self-determination.

We return, then, to the fact that every patient who enters psychotherapy does so with a divided mind. Part of us seeks limitless contact apart from rules and boundaries; every frame deviation becomes a sanction of illusions of immortality. But the hope for sanity, stability, and insight lies mainly with the deep unconscious wisdom system. It is this system, expressing itself with encoded messages such as we saw in Herbie's dream, that reveals the dangers of frame violations, of their ultimately destructive elements, and of how they evoke a deep sense of mistrust and danger that colors the entire therapeutic experience. And it is the deep unconscious system, as we will see, that directs the therapist to maintain or secure the frame—to stick to the rules despite all temptation.

◆　◆　◆

Let us go back for a moment to Herbie, who dreamed about a shark chasing him and his girlfriend, Viola. In the session preceding this dream, the therapist had offered the use of his beachfront home to Herbie and Viola. On the surface, this seemed like a generous offer of support to both his patients. But Herbie clearly experienced it as dangerous and frightening. One might suggest, as an alternative explanation, that Herbie's unconscious view of his therapist was part of his overall problem: He felt competitive with his therapist for Viola's affections and was experiencing the offer as castrating and out of his control.

I would not quarrel with an interpretation of this sort—as an implied subtext of the manifest dream—but this is hardly the source of the dream. To someone of psychoanalytic orientation, the images may *imply* castration fears; but this interpretation warrants a set of assumptions about images involving mouths and teeth and their relationship to unconscious male terrors. And once we've decided that the shark "means" castration fears, we've truncated Herbie's other associations about loan sharks and professional courtesy. We don't need to be that clever about the dream.

The images don't say anything directly about fear of castration, but they quite straightforwardly indicate Herbie's unconscious sense of being pursued and in danger. Herbie's deep unconscious system accurately discerned the therapist's sharklike pursuit of Viola—which Viola ultimately confirmed; and it accurately perceived the therapist's offer as an infringement on his and Viola's personal lives. In other words, the therapist *was* pursuing Herbie and Viola in a sharklike way. If Herbie was contending with unconscious castration fears, it was the therapist's offer that brought them to the fore. Dr. Rumford had already violated the secure frame by accepting Herbie into therapy at all. This was an infringement of both his and Viola's right to privacy and confidentiality in the therapeutic space. His offer of a beach house abridged their right to his neutrality and anonymity, and to the priority of their own material.

Herbie's limited surge of potency after two sessions suggests that he was experiencing the sense of power that frame alterations can offer. One might suggest further that the therapist's offer of his beach house was manifestly designed to make Herbie feel special and powerful. This appeal to the conscious system might well have supported Herbie temporarily. But it is clear that the unconscious wisdom system recognized the destructive nature of such a defense. In that respect, the shark also represents the aspect of Herbie that the therapist was attempting to encourage—the unthinking will to triumph by destroying others. This is, in a sense, to incite sexual desire by way of violent self-declaration. Such a course might well have revived Herbie's potency, but it would also eventually have destroyed his relationship with Viola.

Again, the dream narrative itself, the tendencies to violence and self-damage—they belong to Herbie's psyche. But the broken frame of therapy provided the source image from which old pathologies could spring and come to the surface in encoded form. If Herbie had ignored the encoded level of his dream and continued with therapy, these pathological tendencies would have been encouraged. And perhaps the conscious system ultimately would have welcomed the therapist's sanction of violent self-assertion as an emotional symptom more palatable than impotency.

Let's take a look at another example. Mollie is a young woman in her twenties suffering from depression and severe weight swings—from obesity to anorectic thinness. A friend told her about a clinic that she herself had been to, one that specialized in weight problems. Mollie went to the clinic and was seen by a social worker who took a detailed history. Therapy was recommended and Mollie was assigned a female therapist, Dr. Tudor.

What we are concerned with here are the *conditions* of Mollie's therapy. If the deep unconscious system monitors boundary conditions, then Mollie's dreams and narratives should reflect its point of view on the frame created and maintained by Dr. Tudor.

As I have suggested, positively toned and constructive stories generally follow when a rule is held despite pressure to break it, or when an ideal condition is instituted, rectifying a deviant frame. Such stories speak indirectly for deep unconscious support and validation of the therapist's behavior. Negatively toned and destructive stories characteristically follow lax ground-rule management. Such stories speak indirectly for deep unconscious recognition of destructive behavior on the part of the therapist.

In the first month of her therapy, Mollie was seen briefly by two other therapists—the chief of the clinic and a psychologist who gave her a battery of tests. She also saw a clinic comptroller who negotiated a reduced fee for the therapy. In addition, Mollie signed a statement she prepared with Dr. Tudor, stating the goals and risks of the therapy. Mollie's mother was seen once by Dr. Tudor, and Mollie was told she could cancel sessions without being charged a fee by giving twenty-four-hour notice.

If you will take another look at the list I provided, you will see that all of these conditions to Mollie's therapy are departures from the ideal framework sought for her by her deep unconscious system. On the surface, these conditions seem quite practical and straightforward; they take place every day in clinics all over the world. Mollie had no conscious reason to object to any of them. She was relieved by the sliding-scale fee arrangement, and she had no problem with the number of people she saw at the clinic.

During her first few appointments with Dr. Tudor, however, Mollie spoke quite a bit about people spying on couples, her mistrust of people who intrude on relationships, and her sense that she was being victimized by her mother at home because she couldn't afford to live elsewhere for the small sum her mother accepted.

These stories can be decoded in the same way that Herbie decoded his shark dream. They are deep unconscious reactions to the frame breaks that Mollie had accepted consciously. The many third parties to Mollie's therapy were a violation of her right to privacy and confidentiality, and her deep unconscious system portrayed this frame break by prompting her to talk about spies and intruders being a cause for mistrust. The story about her mother indicates that Mollie unconsciously accepted intrusion and violation because the fee was low and she had no alternative.

Mollie also spoke about her mother being away. She said that in her mother's absence, their apartment had been invaded by hordes of unwelcome friends—including a man she did not want to see because she hated his small talk. Again, to decode the unconscious messages, all we need to do is extract the themes from Mollie's images and place them in the context of therapy. Before this particular session, Mollie had been interviewed by the chief of the clinic. Consciously, Mollie had been gratified by his interest in her case; but unconsciously, her view was dramatically different: The man was an unwanted intruder into the space Mollie shared with her therapist—someone who had entered in Dr. Tudor's absence and barraged her with small talk.

In actual fact, the clinic chief was the butt of many jokes among the staff that alluded to his incessant, empty chatter. It was well known that he carried out very active interviews with the patients he saw at the clinic, and that much of what he said was meaningless and boring. It is clear that the man Mollie mentioned was an encoded representation of this doctor.

The introduction of third parties into any therapy, in-clinic or private, always elicits from a patient the unconscious reaction of intrusion. This is so consistent that whenever I hear intruder imagery in supervision, I unfailingly ask my supervisee where the third party came into the therapy—and there is always a confirming story to support the patient's encoded message.

Mollie went on to talk about her car; lately it hadn't been handling well. She'd had an accident right after beginning therapy. And now she'd found out that the frame was damaged in the accident and couldn't be straightened out. It was damaged for good, and she couldn't steer the car, because it kept veering off. "It's almost as though I have to go where the car wants to go," Mollie complained, "so trying to go anywhere in it is going to be hell."

Near the end of this session Dr. Tudor asked her how she felt about the therapy so far. Mollie said everything was just fine. She especially complimented Dr. Tudor on her warmth and concern.

Again, if we transfer the themes of Mollie's narrative to the situation of therapy, we can see that her unconscious perceptions were quite different from her conscious assessment of the relationship. Mollie's car-frame story may seem too perfect an image to be believed, but I assure you that this is a genuine transcription of her words. This narrative is an exquisite expression of Mollie's deep unconscious picture of the damaged framework of her therapy—damaged, as she rightly portrays it, by serious, unrectifiable alterations. And although it is entirely without awareness of what she herself perceives and understands, Mollie realizes that trying to undergo therapy under these conditions is likely to make matters worse—without the right conditions, the therapy is likely to veer out of control and make her life miserable.

If Mollie had been rating her therapy based on the assessment of her deep unconscious system—as an evaluation of her displaced and disguised stories—she would probably consider leaving. But because she could access only her conscious appraisal—that Dr. Tudor was warm and concerned—she continued on, unmindful of the risks.

The means by which you rate your psychotherapist is crucial to the conclusions at which you will arrive.

Let's look more closely at what we have been doing with Mollie's stories. Essentially, we have taken the implications and meanings of Mollie's experiences in the clinic as our guide in decoding her stories. But we have also lifted the *themes* in Mollie's surface tales of events *outside of therapy* and relocated them *into the therapeutic situation*. The logic in this, of course, is that the perceptions and reactions being expressed unconsciously in this material were originally triggered in the therapeutic situation. As such, we can understand these images as *valid* perceptions and assessments of the conditions of Mollie's therapy. Throughout this book, we will use this method as a basis for rating psychotherapists. The ratings obtained in this way are not the sort you may be accustomed to, but they are quite accurate.

In a therapeutic situation, the patient invariably works over his or her emotional problems unconsciously in light of the ground rules of the psychotherapy. If Mollie's therapist had decoded her stories and shown her their unconscious meanings, she might have gained insight into the unconscious roots of her depression and weight swings. A patient will always select for expression those aspects of the ground rules that relate to his or her own psychological problems. For example, Mollie's mother had had several affairs that Mollie knew about. One thinks again about Mollie's narratives and their concern with spying on couples, intrusion, and damage. The frame problems in her therapy might have given Mollie a chance to come to terms with the frame problems in her life, which in turn were a major factor in her emotional ills.

In summary, adhering to the ground rules required by the deep unconscious system creates what is called *secure-frame therapy*. The patient experiences a sense of safety and support from a secure frame. A space is created in which it is safe to express disguised images from the deep unconscious system. But the secure frame also creates a constricting, closed space—a claustrum—and this evokes anxiety in both parties to therapy. The secure frame creates an irresolvable paradox—the danger of annihilation in the experience of security—which is fundamental in everyone. Thus the material generated in a secure-frame therapy is important to analyze and resolve.

In what we call *deviant-frame therapy*, one or more ground rules are modified for the therapy. The time of sessions is changed, a fee is reduced (or raised), there are third parties, such as insurers, involved in the therapy, and so on. In these instances, the basic hold is impaired, there is reason to mistrust the therapist, and feelings of persecution—however unconscious and displaced ("taken out" on others)—are common.

Deviations offer a defensive gain, however, in overgratification. Breaking a rule is tantamount to defying death. The sense of satisfaction, however, can be sustained only with deviations in the ground rules of the patient's daily life.

These propositions are supported consistently by the expressions emanating in displaced and disguised form from the deep unconscious system. As we have seen, interventions that involve ground rules are invariably followed by stories that offer encoded commentary on the therapist's management of the rules. It is also true that interpretations of these encoded commentaries, in which the therapist decodes the patient's unconscious message, are followed by stories that offer encoded validation or nonvalidation of the interpretation as well.

When a therapist responds to an encoded message that objects to a frame deviation by interpreting the message and securing the frame, the patient often produces narratives about situations outside of therapy in which people are helpful, understanding, strong, or otherwise positively portrayed. I call this *interpersonal validation*. In response to a frame-securing intervention, the patient may also produce material that encodes new information about the unconscious basis of his or her emotional problems. This is because the patient now unconsciously feels understood and supported and sees that it is safe to reveal further unconscious material. This is called *cognitive validation*.

Another illustration will show you what I mean: Mr. Fredericks, a homosexual man, was in private therapy once weekly with Dr. Clark, a female psychiatrist, for bouts of depression. The frame was relatively secure.

Mr. Fredericks began one hour by asking Dr. Clark to change the time of the following week's session because he needed to see his internist, and this was the only hour his internist was available. Dr. Clark responded by suggesting that Mr. Fredericks continue to say whatever came to mind.

Mr. Fredericks was somewhat puzzled by the suggestion, and tried to turn his mind to other things happening in his life. He began to talk about work and soon got caught up in describing the schedule instituted by his new supervisor. The new boss was intent on establishing a staggered work schedule, and in a misguided attempt to be fair to everyone, had arranged things so that each person in the department came to work and left at a different time every day. The whole thing was driving him crazy, he said. Either things should go back to the way they were, or everyone should be given a set time to come to work each day.

After hearing a bit more, Dr. Clark intervened. She suggested that the story about the work schedule was Mr. Fredericks's indirect and unconscious way of telling her that changing the hour would be like doing what the boss had done at work: creating a chaotic arrangement that would drive Mr. Fredericks crazy. Indeed, the indirect advice (of his own deep unconscious system) was actually quite direct: Keep the schedule fixed and clear. And that was exactly what Dr. Clark proposed to do.

Mr. Fredericks thought about this for a minute, nodded, and then began to talk about a man he had once been involved with. He was the only man, he said, with whom he'd ever lived that he felt he could rely on and trust. If he said he'd do something or be somewhere, he'd do it as promised. It was a pity there weren't more people like him.

We can see here the typical split between the conscious and deep unconscious wisdom systems. The conscious system is motivated by expediency and convenience; the deep unconscious system says that breaking the frame would be destabilizing and shouldn't be done. When the therapist interpreted this to the patient and used his encoded directive to keep the schedule as arranged, there was strong interpersonal validation from the deep unconscious system—a displaced story of someone reliable and trustworthy. Notice how different this encoded image is from Herbie's and Mollie's encoded images of their therapists.

This book is asking you to accept responsibility for the way in which therapy is often conducted today. The specific ramifications of a particular rating for your own psychotherapy is a matter of interpretation, however. That is, this book offers general guidelines—strong support for therapists who rate high, and fair warning with respect to those who rate low. But in the last analysis, the reader must make the ultimate assessment in the context of his or her life, emotional problems and needs, and available therapy resources.

In general, it is in recognizing the continued pain and malfunctioning that results from the work of low-rated therapists that the value of high therapist ratings takes hold. Such recognition is not a simple matter, for a low-rated therapist may offer a patient a defensive strategy that may initially appear helpful. But it is also true that a poorly rated therapist is likely to have an effect on a patient's interactions with others that is problematic, if temporarily relieving. A high-rated therapist may usher you through a long period of feeling even worse than you did before you began to see him or her, but ultimately will help you to construct a sounder way of living your life.

In rating psychotherapists, I will make use of a four-point scale, as follows:

Sound Interventions that are basically constructive and not damaging to either patient or therapist.

Questionable Interventions that are likely to be, but are not necessarily, hurtful. Interventions that may be both helpful and harmful.

Unsound/Reconsider Your Choice of Therapist Highly questionable interventions that are likely to be damaging.

Dangerous/Beware of This Therapist This is a highly damaging position or intervention, and should lead to serious thought of termination.

Rather than applying these ratings to a therapist's philosophical position, evaluation will be made with respect to specific practices. In other words, rather than rating a therapist's school of thought—be it psychoanalysis, Gestalt, cognitive psychology, or whatever—this book will simply rate a therapist in terms of what he or she actually does in interacting with a patient. Much of the structure of the various schools of psychotherapy are rationalizations for techniques that have not been examined in the light of patients' deep unconscious responses.

Again, the deep unconscious system has no interest in a therapist's school of thought—only in his or her ability to maintain a secure frame and to understand the meanings of unconscious communication. Therapists from the same background show enormous differences in technique and in ratings, whereas therapists of different backgrounds often share common beliefs and techniques and may receive comparable ratings. In the last analysis, it is how a therapist does and does not intervene that creates his or her part of the therapeutic experience and cure, and it is on these behaviors that his or her assessment must stand or fall.

In most instances, you will find that a therapist who scores low on one or two items will tend to score low on many items. The reverse is also true: the therapist who scores high on one or two items will typically score high on many. There are other possibilities, of course, but the main point is this: The items being rated are not independent of each other. A therapist inclined toward verbal interventions rated *Unsound/Reconsider Your Choice* will be inclined toward a loose frame altogether and likely to do the kind of therapeutic work that leads to an overall low rating.

In general, an accumulation of many *Unsound/Reconsider Your Choice* scores is a cause for concern, though as said earlier, the ultimate assessment and conclusions will be left to the rater, so, too, with even one *Dangerous/Beware* rating. In many cases, however, less-than-*Sound* therapeutic behavior will fall somewhere between *Questionable* and *Dangerous/Beware*; only you can determine, by the nature of your own unconscious responses, how negative a rating should be assigned.

It is necessary to remember, however, that there is no such person as a perfect psychotherapist. Given today's teachings and thinking, a therapist who will consistently score high ratings on a variety of scales is extremely rare, and your expectations must for the moment be in keeping with this likelihood.

One final point: The ratings that I am using in this book are based on the deep unconscious experience of former patients. Although they are a valuable instrument for assessing a psychotherapist, the aim of this book is to encourage you to decode your own stories and dreams as they are mobilized in response to working with an actual psychotherapist. In principle, every time you have a notable contact with a therapist, allow for the spontaneous emergence of dreams and narratives.

For example, on the evening after your session, pay some attention to the anecdotes you tell—to a spouse, a friend, in a letter. Catch yourself and see whether these stories have themes that are relevant to the recent interaction with your therapist. If you have an argument with someone soon after your session, notice the content of it; can you transpose the argument into the therapeutic situation and make sense of it there? Try to remember your dreams. And allow time, too, for some loose, unencumbered free-associating to this material. Once all this has been developed, take some time to examine what you've been thinking about.

In general, the more negative the tone of this imagery and the more distressing the themes and feelings, the greater the likelihood that the deep unconscious system is attempting to communicate a distinctly low rating for a particular psychotherapist. And of course the opposite is also true: the more positive the imagery, the more constructive the themes, the more prominent the subjects of conflict resolution and growth, the greater the likelihood that a psychotherapist rates high and is carrying out sound therapeutic work.

Like psychotherapists—and their patients—no rating scale is infallible. Ratings, whether drawn from the details of this book or from the wisdom of your own deep unconscious system, must be weighed and evaluated, viewed in context, and accumulated over a period of time. There can be no substitute for reasoned judgment that maintains a wary eye toward disruptive, unconscious influence. Yet, by and large, in most situations it will prove possible to develop a reasonable and fairly accurate assessment of a psychotherapist, once all the ratings, personal and impersonal, have been completed.

It is important, too, that we approach the rating of a psychotherapist with a measure of humility, an acknowledgment of his or her humanness, an expectation of inevitable strengths and weaknesses, and a realization that we are all inevitably part of the vulnerable human condition. At best, we can hope for a therapist who both understands his or her limitations and is capable of forgoing the standard defenses against emotional distress.

PART II

• • •

Rating Your Psychotherapist: Past, Present, and Future

·5·

The Referral

Rating the way in which you discovered your therapist may at first seem an odd thing to do. After all, you can't actually rate a therapist until you meet him or her. Essentially, you're rating the person who recommended the therapist, or the manner in which the therapist first came to your attention. Is this logical?

In a word, yes—but we are not talking about conscious-system logic here; we're talking about deep unconscious logic. You may recall my mention in chapter 3 of the premise held by the deep unconscious system: A part of something equals the whole. I used the example of a piece of clothing being equivalent to the person who wears it. This is not really so farfetched a concept. Think about pop culture, for example. For a generation of rock fans, a single glove immediately conjures up Michael Jackson. Advertisers can suggest a Lincoln's birthday sale with the image of a stovepipe hat. For that matter, J. R. Ewing's hat is in the Smithsonian. The Baby Boomer generation grew up with Bat Masterson canes and Davy Crockett coonskin caps.

The deep unconscious mind is so steeped in this kind of associative thinking that all manner of related stimuli become part of the way in which one unconsciously assesses a therapist. For the deep unconscious system, nothing happens in isolation. How you know your therapist—and *what* you know about him or her—becomes part of your therapy and will necessarily affect not only the course of the therapeutic relationship, but the actual outcome of the treatment.

Think again about pop culture. Advertisers and marketing experts use the effects of deep unconscious associative thinking to great advantage. An obvious example is the use of TV celebrities to market products on television. If you grew up with the programs "Father Knows Best" and "Marcus Welby, M.D.," it is impossible to see Robert Young do a commercial for a medicinal product without being subject to the sense of him as a paternal authority figure with medical knowledge. Rock songs are consistently appropriated for commercial advertising because of the conscious and unconscious associations they carry for the target audience. These associations happen with or without our volition.

In the same way, if your therapist is recommended to you by another of his or her patients, the deep unconscious mind cannot help but work over the sense of a third party being involved in the therapy. For the unconscious system, the therapeutic space will always hold three, not two, participants—you, the therapist, and the patient who referred the therapist to you. This is one of the reasons my list of ground rules includes the dictates of privacy, confidentiality, and therapist anonymity.

How a therapist first comes to your attention is not simply a matter of who recommends him or her, however. This rating category includes your knowledge of the therapist's qualifications and/or personal life; whether you decided to see a therapist yourself or were required to by law or corporate recommendation; and whether you yourself have had prior contact with the therapist under other circumstances.

Of course, I am using the term psychotherapist generically. People seek help for emotional difficulties from many different kinds of mental health practitioners—ministers, psychoanalysts, family therapists, biofeedback practitioners, encounter-group leaders, social workers, psychiatrists, psychologists—even spirit channelers and Tarot-card readers. My use of the term psychotherapist assumes only that you are seeking an implicit or explicit contract with someone for the relief of emotional suffering—whether physically or mentally expressed.

And this is one of the difficulties of the field. The criteria for training and treatment for psychotherapeutic practitioners are loose at best. In many states, virtually anyone can claim to be a psychotherapist and take on clients. Despite the interplay between the psychological and physical aspects of many emotional dysfunctions, the field of psychotherapy seems to be considered less a healing profession than a kind of luxury or a way to learn how to be "fulfilled" and "happy." One goes to a therapist to "explore one's feelings" or to get advice. The problem is that the public mind functions in this respect as a collective conscious system. The conscious system has a "so I'll try it" attitude—"If it doesn't work, what have I lost? I can always find another therapist." In contrast, the deep unconscious system takes therapy seriously indeed, and recognizes the great harm that a well-meaning but naïve therapist can do.

Unfortunately, as I have said, the deep unconscious memory system will collude with the conscious system's need not to know, and therapy can provide the perfect route to assuage unconscious guilt by embarking on a course of self-damage—all under the guise of wanting to know more and wanting to achieve optimal emotional functioning. Often, a person unwittingly will choose a therapist who is capable of repeating the very traumas that the conscious mind is defending against. This kind of repetition, in one respect, can be considered a drive toward health—a way of working through the traumas once and for all. But the sad truth is that patients tend to choose therapists who will repeat the old traumas without offering any insight into what is happening. This is why it is so important to access the deep unconscious response to a therapist.

Let's consider an illustration of a low-rated referral: Mrs. Hoffman was seated next to Dr. Victor at a social dinner. As soon as she learned that Dr. Victor was a clinical psychologist, Mrs. Hoffman started a conversation with him and told him that she'd like to see him as a therapist. Flattered, Dr. Victor gave her an appointment in his office for the following Monday.

You will see in the checklist at the end of this chapter that this kind of a referral would rate a *Dangerous/Beware* score. The reason for this is not clear on the surface. But in the deep unconscious system, once a person is a social acquaintance, he or she can *never* be a therapist to that individual. A therapist who attempts to cross that boundary is universally seen in the deep unconscious system as incestuous. The violation of professional boundaries in the therapeutic relationship consistently results in imagery involving the violation of sexual—and aggressive—boundaries in the family. Thus a patient's deep unconscious response to a therapist who accepts this kind of referral will involve memories, fantasies, experiences, and wishes involving breaks in the family sexual boundaries. The deep unconscious memory system will take advantage of the therapeutic frame break to collude with the conscious system in keeping the patient's inner "frame break" out of awareness.

I'm going to show you how this happens. On the night before her session with Dr. Victor, Mrs. Hoffman dreamed that she was in bed making love to her father. She was appalled and wanted to run away but remained half-paralyzed as her father began to caress her.

Mrs. Hoffman found this dream so disturbing that she told it to Dr. Victor the next day in their session. Dr. Victor, rather predictably, told her that the dream indicated that she had unresolved incestuous and oedipal wishes toward her father. He linked these needs to her frigidity with her husband, which was one of the reasons Mrs. Hoffman had sought therapy.

Mrs. Hoffman told Dr. Victor that she was having difficulty believing this interpretation, because she didn't even respect her father very much. He was a man who preached righteousness and social propriety but had several mistresses whom she knew about.

Take a close look at what is happening here. Mrs. Hoffman's dream was encoding her deep unconscious perception of Dr. Victor in light of her prior contact with him. The deep unconscious system was registering this confusion of social and professional boundaries as illicit and incestuous. However, the specific images that were chosen for the disguised expression of these perceptions were not arbitrary. They were clearly part of Mrs. Hoffman's psychological makeup. She did have unresolved problems in her relationship with her father, and these problems were, indeed, contributing to her frigidity with her husband.

In other words, Dr. Victor was not misreading Mrs. Hoffman's dream. But he *was* overlooking his own contribution to its formation. The image of incest had been precipitated by Dr. Victor's illicit acceptance of Mrs. Hoffman into therapy as a social acquaintance. Thus, when Dr. Victor tried to focus on the question of having to resolve incestuous desires, Mrs. Hoffman responded with an encoded perception of the therapist as a hypocrite. Essentially, she said: You're just like my father; you preach righteousness, but you yourself are violating the proper boundaries for our relationship.

Why, you may ask, is this a problem? The answer is that Dr. Victor was not paying attention to Mrs. Hoffman's deep unconscious communication. Thus Mrs. Hoffman's deep unconscious memory system was able to use the therapist's unwitting frame break to collude with her conscious system. Look at it this way: The emotional symptom that Mrs. Hoffman was trying to resolve was frigidity—her inability to respond sexually in the most appropriate of situations: in her marriage to her husband. But in her conscious attempt to deal with that problem, she sought therapy in a manner that actually duplicated unconsciously the insecurity of sexual boundaries in her childhood family.

This may sound like an utterly convoluted way to proceed—as though the mind actually worked to its own detriment. Again, however, what we are seeing is a conscious/deep unconscious memory collusion against awareness. What seemed to be an expedient, if impulsive, decision to get therapy from a psychologist fortuitously met at a dinner party actually functioned as a new way to avoid painful self-knowledge. The deep unconscious memory system struck a deal with the conscious system: I'll let up on the frigidity if you'll partially gratify the incest fantasies you don't want to know about. The result was the selection of a therapist whose violation of professional boundaries could partially gratify and sanction unconscious incestuous fantasies in the patient.

Notice that this kind of collusion doesn't blind the deep unconscious wisdom system to what is going on. It only blinds the conscious system. And it keeps alive—if it does not exacerbate—the problems that could be resolved through a process of self-discovery and understanding. Mrs. Hoffman's deep unconscious wisdom system registered quite accurately the conflict between what the therapist was saying and what he was doing. How can a therapist help a patient to come to terms with inappropriate and illicit wishes when his very decision to see the patient is helping to gratify these wishes? In the language of Mrs. Hoffman's encoded portrayal, Dr. Victor was perceived unconsciously as a hypocrite who was saying one thing and doing another.

Had Mrs. Hoffman gone to a therapist with whom she had no prior relationship, an interpretation of her incestuous conflicts would not have been contradicted by the conditions of treatment. The therapist who knows something about maintaining boundaries and sexual/social barriers is in a position to help the patient understand his or her own difficulties in maintaining ground rules extratherapeutically.

Let's look at another example. You'll recall Herbie, who decided to see his girlfriend's therapist. This is another referral source that the checklist rates as *Dangerous/Beware*. In fact, Dr. Rumford well illustrates the tendency of a therapist who would accept a referral of this sort to rate poorly in other aspects of his or her work with the patient: He violated ground rules involving privacy, confidentiality, neutrality, and anonymity.

With regard to the problem of the referral, however, let's look at another of Herbie's dreams. He dreamed it the night he made the decision to call Dr. Rumford for therapy. In the dream, a man is escorting him into a room in which his oldest sister, who had died several years earlier, is lying in bed. Herbie gets into bed with her but then runs out in revulsion.

If we take the dream and put its theme into the context of Herbie's decision to see Dr. Rumford, we quickly see that this referral, so acceptable to Herbie consciously, was portrayed by his deep unconscious system as an invitation to commit incest. I have included this illustration because I want you to notice how strikingly like Mrs. Hoffman's dream this dream is. Where ground-rule issues are concerned, deep unconscious perceptions are remarkably consistent from one patient to another. Note, also, the similarity of emotional symptoms: impotence and frigidity. Both Herbie and Mrs. Hoffman selected a therapist in terms of the same kind of frame-break issue. This particular kind of frame break lends itself to a conscious/deep unconscious memory collusion involving unresolved issues around sexual boundaries in childhood.

In Herbie's dream, the emphasis is on his deep unconscious perception of his relationship with Viola as a fellow patient. By selecting Viola's therapist, he unconsciously amplified the brother/sister incestuous aspects of his relationship with her. Dr. Rumford, for his part, was much inclined to play the benevolent but pruriently interested father—inviting Viola into Herbie's first session and offering to lend them his beach house for sexual purposes. Dr. Rumford's acceptance of Herbie into therapy was tantamount to a sanction of the very problems that Herbie should have been trying to solve.

And, again, we can see that the deep unconscious wisdom system was not blind to any of this. Herbie's first dream was already advising him against seeing Dr. Rumford long before he called me and told me his shark dream. If he had decoded this first dream and heeded its warning, he never would have made that first appointment.

The need to separate the therapeutic from all social relationships was brought home sharply by another female patient, Mrs. Arthur, who saw a male therapist whom she knew socially from church-related activities. In her first session, she spoke of a painful conflict with her boss at work, who openly indicated his wishes to have an affair with her. Because her own marriage was unsatisfying, Mrs. Arthur found herself flirting with the idea of this relationship. Finally, however, she said she couldn't do it. It was a matter of principle, she explained: "He can be my boss or my lover, one or the other, but not both. To try to be both is to surely fail at both. I don't need that kind of grief."

Once again, we have a displaced story—the voice of the deep unconscious wisdom system—that belies a patient's conscious preference to see a therapist she has already met in a social context. Mrs. Arthur felt guilty over her wishes to have an affair with her boss, and she selected a therapist whose own unconsciously perceived behavior would sanction such an affair. To proceed with this conscious/deep unconscious memory collusion might have brought her relief, but without insight and without constructive merit. Thus the very low ratings afforded this not uncommon means of finding a psychotherapist.

To repeat: By rating the way in which a therapist first came to your attention, you can often predict the kinds of ratings that he or she will receive for other categories. The unconscious power of the selection process is so great that it correlates with your overall unconscious intention: to select a therapist who can provide a reasonably secure frame for therapy or, in contrast, unwittingly to select a therapist who will support a collusion between the conscious system and the deep unconscious memory system. Conversely, the unconscious power of the selection process is such that the rating it receives will generally correlate with the selected therapist's ratings across the board. In other words, a therapist who would accept you as a patient under circumstances that would give the referral a low rating is likely to be rated low on many aspects of his or her work.

There is a real advantage to rating your psychotherapist before you actually have contact with him or her. The deep unconscious system is very sensitive to every nuance of any contact with a therapist, even where the conscious attitude is casual or even cavalier. This rating—of who the therapist is, who recommended the therapist, the nature of any prior relationship with him or her, and, if you've made contact by phone, what that conversation was like—can prevent you from becoming involved with a therapist whose deep unconscious effect on you will be problematic from the outset. Many unconscious influences operate outside of awareness in a way that is hard to recognize, particularly the extent to which they play a role in how you feel and behave. It is better to rate your psychotherapist in advance by assessing the nature of the referral source. A list is provided at the end of this chapter, that will enable you both to rate the referral to your current therapist, and, if the rating is low, to find another therapist by a more sound method.

Having located a psychotherapist, then, you should be concerned with the following questions:

1. How did you become aware of this psychotherapist?
2. Did someone else tell you about him or her? What relationship does this referral source have to the psychotherapist?
3. Have you yourself had any prior relationship or contact with this psychotherapist?
4. Do you have any knowledge of this psychotherapist's personal life? That is, what did you know about this psychotherapist before deciding to see him or her for therapy?
5. Does anyone you know have professional or personal contact or a relationship with this person? For example, do you know another of this psychotherapist's patients? Do any of your friends know him or her socially? Do you know someone related to the psychotherapist in some way?
6. Do you know any close friends, colleagues, or the spouse of this psychotherapist?

It should be clear at this point that we are looking for a therapist who will rate highly in terms of the deep unconscious search for a secure-frame therapy. A secure-frame therapy ensures anonymity, privacy, confidentiality, and therapist neutrality. The "cleanest" referral, therefore, is one that has been made by a healing professional—a physician, another therapist, a representative of a professional organization, and the like. No prior knowledge of the therapist should exist for the potential patient, nor any knowledge of the therapist's personal and professional life.

Low ratings generally indicate prior personal knowledge or actual personal contact with the psychotherapist, even as a minister or rabbi or teacher; a referral from a friend who currently is or was a patient of this psychotherapist; or access to personal information about the therapist's life or family.

You may well have questions about this rating system. Perhaps it seems too oriented toward an unyielding psychoanalytic posture. Given your own preferences and inclinations, you may believe, for example, that strong professional qualifications indicate, above all, a doctrinaire approach to therapy. You might argue that professionals generally operate as an old-boy network, referring patients essentially to one another.

I want to be honest about this. It is true that many medical people know little or nothing about the optimal qualifications of a psychotherapist. Often a referral source will have a general impression, based on feedback of some sort, that the therapists to whom he or she has referred patients are satisfactory or successful in their work. Furthermore, certain individuals have a strong belief in one particular kind of therapy; others may be inclined to refer to friends or colleagues with whom they have a special relationship. This is especially common among psychotherapists, who typically refer only to those therapists who have been trained the way they have. And, yes, therapists often make referrals to therapists who will refer cases to them in turn. It's a bit of a hornet's nest, so you need to stress to your referral source that you want and deserve the best available therapist in your area. Getting a referral from a professional you trust and respect can increase the likelihood of the therapist being competent. Although a professional referral cannot ensure excellence in the therapist, it can guarantee the absence of the therapist's prior contact with you, confidentiality, and your sense of the therapist's full commitment. The best route to these aspects of the secure frame is the professional referral.

It is entirely possible, of course, that a professionally referred therapist may in fact turn out to be a poor therapist. In that case, other factors used to rate a therapist will help you to discover that possibility. There is no referral that can *guarantee* you an excellent therapist. When I say that the cleanest referrals are professional ones, I do not mean that such referrals are certain to be the ideal conditions under which to begin a treatment experience. They are simply better than other possible avenues to therapy.

High (*Sound*) ratings, therefore, go to referrals from:
   a. Physicians, other therapists, mental health practitioners, nurses
   b. Professional organizations, such as psychiatric, psychological, social work, psychoanalytic, and other local or national organizations
   c. Self-help groups, such as Alcoholics Anonymous, Overeaters Anonymous, and the like
   d. Professionals who are not in the health field: attorneys, religious leaders, school and job counselors, etc.
   e. Friends or relatives whose contact with the therapist is professional, nonpersonal, and does not include a therapeutic relationship

Somewhat lower ratings (*Questionable*) go to:
   a. Compromised professional referrals, those from:
      Judges and officers of the court
      Employee Assistance Programs
      Anyone who mandates therapy as a condition for continued employment, matriculation, or parole
   b. Therapists about whom you know something minor person-

ally, even though you yourself have had no personal contact with him or her

c. Arbitrary referrals, such as listings in telephone books

Unsound (Reconsider your choice of therapist) or *Dangerous* (Beware of this therapist) ratings go to referrals that are:

a. Obtained from a public source, such as:
   Books by therapists, news articles, and other written materials
   Appearances on television and radio
b. Contaminated, such as from friends or relatives whose contact with the therapist is social and personal
c. From present or former patients of the therapist in question
d. Based on your own personal or social contact with the therapist

In principle, compromised professional referrals create initial conditions of therapy that are likely to have hurtful aspects—it is far from ideal to mandate a psychotherapy. This is especially true if there is any requirement that the therapist report back to the referral source. Insightful psychotherapy in which deep secrets must inevitably be revealed cannot take place in the presence of extraneous witnesses to the proceedings.

Knowledge of a therapist's personal life from any source can also compromise a therapy, since anonymity is an element of the ideal frame. In small communities, this compromise may prove to be unavoidable. Still, extensive knowledge of a therapist's personal life will be problematic for the therapy. Lesser bits of information can be brought up with the therapist and properly explored and interpreted so that the unconscious effects of such knowledge are kept to a minimum. However, were the therapist to reveal anything further about his or her private life or personal opinions, the situation would call for a *Dangerous/Beware* rating (see chapter 10).

Arbitrary referrals—such as taking a name from the telephone book or an advertisement of some sort, or going to a therapist because you pass by his or her shingle—are what one might call potluck choices. It may be that under unusual circumstances you, as a prospective patient, have no other choice; but this type of selection is more often careless and unthinking. It speaks for a willingness to risk your mental well-being with an entirely unknown figure. All too often, therapists found in this way warrant low ratings on other aspects of their work as well. At the very least, you should suspect that behind a choice of this kind lies an unconscious wish to hurt yourself. Of course, the odds have it that you may blindly choose a sound and helpful psychotherapist. But the latter possibility is least likely with a therapist who is comfortable advertising his or her services.

Public-source referrals violate a therapist's anonymity, even if the public situation has been such that no personal information about the therapist has been revealed. In the deep unconscious system, any view of a therapist outside his or her office is experienced as personal exposure regardless of its nature. If you are drawn to such a therapist, unconscious factors involving the issue of exposure are likely to be playing a role. When a therapist's anonymity has been compromised, the effects cannot be analyzed away, and the ensuing therapy is likely to leave part of your emotional problem quite unresolved. Perhaps the best compromise— if you feel strongly that the therapist in question has expertise in the area of your difficulty—is to seek out a referral from this individual. Still, the deep unconscious memory system is clever in its ways of influencing our thinking and leading us toward misguided choices. Be careful of any referral that departs from the ideal—no matter how tempting or strongly rationalized.

Referrals from friends and relatives, as long as they do not have any ongoing personal or professional contact with the therapist, rate highest after professional referrals. However, a referral by a friend or relative to a therapist who is in close contact with that person would be rated lower.

The lowest ratings are those of patient referrals and self-referrals based on hearsay comments and social contact with a potential therapist. During my many years of investigating the deep unconscious system's reaction to violations in the ideal-frame conditions, referrals from current patients of a psychotherapist have repeatedly generated some of the most vicious, selfish, self-serving imagery that I have seen—much of it laced with themes of betrayal, inconsistency, exposure, and more. We have already seen images of this kind in Herbie's shark dream.

There are other strong reasons that mitigate against referrals from patients. Very often, such referrals are made by patients for whom death anxiety and loss are major issues. This was true of Herbie. You'll recall that his incest dream was about his sister, who had died when Herbie was ten. (This was true of Viola as well; her mother had died when she was four.) In the deep unconscious system, a threesome will prevent the experience of being left alone—if one member dies, the other two can deny the loss, because they have each other. Since a patient referral is experienced by the deep unconscious system as a threesome—the other patient becomes part of the therapy—death anxieties are mollified, but in a maladaptive, uninsightful way.

Patient referrals also lessen unconsciously a patient's anxieties related to being alone with a therapist. Conversely, they can lessen a therapist's anxieties about being alone with a patient. Often this kind of situation creates unconsciously for both patients an illicit triad that repeats earlier disturbing threesomes. Again, insight is bypassed in favor of an enacted attempt at relief—an enactment that then must continue to be dramatized in the outside life of the patient. This is a high price to pay for a moment's risky respite.

Beverly, a woman in her twenties, was referred to Dr. Arnold by her close friend, Nancy, who was in therapy with him at the time. On the night before Beverly's first session, Nancy told her a dream that she had had about sexual exploitation. When Beverly saw Dr. Arnold the following morning, she told him about Nancy's dream. Dr. Arnold became completely confused, and even had some difficulty in keeping track of who he was talking to about what.

Apart from the confusion and lack of boundaries produced consciously by this kind of departure from the ideal ground rules, in the deep unconscious system a referral of this kind is always viewed as a kind of sexual exploitation. Nancy's dream reflected her perception of Dr. Arnold in light of his taking on her friend as a patient.

Let me give you another example of this kind of imagery. A young man I know named Philip recommended his therapist, Dr. Spinelli, to Ron, the brother of the woman he was dating. Dr. Spinelli accepted Ron as a patient and scheduled him for Tuesday evenings. Philip was seeing Dr. Spinelli on Wednesday mornings. The first week that Dr. Spinelli was seeing both Philip and Ron, Philip had a dream: He is in a hotel room, and a middle-aged cleaning woman comes to his open door. She asks if he'd like his room serviced. Philip impulsively says, "No, but if you provide sexual service, why don't you come back after work?" To his surprise, the woman says yes—she'll be back in an hour. Just after she leaves, another middle-aged cleaning woman comes to the door and asks him the same question. He again responds with a sexual proposition. This woman also says yes—in fact, she's getting off work right now; why doesn't he come to her place in about ten minutes? After she leaves, Philip thinks: What am I doing? I've managed to schedule two liaisons back-to-back, and if someone else came to the door, I'd probably ask her, too. Am I crazy or what?

There are many levels of meaning in this dream. For the moment, however, we are interested in the imagery as a response to a deviant referral. The images very clearly involve the personalization of a professional service, lack of discrimination, and scheduling meetings back-to-back with two people who know each other. We can easily decode these images as references to Dr. Spinelli's having scheduled Ron for therapy on the night before Philip's own weekly appointment. The dream suggests that the therapist's acceptance of Ron has led to unconscious questions involving Dr. Spinelli's commitment and attitude toward Philip. Unconsciously, Philip has experienced Dr. Spinelli's behavior in sexually exploitative terms.

Notice that in the dream, it is Philip who has scheduled these meetings and violated the boundaries of a professional service relationship. And it is Philip who is guilty of a form of sexual exploitation. In one respect, Philip unconsciously felt guilty about having referred Ron to his own therapist and broken the secure frame; but it is also true that Philip identified with Dr. Spinelli's behavior in this regard. Philip was seeing his current girlfriend while trying to decide whether to separate from his wife. (Note the dream's reference to his seeing one woman in his own room and the other at her place.) Both women in fact were middle-aged, and each was aware of the existence of the other in his life. Philip had gone into therapy to resolve his feelings of guilt and indecision with respect to this situation.

So again we have a situation where a frame break became the occasion of collusion between conscious and deep unconscious memory. Unconsciously, Philip had introduced Ron into the therapeutic relationship in order to duplicate the very situation he was consciously attempting to resolve. Instead of coming to terms with the deep unconscious sources of his emotional problems, he felt unconsciously justified in the way he was handling his marital and social life, because his therapist's behavior served to sanction it.

As I have said, high ratings on a referral source cannot guarantee a sound therapeutic experience; it simply provides a foundation on which an experience of that kind can be built. On the other hand, low ratings on this item tend to predict further ratings of like kind, leaving a patient with nothing but the hope of some kind of uninsightful cure.

With all that said, you may still be wondering why it wouldn't be an advantage to have a firsthand account of a therapist's work from a friend or relative who had already been in therapy with that person. Wouldn't it make sense to see a therapist who came highly recommended both personally and professionally?

My answer to this is yes, all of these questions make sense; they are logical, practical, and direct—as befits the efforts of the conscious system. However, we are dealing here with the ratings brought to bear by the deep unconscious system, whose priority is a secure-frame therapy.

A secure-frame therapy assures the patient, among other things, that the therapist will not react personally to what the patient is saying or feeling. If the patient reveals a seductive fantasy, the therapist must be trusted not to respond behaviorally—either by acquiescence or repudiation. If the boundaries of the relationship between the patient and therapist are blurred or damaged, the patient may well feel endangered even at a conscious level of experience. The ground rules commit the therapist to treat whatever the patient says and feels not as an incitement to direct response, but as material for analysis, synthesis, and insight.

In other words, the ground rules establish the distinction between a social and professional relationship with your therapist—a vital difference that establishes the therapist as a *therapist* from whom a patient can unambiguously expect a therapeutic rather than social response.

The ground rules also create a context for what is being said and felt. It can be shown that the setting and the overall relationship with the person to whom we are speaking give as much shape to the meanings we are conveying as do the separate words and sentences they compose. For example, suppose someone were to say, "Get in line, buddy!" The impact of these words would be quite different if they were spoken by a prison guard to a prisoner, an usher to a movie patron, or a woman to a man making an untoward sexual advance. There is no single meaning to most sets of words. The specific meaning is given by the context.

When the conscious system assesses a therapist, its focus is usually on the therapist's attitude and on what he or she has to say. But all the while this is happening, the deep unconscious system is assessing these factors in its own way, along with the context. In particular, the deep unconscious system is sensitive to the correlation of the therapist's words with his or her behaviors. A therapist who does not maintain a consistent therapeutic frame has no basis on which to help a patient with frame-related issues in his or her life. The deep unconscious system registers the therapist's behavior as a contradiction of his or her words. "Don't do as I do, do as I say" has no meaning for the deep unconscious system. The patient will in all likelihood do as the therapist does, for good or ill.

As I have pointed out, a contradiction that occurs between a therapist's words and his or her behaviors is registered by the deep unconscious system selectively—in terms of memories, experiences, fantasies, and problems involving similar contradictions in the patient's extratherapeutic life. This is why a frame break always involves unresolved emotional difficulties in the patient, which are reflected in the kinds of imagery used to convey the perceptions registered. Living one's life is fundamentally about the interface between one's own individual endowment and the outer context in which one is operating. The therapeutic relationship becomes a microcosm of that psychic battleground.

Underlying this discussion is, of course, the issue of just how competent is the psychotherapist you have chosen to see. Given the literally dozens of avenues to becoming a psychotherapist and the seemingly endless debates as to the best method of cure, this is a complex problem—one to which I will return throughout this book.

Here I offer a simple, if disquieting, answer: There is no means by which you can assuredly assess the competence of your psychotherapist, short of seeing him or her for a while, and using the ratings discussed in this book. All you can do initially is to contact a referral source who will presumably recommend someone with basically sound training in doing psychotherapy. If you are contacting a professional in the mental health field or an organization, your referral source will recommend someone with a professional degree, perhaps some additional specialized psychotherapy training, and a strong sense of concern and responsibility as a therapist.

You might well ask your referral source briefly about the qualifications of the therapist recommended. But it is important not to ask too much—because what you are told is only minimally helpful, if at all, and it is too easy to compromise the anonymity of your therapist, which is part of the therapeutic frame.

For these reasons, there is little value in looking up the credentials of your potential therapist. They can tell you only that he or she has a "proper" degree, and beyond that, they may compromise the anonymity your deep unconscious system advocates. Knowing your therapist's date and place of birth, the books or papers he or she has written—and whatever else—does not meaningfully inform you as a potential patient. There is no substitute for learning firsthand how your therapist works.

We come back again to the difference between simple but deceptive conscious-system logic and deep unconscious wisdom. Consciously, you feel entitled to know more, not realizing that the knowledge you seek is unwittingly designed to undermine your therapy. Adhering to deep unconscious preferences is sometimes bewildering and difficult, but it serves you very well in the long run.

Let's look at one more example of a low-rated referral source. Mr. Hardin, who worked in the billing department of a large corporation, made plans to see a therapist through his Employee Assistance Program (EAP). The program guaranteed him a six-session psychotherapy with a therapist selected by the program; this person would provide a brief progress report on the therapy. Dr. Gordon, a female psychologist, was a therapist with whom the program had established a standing referral relationship.

Mr. Hardin called Dr. Gordon and arranged a consultation session. On the morning of the consultation, he called to cancel because he was ill. When the session was rescheduled, illness again interfered with his appearing for the hour. Finally, given a third appointment, he appeared.

In the session, he began by saying that part of his problem was his inability to trust anyone. There were times when he was convinced that people were talking behind his back. It made him very anxious.

"At work," he said, "people will do anything for a buck—even cheat and lie. Recently, my section head hired his own nephew but didn't tell the company who the new man was. When the bosses found out, they fired the nephew and demoted the section head. But that's what I mean—there's no integrity left in this world.''

We are focusing narrowly on what this excerpt can tell us about the patient's response to the frame of therapy. We first identify the stimulus for the patient's material in his relationship and inter-action with the therapist. Then we identify *themes* in the patient's material relevant to this stimulus. In this way, we can decode the material to reveal the patient's disguised perceptions of the ther-apist's interventions—broadly defined. It is this kind of decoding that any potential patient should carry out as often as possible with his or her dreams or invented stories in light of the triggers created each step along the way in selecting a psychotherapist.

In the situation with Mr. Hardin, the stimulus—the intervention that triggered his response—involved the conditions of his referral: being sent by someone in the EAP to a preselected therapist, who would in turn report back to Mr. Hardin's employer. This may not sound like much of an infringement on the patient's confidentiality and privacy; however, in the deep unconscious system, *how much* plays only a small role, while *has it happened at all* is critical—that is, there is no concept of the frame being just a little bit broken. Broken is broken, and the patient's encoded messages will indicate a view of the therapist in terms of that alteration in the ideal ground rules. True, a serious frame break will engender a more serious unconscious reaction; but any alteration in an ideal ground rule will have a great impact on the patient's view of the therapist and on the nature of the possible cure.

The fact that Mr. Hardin fell ill and canceled his first two ap-pointments is not arbitrary. It suggests that there was something wrong with the holding qualities of the therapeutic situation that he accepted for himself. Take a closer look at the nature of the referral situation. My list of ground rules required by the deep unconscious system indicates that the ideal frame involves a one-to-one relationship with the therapist. In Mr. Hardin's situation, the therapist was referred by an employee in the EAP. The ideal frame also involves privacy and total confidentiality. In Mr. Hardin's situation, the therapist was required to release information to the patient's employer.

Using these alterations of the ideal conditions of therapy as our organizer, it is easy to decode the themes in Mr. Hardin's material. Where Mr. Hardin was talking about work, beneath the surface he was talking about the psychotherapy. Where Mr. Hardin was talking about the section head, beneath the surface he was talking about the psychotherapist.

What was Mr. Hardin saying? He began by complaining about people talking behind his back; he said that he couldn't trust anyone; people will do anything for money. The section head had unfairly preselected someone for a job. The situation lacked integrity and warranted correction.

Consciously, Mr. Hardin was feeling relieved that there was someone he could talk to. He had no concern about the report the therapist was obliged to write. Nor was he disturbed to learn from the therapist that she and the EAP employee had been talking about him. After all, Mr. Hardin claimed, it's not every day that you can get free therapy.

This, then, was Mr. Hardin's conscious perception of the situation with Dr. Gordon. But his deep unconscious perceptions were dramatically different. On that level, as his encoded material makes clear, he experienced Dr. Gordon as someone not to be trusted, without integrity, preselected in a dishonest way.

This condemnation may seem extreme. After all, you might argue, Mr. Hardin was entitled to this referral; where is the harm in an essentially nominal report? People work hard for their money, the cost of living is high, so why should he pay for brief psychotherapy when he can get it for free through his EAP? Is psychotherapy only for the rich? So what if the deep unconscious system has a different point of view? Maybe that view is part of his problem and he should solve it.

The rejoinder to this argument lies in the substance of this book. There are times when I think of psychotherapy as the eleventh plague. I don't know why the deep unconscious system works the way it does. I know what I know from years of clinical experience and of decoding unconscious messages. And it is more than clear that the deep unconscious memory system will use any kind of deviant-frame arrangement to collude with the conscious system in avoiding self-awareness and in creating self-defeating reenactments of past problems. Part of Mr. Hardin's fundamental problem *was* in fact that he couldn't trust people and suspected everyone of dishonesty. How would Dr. Gordon help him to winnow fact from fantasy when she herself was unconsciously experienced as untrustworthy?

Apart from Mr. Hardin's unconscious communication, we have the fact of his illness and inability to keep the first two appointments he made. This is also a frame issue. You may not want to understand these episodes of illness as related to the conditions of therapy, but my own studies have convinced me beyond a shadow of a doubt that we pay a price for every frame break that we accept. We get physically ill, we file for a questionable divorce, we manage to get ourselves fired. We simply don't realize the direct line between the deviant condition of a psychotherapy and various forms of self-destructive behavior.

What, then, does a sound referral look like and evoke? Mr. Manning was depressed and suffering from psychosomatic physical symptoms. He asked his internist for a referral and was given Dr. Shipley's name, address, and telephone number.

"Is he a good therapist?" Mr. Manning inquired.

"So far as I know, he is," replied the internist. "He's a fully trained psychiatrist and he's had some training at a psychotherapy training program in the city. He's the best I know of."

Mr. Manning let it go at that and decided to call Dr. Shipley the next day. That night he had a brief dream: He was with his Aunt Sally. She was putting a soothing ointment on a burn on his left arm.

The dream led Mr. Manning to recall an incident in his early teens when he was playing with firecrackers one July 4. One of the firecrackers had exploded in his hand as he tried to throw it. His hand had been burned, though not irrevocably. In severe pain, he was afraid to go to his parents for help because he didn't want to tell them what he had been doing. Instead, he had gone to his Aunt Sally, whom he knew to be understanding and worthy of trust. She had treated and bandaged his wound, even encouraged him later to tell his parents the truth of what had happened.

We are familiar now with the decoding process: We take the dream and Mr. Manning's associations and place them in the context of his referral to Dr. Shipley. The image is one of being damaged and needing help but being afraid to tell someone. The image also involves a trusted person to whom Mr. Manning turned—one who eventually soothed his wound and helped him to reveal the truth. These themes are highly positive and in striking contrast to those we saw with low-rated referrals. They speak for the strong sense of holding and trust that is inherent in a high-rated referral experience.

We can now see that before we pick up the telephone to call a psychotherapist, we have made a most important choice. We have learned of the existence of a particular therapist, thought over the situation, and decided to give it a try. We have made an evaluation.

Sometimes a potential patient will give very little thought to this fateful choice. But there is good reason to pause and reflect, and to rate the potential psychotherapist on these initial scales. And when the ratings are completed, the highs will need to be weighed against the lows in the context of possible alternatives.

In summary, there are two *Dangerous/Beware* groups of items in this first list that should sound a warning: *Not this one; find another therapist.* They are prior social contact with the therapist, and referral by one of his or her patients. In this kind of situation, the conscious system will say, "Go ahead, why not?" But the deep unconscious system says, "Never. This person cannot be your psychotherapist. He or she may be your lover, betrayer, or partner in incest, but not your therapist.''

Beyond these two danger situations, you should pay attention to whether you have personal knowledge of the therapist or prior professional contact with him or her. Be wary of public and impersonal selections, and of therapists to whom you are mandated without personal choice. Wherever possible, seek out a referral from another professional, even though this situation may not be ideal.

In the end, it comes down to this: A professional referral gives you a chance at something constructive, the best possible point of departure, but it offers no guarantees. What you really need to do is to look at your dreams the night after you have considered a particular therapist for your psychotherapy. Allow yourself to think about the images in the dream, and the themes that these images bring to mind. Then take a look at the conditions of the referral you are planning to accept. How do those themes relate to this referral? Are they negative and frightening? Or are they positive and encouraging?

You may believe that negative and frightening dream images mean only that you're frightened of starting therapy. But the deep unconscious mind doesn't work like that. It reflects the destructive implications of what it perceives, or it reflects the positive implications of what it perceives. If you're on the right track, your dream images will be hopeful and constructive.

Even though the referral comes from outside of yourself through a professional, the ultimate decision is yours and yours alone. When you make this decision based on the intelligence of your deep unconscious system, you'll be adopting a course that has made use of your most profound resources and gifts.

Table 1: The Referral

I know of this therapist because:

Sound Answers
- My local Medical Society/Mental Health Association/professional organization recommended him/her.
- My family doctor recommended him/her.
- He/she came to see me for a consultation when I was in the hospital.
- A friend who's a psychiatrist/psychologist/social worker/mental health professional recommended him/her.
- A coworker/social acquaintance/relative knows him/her professionally and recommended him/her.
- My employer/principal/lawyer recommended I see him/her.

Questionable Answers
- My former/present therapist recommended him/her.
- He/she is the therapist I was assigned to in a group practice/clinic.
- He/she is at the clinic where my health plan requires me to go.
- I picked him/her out of the phone book.
- I pass his/her office on my way to work.

Unsound Answers: Reconsider Your Choice of Therapist
- I saw his/her ad in a telephone book/on television/in the paper.
- He/she works in a different section of my office complex.
- His/her office is in my apartment building.

Dangerous Answers: Beware of This Therapist
- A coworker/social acquaintance/relative sees/used to see him/her and says he/she is good.
- I used to see him/her with my parents/children/spouse in family therapy and I liked him/her.

- My daughter/son goes to school with his/her daughter/son.
- I've heard him/her lecture and he/she sounds like a good therapist.
- He/she is my minister, so I know him.
- I've read his/her books/seen him/her on television/heard him/her on the radio.
- His wife/her husband is one of my friends.
- I met him/her at a party and he/she gave me his/her card.
- I took a course from him/her and he/she seemed really insightful.
- I used to date him/her/I'm currently dating him/her, so he/she must know me pretty well.
- He/she is one of my father's/mother's colleagues.
- He/she is a coworker and seems bright and helpful.
- He/she is a friend/used to be a friend of the family.

·6·

The First Contact

You don't get a second chance to make a first impression. That's what the commercials tell us, anyhow. Whether it's a job interview or a first date, we're advised to make that first contact count: dress for success, register enthusiasm, ask questions, avoid dandruff. Unfortunately, we tend to use pretty much the same standards to assess a first meeting with a psychotherapist: Is he or she congenial? Does he or she appreciate my situation? Is he or she asking helpful questions? Does he or she look like "a therapist"? On the surface, these seem like the right criteria for judgment. On the other hand, people very often consider psychotherapy because they are unhappy with their current pattern of choices and relationships. How can you be sure that your choice of a therapist isn't one more reflection of the very pattern you hope to change?

This apparent paradox has troubled a great many people. In answer to a woman who described her experiences with three successive abusive therapists, Ann Landers counseled, "If [your relationship with your therapist] feels icky, it probably is." The undeniable wisdom of that advice unfortunately suggests that the converse is true as well—"If it feels good, it probably is." But the fact is—as we have been discussing—that feeling good and being healthy are not necessarily synonymous. The conscious system often feels good when unconscious information is badly influencing behavior outside of awareness. It is instructive, however, that the "feeling icky" standard of judgment is the best the conscious system can offer in a moment of doubt.

By contrast, the deep unconscious system is registering impressions of a therapist long before the conscious system is contending with presentiments of "ickiness." In fact, the deep unconscious system is registering these impressions even before the first consultation. Perhaps this sounds impossible. It is true nevertheless. The deep unconscious system has no particular interest in the hail-fellow-well-met standards of the conscious system; it is taking in information as soon as we are aware of the therapist in question, and it is registering extensive impressions even on the basis of the initial telephone call. So when I talk about rating your "first contact" with a therapist, I mean exactly that: not the first session, not the first consultation, but the first *contact*.

In a pattern that is now familiar to us, prospective patients typically pay little conscious attention to just how this contact is made. As a result, that first contact usually leaves a person quite unprepared for the psychotherapist encountered week after week in the office. The deep unconscious system, however, by the end of the initial exchange, already knows a great deal and is seldom surprised by the relationship to follow. In fact, the decision we make about seeing a psychotherapist (or continuing to see him or her) is greatly influenced by the processing of the first contact carried on in the deep unconscious system.

It is important to understand that this processing is occurring on two levels. One part of your unconscious system sensitively processes the implications of virtually everything your therapist does and does not do in the first contact. But another part of that system, which contains the residuals of our most awful experiences and needs, incessantly presses for compromise with the conscious need not to know—thus sparing us the awareness of intolerable information. This part of the unconscious system exerts a silent power on our conscious thinking and behavior that far exceeds our conscious ability to analyze and reason. Sometimes it is even stronger than our own unconscious wisdom. Again, the result is a paradoxical and consciously rationalized search for a therapist more likely to hurt us than to help us. Many of the awful experiences we tolerate in therapy could not occur if this were not the case. Thus we need to become aware of the unconscious perceptions that are informing our decisions—and we can do that, initially, by listening to the unconscious wisdom of patients who have gone before us.

Quite often it is the referral source who suggests the form of the first contact. (Try Dr. So-and-so; here's the phone number.) Nonetheless, your choice of how to make the first contact says quite a bit about yourself and your own conscious and unconscious needs and inclinations—probably as much as your choice of which therapist to contact. For this reason, we will rate not only how the psychotherapist handles the first contact but also the nature of your own preferences. This will alert you to both questionable therapeutic practices and to self-endangering needs of your own.

When you begin to treat the first contact as an entity in its own right, you will see that it is a two-person exchange, and that it shares properties with other two-party conversations. If you were attempting to define the nature of the contact and its boundaries, you would ask perhaps six basic questions:

1. How and where was the contact made?
2. Who made the contact?
3. What transpired in the contact—comments, demeanor, manner of relating of both parties?
4. Were there any problems that arose for either party, and how were they handled?
5. What advice, instructions, and directions did the therapist offer?
6. How was the contact ended?

Unquestionably, the most common form taken by a first contact between a patient and therapist begins with a phone call from the former to the latter. Sometimes first contact is made directly, either in a social or professional setting, or, more indirectly, by mail. And sometimes the therapist will call the patient—for example, in a clinic where a patient is screened by an intake worker and then assigned to a particular treating person. From the point of view of the deep unconscious system, however, a telephone call from patient to therapist is the ideal form for a first contact to take. And since this is the normal course of events, we will initially examine in detail the various aspects of such a telephone call that are invariably rated unconsciously in the first contact situation. Following that, we will consider other types of contact—some inevitable and acceptable, some unacceptable.

I should preface my discussion by saying that, as a matter of principle, all patients tell two stories in their first hour with a psychotherapist: a surface or manifest (conscious) one, giving the nature and history of their emotional problems; and an encoded or disguised one, a portrayal of their unconscious experience of the therapist during the first contact. This portrayal includes unconscious perceptions of the therapist in light of the nature of the referral and/or the existence of any prior contact with him or her.

Let's take a look at an illustration of a positive portrayal:

Mrs. Lobel had decided to see a therapist because she was becoming obsessed with the cleanliness of her house beyond all rationality. She was referred to Dr. Egan—a male therapist—by her internist, who gave her the therapist's phone number and address. With some anxiety, she telephoned Dr. Egan one afternoon and was relieved to hear him answer the phone personally. "Hello," he said, "this is Dr. Egan speaking." Mrs. Lobel identified herself, said that she'd been referred by her internist, Dr. Black, and asked Dr. Egan if he could see her in consultation. As she spoke, it was clear that the therapist was listening and free to talk—there was no sign that he was with a patient or with anyone else. Dr. Egan responded by offering an hour early in the following week, at a time that was good for Mrs. Lobel. She therefore agreed to see him at that time and said no more, since she was familiar with the location of Dr. Egan's office. In response, the therapist confirmed the appointment, stated that he would see her then, and offered his good-bye. Mrs. Lobel said good-bye as well and hung up the telephone. Well, she thought, Dr. Egan certainly gets right to the point.

The first contact ideally should be by telephone, should be with the therapist in his or her office, should be brief and professional, and should be without evidence of the presence of others. The therapist should make no extraneous comments other than those needed to define the nature of the referral source, set up an agreeable time for the first appointment, inquire whether any emergency issue exists, and offer directions to his or her office. Your conscious system may well regard this sort of contact as perfunctory at best, and cold at worst. But it is the deep unconscious system that is at issue here, and it registers this kind of contact as an expression of deep concern and warmth.

Although Mrs. Lobel thought no more during the week about the therapist's manner on the phone, her deep unconscious system had registered every nuance of the contact. When the day came for her consultation, Mrs. Lobel spent the opening minutes outlining the problems that had led her to contact Dr. Egan. She was trying to pinpoint what seemed to her the beginning of her obsession with cleanliness, and by way of explanation, recalled her first apartment away from home. This memory brought to mind the friend with whom she had shared that apartment immediately after graduating from college. Mrs. Lobel spoke of this friend with enthusiasm and animation; this was a woman, she said, on whom she could rely. She was always there when you needed her, gave more than she asked for, and never wasted words. In this story are the positive unconscious perceptions that Mrs. Lobel had registered from the manner in which Dr. Egan handled the first telephone call. This kind of deep unconscious experience provides a secure hold and foundation for the psychotherapy that is to unfold.

From this illustration, we can again define the ideal first telephone contact as one in which the patient calls the therapist. The ideal therapist will answer the phone in a manner that indicates his freedom to talk under conditions of total confidentiality. Of course, if a therapist is with a patient when the phone rings, a telephone answering machine may intercept the call. Under these circumstances, the therapist's message should be brief and professional, indicating only that he or she is not available to answer the telephone at the moment, and will return the call as soon as possible if the caller will leave his or her name, telephone number, and a brief message. Many therapists employ a professional answering service, in which case the person receiving the call should simply take the caller's name, number, and a brief message that indicates availability for the therapist's return call.

It is important to realize that in the deep unconscious system, the manner in which the answering-service operator handles your call will be experienced as an intervention *from the therapist*. Of course, you are consciously aware that your prospective therapist and an answering-service employee are two different people; but in the deep unconscious system the two are fused. Thus the behavior of an individual that barely impinges on one's conscious awareness can have an unconscious influence on the course of your therapy. Ideally, the person taking your message will say nothing more than to indicate when the therapist will be available to return your call (if this is known) or that the message will be given to the therapist as soon as possible. Comments as to the therapist's whereabouts or details about any aspect of the therapist's personal or professional life—or anything else that is extraneous to essential information—are departures from the ideal. In the deep unconscious system, they are experienced as self-revelations by the therapist and as modifications in the ideal framework or conditions of the therapy.

All departures from the ideal frame that take place in the first contact with the therapist or his or her surrogates will have a strong effect on both yourself as patient and on the course of the therapy. Nothing about psychotherapy can be taken too lightly.

In general, the use of an answering machine by a psychotherapist receives the highest possible rating, because it promises total privacy and confidentiality between patient and therapist. Since the taped message can be brief and to the point, extraneous comments and self-revelations are largely avoided. Answering-service personnel who are inclined to say too much or to make an error in the transmission of a message can unnecessarily complicate the first consultation. The patient will spend a great deal of time communicating unconscious perceptions of the therapist in terms of the lapses involved, and will have the sense of an insecure therapeutic hold.

When the therapist has been reached by phone—has answered the phone or returned the call (ideally, within a few hours from the time you left your message)—he or she should make some formal identification: for example, "Hello, this is Dr. Arbus." If the therapist does not have a doctorate or a medical degree, the greeting should involve the person's last name only: "Hello, this is Mr. Arbus." The use of first and last names is acceptable but not preferable. A therapist who answers the telephone using only his or her first name—"Hi, Al here"—would be rated as using a questionable approach, whose deep unconscious effects should not be underestimated. A person who maintains boundaries that are less than professional on the phone will very likely maintain relaxed boundaries in the therapy itself—engaging in mild forms of physical contact, spending the hour talking about himself or herself, reacting personally to what you are communicating as a patient, and so forth. An event of seemingly minor import that occurs during the first contact is always part of a greater whole whose adumbration the deep unconscious system fully appreciates. Even the therapist who answers with a simple hello is communicating an impersonal and somewhat nonprofessional standard of operation, given the fact that he or she is a psychotherapist receiving a call in his or her professional office.

You have dialed your prospective therapist's professional office, and been greeted by him or her. It is now your turn to speak. Ideally, you should immediately identify yourself, mention your wish for a consultation, and indicate the source of your referral.

(If you fail to mention how you obtained your therapist's name, he or she should ask that question early on.) Short of an emergency or urgent need, this is all that need be done. However, if there are strong constraints on when you can see the therapist, it is also advisable to indicate those limited times during which you can be seen.

In response, the ideal psychotherapist should simply indicate a willingness to see you and propose a day and time for the consultation. The day proposed should not be more than a week after the day on which the telephone discussion is taking place, and preferably it should be within two or three days of that call. If the appointment offered is one that you cannot make, the therapist should offer another alternative (this is to be preferred to the offer of several possibilities, a practice that is nonetheless acceptable). Once a suitable time has been proposed, you should agree to it and ascertain the address of the therapist's office and/or obtain directions. Beyond that, there is nothing for you to add.

If plans for the consultation have been made in a direct and proficient manner, the therapist will recognize that no emergency exists and that you can handle your problems until you see him or her. On the other hand, if you have been indicating a notable state of distress, depression, or any other type of acute disturbance, the therapist will generally inquire as to whether you can manage things until the hour appointed for the consultation. If you indicate that you think you can do so, the therapist may indicate that he or she will be available by telephone if the situation should deteriorate.

If you have said nothing about the matter, the therapist should inquire as to whether you know how to reach his or her office. If you do not, simple directions should be given on the telephone (nothing, for example, should be sent to you in the mail). With the day, time, and place established for the first consultation, the therapist should then end the conversation with either a simple good-bye, or with a final comment that he or she will see you at that time. Your own response should be comparable.

◆　◆　◆

Having identified the ideal initial contact, we should now consider the most common variations on or departures from this ideal.

1. How and where the first contact is made

By phone: If a therapist does not immediately answer your initial call, you will, as a rule, leave a message—either on a tape or with an answering service. If there is no answer at all—if the phone keeps ringing without response—you might first allow for human error: an answering service too busy to pick up, a lapse in which the therapist forgot to turn on his or her answering machine, a line problem, etc. However, if it becomes clear that the therapist lacks twenty-four-hour coverage, a questionable rating must be given because of the lack of availability implied in this situation.

Having left a message, you will want to rate the speed of the therapist's response. The sooner the therapist calls back, the better. A return call delayed beyond the day of your own call points to more questionable ratings—provided, of course, that you have remained available to receive the call or have an answering machine of your own. (It is preferable that you be there for a return call. It may be inconvenient, but a recorded message from the therapist has some potential for third-party involvement to therapy, which would frustrate your deep unconscious needs for total privacy and confidentiality.)

If you have called a therapist in the evening, it is acceptable for a return call to be made the following morning. However, a daytime call should be returned within the same day. A return call that is delayed more than twenty-four hours must obtain a doubtful rating, and if the call is postponed more than a day and a half, you should consider a *Dangerous/Beware* rating, unless there is a suitable explanation. An undue delay by a therapist in responding to a call for a consultation suggests that he or she is too busy or preoccupied with other patients and matters. Such a therapist is likely to be insensitive to the delicacy and possible seriousness of the situation and to the anxieties inherent in calling for a first appointment. Typically, a delayed telephone response indicates a tendency to other kinds of low-rated comments and behaviors if the consultation and psychotherapy are pursued.

At times, a therapist will answer the telephone while in session with another patient. If this happens when you call for an appointment, you should question the therapist's regard for his or her patients. The rating becomes even more doubtful if the therapist proceeds to discuss an appointment with you under these circumstances. The misuse of the other patient, your involvement with a third party to your own therapy, and potential violations of total confidentiality—all are incisively perceived by your deep unconscious system, even though you may hardly question the situation consciously.

On occasion, the therapist will have an extension of his or her office phone at home or in a second office. As long as the telephone is answered in a manner that is comparable to the way in which this would be done in the privacy of the therapist's consultation room—i.e., you have no way of knowing that the situation is otherwise—this is an acceptable practice. However, if you are directed by the therapist's answering service or answering machine message to call the therapist at some other location, such as another office or outside work setting, this directive should be given a *Questionable* rating.

The rating is even more doubtful if the second setting is more personal than private, such as the therapist's home or the occasion of a social visit. Practices of this sort violate the necessary relative anonymity of the therapist, in that they provide you with superfluous information about his or her professional and/or personal life; they also extend the boundaries of the therapeutic setting beyond the consultation room in ways that have detrimental consequences. Ideally, psychotherapy should be confined to the therapist's office; any other arrangement is experienced as lack of containment, as confusing and disorienting, and often as seductive or elusive—much of this depending on the nature of the extension of the frame. The existence and implications of deviations of this kind are tellingly perceived by the deep unconscious system.

In person: There are, of course, some circumstances under which a person-to-person initial meeting is not uncommon. Certain types of walk-in clinics encourage clients to come directly to the clinic rather than make an appointment by telephone. In situations of acute emergency—for example, severe depression, suicidal thinking, or overwhelming paranoid ideas—the patient or a concerned relative or third party may well opt for a visit to a psychiatric emergency room where the first contact is direct. A similar situation exists for psychiatric/psychological consultations with patients hospitalized for medical or surgical reasons. Most often, the attending physician will request a consultation for the patient, and the consultant will make his or her first appearance in the hospital, at the patient's bedside. (Even so, the actual consultation is best conducted in an office rather than at bedside—if this is at all possible.) A therapist who allows direct first contact with a patient under any of these unusual but necessary conditions can be rated as quite acceptable.

However, under conditions short of an emergency, a private consultation should not be arranged through a visit to the therapist's office. The therapist who accepts a surprise visit of this kind and makes an appointment with a patient rather than suggesting that the individual call for such appointment must receive a doubtful rating. As far as the deep unconscious system is concerned, such a therapist allows intruders into the treatment space, has failed to maintain the necessary interpersonal boundaries between therapist and client, and has, in this sense, overgratified the patient. Only a dire emergency might suitably lead a therapist to hold a consultation at that very moment. And even this kind of conscious and direct justification will have a measure of detrimental unconscious ramifications that will influence the patient and the therapy.

To illustrate: Mr. March began to experience intense suicidal impulses after the death of his wife. One afternoon, as he left his dentist's office, Mr. March became frightened that he might lose control when he got home. To his great relief, he noticed that a psychiatrist, Dr. Gray, had an office on the same corridor. He entered Dr. Gray's waiting room and sat there alone until another patient left. He then knocked on the door to Dr. Gray's consultation room. When Dr. Gray, who turned out to be a man, answered the door, Mr. March explained why he was there. Dr. Gray said that he had about a half hour available and suggested that they go into his consultation room and talk. Mr. March was consciously relieved and grateful.

In light of what we know about unconscious communication, we would expect that the stories Mr. March told this therapist would reflect his unconscious perceptions of Dr. Gray's decision to see him immediately. One of these stories involved an incident he had seen on the television that morning. A recent hurricane had caused flooding in another part of the country, and several members of the National Guard were singled out for their heroic efforts to rescue flood victims. However, in one instance of apparently marginal danger, a farmer was forced to evacuate his farm, leaving behind his many animals. Although his removal seemed a wise decision in the long run, most of his animals had died, and the farmer felt a great deal of resentment toward the rescue team.

Encoded in this story is Mr. March's unconscious perception of Dr. Gray's decision to see him in emergency consultation. Unconsciously, Mr. March believed that the consultation was only marginally necessary (in fact, Mr. March realized soon after the exchange that he was not as close to suicide as he had imagined). And even though it was clear that the consultation was justified, he felt resentful of the concomitant damage.

Consciously, of course, this emergency consultation was quite justified. However, the deep unconscious system sees both sides of the picture. Unconsciously, Mr. March experienced Dr. Gray's decision as constructive, but appreciated its detrimental aspects as well. The decision, among other things, implied that Dr. Gray would be available at Mr. March's beck and call; it also implied that Dr. Gray did not believe Mr. March capable of managing his impulses. These unconscious perceptions will have effects on Mr. March's experience of himself and any therapy pursued with Dr. Gray. Although such unconscious perceptions can be explored and resolved to some degree, they usually exert a silent influence that goes unnoticed.

That said, it is still true that a therapist who takes suicidal impulses seriously and responds quickly should be rated far higher than a therapist who puts the patient off. I am simply making the point that we often fail to recognize consciously the secondary, but quite definite, detrimental consequences to an intervention by a therapist that is, at its heart, clearly helpful. In rating Dr. Gray's decision acceptable—and clearly preferable to a refusal to see Mr. March—we must be mindful that there will be some negative aftereffects.

Similar principles apply to walk-in clinics where the practice of seeing the patient immediately and directly is acceptable, whatever the unconscious ramifications. Unfortunately, in many of these clinics, the first contact is often made with an intake worker, who may range from clinic secretary to trained mental health professional. An assessment is made and the patient is then assigned to a second therapist for ongoing psychotherapy. Despite their common use in clinics, such practices must be rated as questionable, since the transfer from one individual or therapist to another is always traumatic. Once again, necessity may dictate such a course, and the consequences may be explored once regular therapy is established. We may hope that someday clinics will find the means of enabling a single therapist to see a particular patient so that this complication can be avoided.

In situations of this kind, the first contact with the treating therapist is often directed by the consultant. He or she may introduce the patient to the regular therapist, or may have the therapist telephone the patient for an appointment. The best practice under these circumstances is to have the patient telephone the therapist as a way of initiating the regular treatment.

In considering direct first contact between patient and therapist, we must give a *Dangerous/Beware* rating to the therapist who meets a patient in a social situation and makes the first appointment at that time. As we saw in chapter 5, prior social contact between patient and therapist is a strong indication that the patient should find another therapist. So, too, with arranging for a consultation through any other type of chance or planned meeting with a prospective therapist—e.g., contact made at some kind of lecture or meeting, through an encounter on the street or in a store, and the like. All such practices greatly blur the boundaries between patient and therapist, erase the vital distinction between a social and professional relationship, give an indefinite aura to the physical/psychological therapeutic setting, and considerably modify other basic dimensions of the therapeutic experience. They speak against cure through insight and tend to favor relief through action and inappropriate ways of relating.

Mr. Larkin first met his therapist, Dr. Bessemer, at a lecture given by the latter on mid-life crisis. Impressed with the therapist's ease as a speaker, Mr. Larkin asked him, after the presentation, if he saw patients in his office. Dr. Bessemer said that he did, and suggested that Mr. Larkin call him for an appointment. Mr. Larkin called and they arranged for a consultation.

In his consultation hour, Mr. Larkin said that he'd had a dream. A weird-looking hobo was lying naked in a boxcar. He then thought about a friend of his—a department-store salesman who made a habit of trying to seduce his female customers. It was just a macho game for him, Mr. Larkin said, but the women involved were ultimately humiliated, because they had been led to believe that he was genuinely interested in a long-term relationship. "It's strange, though," Mr. Larkin went on, "it's strange that anyone would believe a man had serious intentions picking up women in a department store. I don't know; I guess lots of people do it, but it's pretty crass. My father was like that—he had all sorts of affairs; I don't know why my mother put up with it. He was a detective; you'd think he'd have had some experience with people's messy affairs. People are strange."

Strange, indeed—especially when it comes to meeting and choosing a therapist. Mr. Larkin had selected a therapist who was the unconscious equivalent of his father and promiscuous friend, then spent the first consultation unknowingly protesting his own choice. In other words, at the very moment the conscious mind selected a therapist from the lecture platform, the deep unconscious mind condemned the practice as corrupt. You might ask: Why did Mr. Larkin become involved in this kind of therapeutic relationship? The unhappy answer is that he prefers unconsciously to prove that all men are like his father—corrupt—rather than struggle with the painful truths evoked by awareness of his own corruption.

2. Who makes the first contact?

In considering this dimension, we must not only rate the therapist but also consider your needs and behaviors as the patient. As long as you have the capacity to dial the therapist's telephone number and to arrange a consultation, it is you, the seeking patient, who should make the first contact with the therapist. Even justifiable exceptions can lend a questionable cast to the therapy. Such exceptions are: a child who is too young to call a therapist personally; a person who is physically or mentally incapacitated; and those who are suffering acutely and extremely and yet adamantly refuse to contact a psychotherapist—for example, people who are suicidal or homicidal, in the midst of a toxic drug reaction, or so severely psychotic that they are paranoid, withdrawn, or otherwise divorced from reality.

In these situations, it is a matter of necessity to engage in a *Questionable* practice—there is no other choice. The constructive side of such a step will register both consciously and in the deep unconscious system, but the latter will also be concerned with detrimental side effects. Although we cannot deceive the deep unconscious system, we can expect it to maintain a perspective, so that what it experiences as manipulation, loss of autonomy, and the contamination of therapy with a third party will be viewed in light of the compelling need. Departures of this kind from the ideal frame may also be "detoxified"—analyzed and resolved through proper therapeutic work that interprets their unconscious meanings.

Not infrequently, the person making the referral to the psycho-therapist will also insist on making the first contact for the patient. Well-meaning physicians, other therapists, and, especially, con-sultants to employee assistance programs are often so inclined. Prospective patients who nonetheless insist on making their own arrangements have sound and healthy inclinations in this regard. The same applies to the psychotherapist who balks at making the appointment with the referring party, and who insists either that the patient be put on the telephone then and there or, better yet, that the patient make the initial call when his or her time permits. The therapist who makes the appointment with the referral source, as well as the therapist who will do so with a parent for a child, a spouse for his or her mate, or with anyone other than the patient in nonemergency situations, obtains an *Unsound/Reconsider Your Choice*–to–*Dangerous/Beware* rating from the deep unconscious sys-tem, depending on just how inappropriate and intrusive the third party to therapy happens to be. Ideally, psychotherapy is a one-to-one private experience without the intrusion of others in any conceivable way.

To illustrate the reaction of the deep unconscious system to a therapist who makes an appointment with a third party, consider this vignette. Mr. Cooper is a young homosexual man in his early twenties whose mother called to arrange a consultation with Dr. Silas, a therapist who had treated him some years earlier. Her explanation for calling on her son's behalf was that Mr. Cooper was currently living out of town and in the process of moving back (a flimsy rationalization at best, since Mr. Cooper could have called the therapist long distance). Dr. Silas suggested to Mrs. Cooper that her son call him directly (thereby earning a *Sound* rating). The mother passed this suggestion on to her son the next time she called him, but Mr. Cooper saw a direct call as unnec-essary. He asked his mother to call Dr. Silas back and to make an appointment for any day the following week, since he planned to be back in town by then.

Mrs. Cooper did as her son asked, and this time Dr. Silas traded his *Sound* rating for a *Questionable* one by allowing Mrs. Cooper to make an appointment for her son.

As we know, a patient's stories in the consultation hour will reflect his or her deep unconscious perceptions of the therapist's behavior in the first contact. This is what Mr. Cooper spoke about in the beginning of the consultation, which did indeed take place the following week. The patient said that he'd done a favor for a friend—he'd picked up the friend's dog on a farm near his parents' house. He then spoke about seeing an uncle, and about telling this uncle how much he wanted to get away from his mother. His mother often complained bitterly that her son spent too little time with her, and that his friend was more important to him than she was. When she was angry with him, she tended to sulk and not speak to him directly, using his aunt as a go-between. His father, on the other hand, always treated him like a hopeless case. Mr. Cooper then said that a friend had recently set him up with a man who wanted to spend the night with him; but once involved, the patient found the intimacy frightening, and he wound up pulling away from the relationship. Now he felt that his friend and the man in question were talking behind his back and spreading rumors and lies about him.

There is a great deal of information in this material. For present purposes, however, I will concentrate on decoding it in light of the therapist's decision to let Mrs. Cooper make the appointment for her son. Each of the themes in this narrative encodes an unconscious perception of the implications of this particular departure from the ideal conditions of therapy.

In sequence: The patient is saying that, unconsciously, his mother's arrangement with the therapist has made him feel like a pet that has been picked up by a third party and delivered as a favor to someone else. He then unconsciously advises his therapist to get away from his mother, adding that by making the appointment as he did, the therapist saw his mother as more important than the patient. In fact, just as his mother has done with her sister (Mr. Cooper's aunt), the therapist has used the mother as an unnecessary go-between between himself and the patient. Unconsciously, the patient sees this decision as a reflection of the therapist's view of him as a hopeless case. By allowing the mother to arrange the hour, the therapist has accomplished something equivalent to arranging a homosexual liaison; further, the patient perceives the therapist as frightened by the intimacy of the one-to-one relationship with the patient alone—so much so that he needed the mother's presence for self-protection. These images culminate in the patient's sense of mistrust and his feeling of being deceived—a type of iatrogenic (therapist-caused) paranoia that is not uncommon in patients when the therapist alters the ground rules and boundaries of the therapeutic relationship.

These are powerful and extensive perceptions and readings of what seems, to the conscious system of many individuals, to be a minor detail. The scope and incisiveness of these images should caution us once again that there is no such element in psychotherapy as a minor detail. On the deepest level, we experience the world with remarkable sensitivity, in ways that unknowingly, but greatly, influence our feelings and actions. The values and sensitivities of the deep unconscious system are such that the least nuance can have extremely powerful effects. It is our respect for these consequences that informs the ratings of psychotherapists presented in this book.

We have established, then, that the ideal person to establish the first contact with a therapist is the patient himself or herself. It should be apparent from this that the other side of the coin is also true: The ideal person to establish the first contact with a patient is the therapist himself or herself. The deep unconscious system is quite clear on this matter. This means that *Questionable*–to–*Dangerous/Beware* ratings are made when a therapist permits a third party to make arrangements on his or her behalf—whether the third party is an answering-service employee, a secretary, a family member, an associate, a friend, whoever. The presence of these parties speaks for a lack of privacy and total confidentiality in the psychotherapy, circumstances that often evoke a wide range of negative images, including variations on the iatrogenic paranoia we saw in Mr. Cooper—reflected in stories of spies, intruders, unwanted company, inept people who can't function for themselves, and so on.

This ideal applies to clinic situations as well as to private practice, despite the fact that in many clinic settings there is no alternative. Very often, a secretary or another therapist will make an appointment with the patient to see a treatment therapist. The fact that there is no alternative makes a difference only in the degree of the disturbance. Nature is nature, and unconscious perception is unconscious perception. The intrusiveness of the procedure will register outside of awareness and have its effects. On the other hand, as we have seen already with other necessary departures from the ideal, in the clinic situation for example, the deep unconscious system will recognize the lack of an alternative and register a lesser degree of disturbance. In private practice, this is never the case. No matter how strongly a therapist rationalizes the practice, allowing someone else to make his or her appointments is a deviation that the deep unconscious system recognizes as unnecessary when the ideal is feasible. Thus, whenever possible, a therapist should make his or her own appointments, as well as his or her own cancellation of hours when need be. The deep unconscious system will have it no other way.

Mr. Fogel was in therapy in a clinic with Ms. Clarkson, a social worker. On one occasion, Ms. Clarkson fell ill; she called the clinic secretary, gave her a list of the patients she was to see that day, and asked her to make the necessary cancellations. Mr. Fogel found the secretary's message on his home answering machine when he checked his calls that afternoon.

The patient began the next session by describing a luncheon appointment with his father earlier that week. I don't mind that he canceled out, Mr. Fogel said, anyone can get too busy. But he didn't have the decency to call me himself; he let his secretary make the call. It's as if he wanted nothing to do with me.

In the deep unconscious system, a therapist who introduces a third party into the therapy in order to cancel his or her hours is seen as rude, lacking in common courtesy, and as wanting to be rid of the patient. These perceptions, and the *Questionable* rating they imply, are reflected in Mr. Fogel's displaced story about his father. On the conscious level, he had actually felt relieved by not having a session. His deep unconscious response—typically—was far different.

3. The substance of the first contact

We have already seen that the ideal first contact is by telephone, handled by the therapist in a manner that is brief, professional, and to the point, with no extraneous comments unless an unusual issue arises. We will look now at some of the main variations and departures from this ideal.

Some departures are clearly due to the needs of the patient, whose ideal behavior would be to indicate as soon as possible that he or she wishes to have a consultation. It is best not to barrage the therapist with extensive details of symptoms and emotional problems. These are matters best worked over in the first session, rather than by phone. In fact, the therapist who goes along with dialogues of this kind deserves a *Questionable* rating, and if the participation is extensive, one might even take a view that there is notable danger. Any attempt by a therapist to offer an opinion, recommendation, interpretation, or any other type of explanation to a prospective patient during the first telephone contact must be seen as quite suspect. *Questionable*, too, are efforts by a therapist to probe the personal life of the caller, to ask irrelevant questions, and to make unneeded comments—this is especially true of personal opinions, self-revelations, recommendations, and even unneeded professional information. An example of the latter would be a therapist who reveals that he has two offices or doesn't have hours on a particular day. The first contact should be honed in on making arrangements for a consultation as soon as reasonably possible. All else is superfluous.

It is common, even for therapists, to misunderstand this ideal as a recommendation of cold and insensitive behavior. What is recommended, rather, is to maintain a sharp focus—and this can be accomplished with considerable warmth, concern, and tact. Patients who seek extensive responses from therapists during the first telephone contact consciously deceive themselves into believing that a therapist who is responsive to such needs is especially helpful. Indeed, the view of the deep unconscious system is far more discerning and accurate: Extended conversations during the first contact often reflect depressive problems in the therapist (a need to cling to the patient), a tendency to wander into tangential matters, a need to be inappropriately overgiving, and a desire to merge with or entrap the patient—to cite a few of the typical encoded perceptions that indicate *Unsound/Reconsider Your Choice*-to-*Dangerous/Beware* ratings from clients who have gone through such an experience.

Consider the first telephone contact between Mrs. Lacey and Dr. O'Hara. Mrs. Lacey told Dr. O'Hara that she had been referred to him by her parish priest, that she was having marital problems, and that she would like an appointment. Dr. O'Hara responded by asking Mrs. Lacey further about her marital problems. Mrs. Lacey's answers were appropriately brief, but as the therapist continued to pursue the issue, she warmed to her subject. She said, with disgust: "You know, it's just that my husband is always after me. If he'd just relax a little and keep his hands off me for a while, we'd be just fine."

The encoded image is clear: Dr. O'Hara's persistent questions are plainly experienced in the deep unconscious system as pursuit and physical molestation. Despite this unconscious view—or perhaps, in part, because of it (Mrs. Lacey had, after all, chosen to marry her husband)—the patient made an appointment and saw Dr. O'Hara in consultation. Her associations in the session were replete with allusions to people who are unnecessarily intrusive.

Having heard that the patient wishes a consultation, the therapist should immediately ask how the caller got his or her name. This is needed because, as we saw in chapter 5, there are some referral sources—such as other patients of the therapist, his or her relatives, and the like—that virtually preclude a therapeutic relationship between the caller and the therapist. It is therefore essential that a therapist clarify this aspect of the situation before proceeding to other issues.

The wait between the call and the actual consultation should, as I said earlier, be no more than one to three days, and certainly less than a week. Longer delays are suspect. Such was the case with Mrs. Taylor, who called her therapist early one Monday morning, only to find that the first available hour for consultation would be ten days later. Because the therapist had come so well recommended by her family doctor, Mrs. Taylor agreed to wait, despite the frequent attacks of anxiety she was experiencing. Not surprisingly, when her consultation finally took place, she spoke of how unreliable her husband was with appointments. He would arrange to have dinner with friends, she said, only to cancel out for some frivolous reason or delay the meeting for a week or two because of some distraction. She concluded, "His selfishness and lack of regard for others seems to know no bounds."

Images of this kind are relatively easily decoded in light of the long delay between call and consultation in this instance. They speak strongly for the patient's unconscious sense of abandonment and feelings of being exploited. Consciously, Mrs. Taylor was impressed that her new therapist was so busy, despite some passing annoyance over having to wait so long before being seen. Overall, she felt quite fortunate to be able to see a therapist so apparently in demand. As we have come to expect, this is far different from the deep unconscious experience of the situation.

4. Problems and the manner in which they are handled

Apart from the therapist's responsibility to arrange for an appointment as quickly and courteously as possible, a number of unusual circumstances may color the first contact and call for special responses from the therapist. Again, the patient also has a responsibility to the therapist. A potential patient should make clear to the therapist the existence of any psychotherapeutic emergency—severe depression; suicidal or homicidal feelings; psychotic breaks with reality, as seen with paranoid or severely withdrawn patients; and extreme symptoms of any kind. The same rule applies where acute interpersonal crises are concerned—the sudden death of a loved one, an unexpected abandonment, a terrifying medical diagnosis, and the like. The sense of urgency should be conveyed as briefly as possible to the therapist, who should respond with due concern.

Most highly rated are those situations in which the therapist responds to this high level of distress by offering to see the patient that very day or, at most, the day following. So, too, with a therapist who indicates his or her availability to the patient if the symptoms worsen, explaining that he or she might not be immediately accessible but would certainly return an urgent phone call as soon as possible.

Unsound/Reconsider Your Choice–to–*Dangerous/Beware* ratings should be given to therapists who completely ignore extreme disturbances in the caller, and to those who offer appointments several days later in the face of an emergency situation. If the symptoms are sufficiently severe, the therapist's insensitivity and delay should be taken as a clear *Dangerous/Beware* sign and as a strong indication that the patient should find another, more available and responsive psychotherapist.

All this granted, it is nonetheless inappropriate for a therapist to overextend his or her exploration of a patient's acute symptom; the best response after definitive clarification is the offer of a quick appointment in an immediate crisis or the assurance that someone is available if the situation were to become an emergency. Of course, it is not always possible for a therapist in private practice to arrange for an immediate consultation or emergency hospitalization. A highly rated therapist, however, will act with all the expediency that circumstances allow and resolve unconscious reactions later.

Not uncommonly, issues during the first contact involve questions raised by the potential patient regarding the therapist's qualifications, fees, and, sometimes, his or her personal opinions and private life. In principle, you should be assured of a therapist's sound qualifications and judgment by the worth of your referral source. After all, a patient is seldom sufficiently knowledgeable to assess the credentials of a therapist. More often than not, the issue involves poorly informed prejudices that are likely to influence your judgment in self-hurtful ways.

Ideally, you should have little or no interest in the personal opinions or life of the psychotherapist. Asking a therapist whether he or she is married, has children, practices a particular religion, knows other therapists, and the like, serves no purpose and is clearly inappropriate. Such questions tend to express antitherapeutic wishes to shift the relationship with your potential therapist from the professional to the personal domain. Be wary of all such impulses.

If you, as a prospective patient, can afford to pay no more than a certain amount, it may be necessary to ask at the outset exactly what the therapist will be charging per session. (This question is covered in greater detail in chapter 9.) And if you do not have any knowledge of your therapist from your referral source—for example, if you got the name out of a telephone book or heard about this person on the radio—you might then be justified in asking the therapist about his or her professional training. On the other hand, as I have just stated, a potential patient really cannot evaluate the competency of a psychotherapist by his or her credentials. The only way to get a sense of the therapist is to rate carefully his or her behaviors during the first contact and first consultation. In addition, there is a great danger of pursuing such questions to the point of persecuting the therapist, thus shifting the psychotherapeutic focus from yourself to him or her. The nuances are such that it is best to make contact with a therapist who comes properly recommended so that these potentially disruptive questions need not be asked or pursued.

Therapists who do not bring up such matters as fees, qualifications, and personal information should be rated highly. All of these issues are best handled during the first hour. If the patient asks questions in these areas, the therapist should suggest that these matters are best discussed during the consultation session. Nonetheless, if the patient has a need to press the issue, the best response from the therapist is to state a single and fair fee, or to briefly indicate the nature of his or her degree and fundamental training.

An especially problematic question arises when a patient has an inappropriate need to ask the therapist if he or she works in a particular way—such as, Do you believe in hypnosis? Do you do behavior modification? and other questions of this type. Patients should not determine in advance the type of therapy that they are seeking. It should fall to the competency and expertise of the psychotherapist to offer the best possible therapy for the particular complaint with which the patient enters treatment. Selectivity of this kind almost always reflects inappropriate defensive needs in the prospective patient. Ideally, the therapist should not respond definitively to such questions, but should leave the matter open for exploration during the first hour.

At times, the patient will call to change the time of the first consultation. Short of a major, unexpected emergency, a need of this kind is usually a reflection of the patient's anxiety and reveals the patient's resistance to the unfolding of the psychotherapy. The ideal response from the psychotherapist is to suggest to the patient that he or she make all possible effort to maintain the hour as set. However, if a true emergency or urgent need has indeed taken place, the therapist has no choice but to shift the appointment. Still, in the deep unconscious system, the patient will feel that he or she has manipulated the therapist and that the sense of definitive hold so necessary for optimal psychotherapy has been modified. The need to maintain a fixed time for all psychotherapy sessions will be discussed further in chapters 9 and 10.

Consider the following vignette: Ms. Wade, a commercial artist at an advertising firm, had gone to a clinic, where an intake secretary gave her the name and phone number of Dr. Bentley, a female psychologist. Ms. Wade was able to reach Dr. Bentley directly by telephone later the same day. In the course of the conversation, Ms. Wade indicated that her problems were work-related and not at all personal—and, in particular, not the least bit sexual. She stated that she couldn't see herself working with some kind of analytic therapist who thought that everything had sexual roots and who insisted on invading the privacy of her personal life. She therefore asked to be assured that Dr. Bentley would confine the therapy to the work issues—her problem with lateness and a tendency to antagonize her superiors. Dr. Bentley agreed to this restriction for the psychotherapy, and arranged for a consultation hour.

In the first session, Ms. Wade told the therapist how much she appreciated Dr. Bentley's willingness to agree to her request. "Now I know I can trust you," she said, "and I can talk freely, knowing that you won't insist on exploring what I say as having a sexual meaning." This comment, even on a conscious level, is peculiarly contradictory. It is clear, however, that the patient felt comfortable with the therapist consciously. Deep unconscious reactions were a different story, however. During the course of this session, Ms. Wade recalled a time when her brother had developed acute abdominal pain and the surgeons were cautious about doing exploratory surgery. As a result, her brother's appendix had burst, and he barely survived the emergency operation that followed. Ms. Wade was furious all over again as she thought about it: Why didn't they carry out the proper therapeutic measures? What was wrong with their judgment? What deplorable incompetence! There is little question that these comments represent Ms. Wade's unconscious perceptions of Dr. Bentley in light of her agreeing to circumvent the patient's sexual life. The human mind is quite remarkable—it is structured in such a way that a patient can speak of conscious trust, all the while conveying pervasive deep unconscious mistrust.

As we will see in chapter 10, a patient sometimes asks a therapist to see him or her along with some other individual—a spouse, friend, relative, and the like. Such a request indicates a wish to avoid the intimacy and directness of one-to-one psychotherapy. A therapist who would accede to this kind of request would receive an *Unsound/Reconsider Your Choice* or even *Dangerous/Beware* rating. In the deep unconscious system, total privacy and total confidentiality are the ideal therapeutic conditions. Yes, it is possible to obtain some measure of help in couple, family, or group psychotherapy; however, many unconscious ramifications of these treatment forms have gone unrecognized by patients and therapists alike. Any therapeutic situation that compromises privacy and confidentiality is experienced by the patient's deep unconscious system as the result of a therapist's fear of being alone with the patient. A therapist who works in this fashion will be unconsciously perceived as needing the protection of others, as being unfaithful, and as being more committed to others than to the patient.

You may recall in this regard the story of Philip in chapter 5, who recommended his therapist to his girlfriend's brother, then dreamed about scheduling two promiscuous liaisons back-to-back in a hotel. A therapist who accepts a third party into therapy, even indirectly, is invariably perceived unconsciously as frightened by intimacy, unable to make commitments, and lacking in morality and discrimination. When a therapist accepts a third party directly into a patient's therapy, these unconscious perceptions are even more pronounced. Other implications of this kind of therapy will be discussed in detail later on. For the moment, however controversial this statement may sound, it must be stressed here that the deep unconscious mind universally prefers a one-to-one psychotherapy to all other treatment forms.

Turning now to other matters, it is *Questionable* for a therapist who is about to take a vacation to see a patient in consultation during the week or two before that vacation begins—and perhaps even three or four weeks before an extended vacation. At the very least, the patient should be informed of the situation and given the option of either seeing the therapist briefly before the interruption or accepting a referral to another therapist. Therapists who fail to mention such vacations to their prospective patients on the telephone are unconsciously—and rightly—perceived as exploitative and abandoning.

What then of a therapist whose schedule is full and cannot offer a regular hour to a prospective patient? What about a therapist who maintains a waiting list? Or a therapist who will see a patient in consultation in order to determine whether he or she wishes to work with that person or refer the patient elsewhere?

Ideally, a therapist will see a patient in consultation only if he or she is quite certain that a regular hour can be arranged for continuing therapy. The practice of seeing a patient in consultation in order to make a referral is at best *Questionable*, and at worst deserves a *Dangerous/Beware* rating. The use of waiting lists should be rated similarly. Given the power of the therapeutic situation, all such practices are seen as exploitative by the patient's deep unconscious system, despite the conscious willingness of many patients to endure such arrangements.

Given the need of the conscious mind to seek out or to overlook seemingly subtle abuses at the hands of psychotherapists, it is important to maintain a sense of conscious vigilance and to give careful measure to everything a therapist says and does during the first contact. Nothing should be taken for granted; everything should be cause for reflection. And even more important, every story you tell and every dream you have after the first contact should be decoded in light of the most striking triggers—specifically, the most notable interventions of the therapist during these first moments—in order to understand the unconscious ramifications of all that has transpired.

5. The instructions that are given

The ideal therapist will inquire if the patient knows the way to his or her office. An affirmative answer can lead to the end of the telephone contact. A negative answer should evoke careful verbal directions. It is highly *Questionable* for a therapist to propose to mail maps or other directions to a new patient.

A therapist who gives advice and other forms of instruction during this first contact should also receive a *Questionable–*to*–Dangerous/Beware* rating. Suggested measures for relief of a symptom that has been mentioned, for example, are unconsciously perceived by the patient as intrusive, manipulative, and destructive of individual autonomy.

At times, a patient will request medication during the first contact. A therapist who would agree to do so based on an initial telephone conversation—or at any time, in response to a telephone rather than direct contact—should receive a *Dangerous/Beware* rating. Medication should be prescribed only after a careful consultation and evaluation of a patient, and its frivolous use by a psychotherapist, no matter how great the apparent emergency, is deeply suspect.

6. How the contact is ended

Ideally, the end of the conversation is simple, a matter of a good-bye or perhaps a reiteration of the day and time of the agreed-upon appointment. As already suggested, neither patient nor therapist should delay the end of the telephone conversation. Further probing of the patient's difficulties, idle conversation, unnecessary questions, and other efforts by a therapist to extend the conversation must be considered suspect and rated as *Questionable*. Once the safety of the patient has been assured and the time of the first appointment established, the call should be terminated.

Here is one final vignette that touches on the nature of the referral source. It also shows how much is revealed in the way a first call is handled, and it anticipates our discussion of several other ground-rule issues in chapters 9 and 10.

When Mrs. Glass called Dr. Cartwright to arrange a consultation, the phone was answered by Dr. Cartwright's secretary. Mrs. Glass asked the secretary if Dr. Cartwright would accept a particular type of insurance coverage, and the secretary said yes. Mrs. Glass then attempted to make an appointment to see the therapist, but the secretary said that she would give Dr. Cartwright the message and have him return her call within the hour.

On returning the call, Dr. Cartwright realized that Mrs. Glass was the chief of nursing at a hospital where he was on staff. Since Dr. Cartwright had been active on the psychiatric unit and on a number of committees, he was quite certain that Mrs. Glass knew who he was. However, none of this came up during his return call to the patient, who simply asked again about the insurance situation. Dr. Cartwright reaffirmed his acceptance of that particular coverage. Mrs. Glass then said that she had been referred by a nurse at the hospital who had given her the name of two psychiatrists to choose from. Dr. Cartwright responded that he had time available and would be glad to see Mrs. Glass in consultation. Mrs. Glass said that she needed time to think about the matter some more. The following day she called back and made her first appointment.

Dr. Cartwright's office is in a professional building, and though he does have a secretary who assists him in completing forms and the like, she cannot be seen from the waiting room or from his consultation room. During this consultation session, Mrs. Glass said that her main problem was the fact that she had become involved in an extramarital affair. Her husband was somewhat aloof, she explained, and she often went to church and other activities on her own. She had met this particular man at church. He was single. She had sought out a therapist because she needed some sense of what she should do. She felt that she loved this man, and wondered if she should leave her husband. She hoped that the therapist would have some answer for her.

The patient then said that her preference was to be honest with her husband; she didn't want to create a complicated threesome. As the hour went on, she began to talk about an uncle who had made overt sexual advances toward her when she was a child. Sometimes this happened in the presence of her mother, who ignored what was going on. She said that she'd been married three times—what worried her was an apparent pattern of becoming involved with other men while married. She'd done this in each of her marriages, and the situation was always quite chaotic and ultimately self-destructive. She wondered if the therapist would agree to see her husband; perhaps this would tell him something. At the very end of the hour, Mrs. Glass made a passing allusion to the hospital and to the unit on which Dr. Cartwright worked.

We see here a rather typical situation in which a patient unconsciously seeks out a psychotherapist who is acceptable to her conscious system but who unconsciously offers a relationship that repeats the traumas of the patient's early childhood. This particular therapeutic dyad embodies the very problem the patient is hoping to resolve—contaminated relationships and incestuous threesomes. It is quite likely that Mrs. Glass selected Dr. Cartwright over the other psychiatrist she knew about because, first, she knew Dr. Cartwright from the hospital (and therefore he was, unconsciously, an incestuous figure for her); and, second, because he had a secretary and would accept insurance (and therefore would create a three-party situation unconsciously similar to the one that Mrs. Glass was already involved in). Much of this was established during the first phone call, which was answered by a secretary who directly—and quite inappropriately—answered Mrs. Glass's questions about insurance coverage and who made clear her role as a third party to the treatment.

Dr. Cartwright himself ignored the fact that he already knew this patient in another setting, which indicated from the outset his capacity to lend himself to the patient's pathological unconscious drama. This drama was enacted in the therapeutic relationship just as it was repeated in the patient's three marriages; yet all the while, both patient and therapist believed that they were trying to solve the problem. Yet another effort at creating a threesome appeared in the consultation session when the patient asked the therapist to see her husband.

You can see from this just how much can be revealed and initiated by way of a deviant first telephone call. The patient's material in the consultation session—her description of the way she was living her life and her dissatisfaction with that way of life—clearly encodes her low rating of the treatment situation. Miraculously, as I have suggested, a patient may obtain a paradoxical cure under such circumstances, essentially by becoming a therapist to his or her therapist and establishing secure-frame life conditions as a curative model of mental health. But the actual likelihood of resolving lifelong problems in a psychotherapy that unwittingly replicates those very problems is quite small. The fact is that people whose lives have been contaminated and disturbed by incestuous experiences and needs unconsciously seek out contaminated and unconsciously incestuous psychotherapeutic situations.

With the first contact over, the prospective patient is moving toward the first session. As this chapter has shown, a psychotherapist makes many kinds of interventions prior to that hour, each of them a trigger for the patient's conscious and unconscious experiences of the therapy. Those interventions that are especially helpful or harmful—especially as they pertain to the framework of therapy—tend to be the most significant triggers for the communications in the hour that will follow. The patient or therapist who understands this principle will be well prepared for much that takes place during that particular session.

Still, before that session occurs, a potential patient can pause and take stock. You have already rated your therapist on the basis of your referral source. To this, add a detailed assessment based on the therapist's conduct during your first contact with him or her. If your prospective therapist has amassed many *Unsound/Reconsider Your Choice* ratings, including even one or two *Dangerous/Beware* items, you would be well advised either to proceed with great caution or to seek out another psychotherapist. The actual consultation experience has even greater power than the proceedings occurring beforehand. Think about it: If there are already strong signs that a hurricane is on its way, you're going to want to protect yourself or get out of its path.

Your decision will be even more clear if you pay attention to the stories you tell and the dreams you have in the days after the first contact. All of these stories and dreams should be decoded— that is, you should pay attention to the themes of these narratives and think about them as descriptions of what your therapist said and did during your first conversation. If these dreams and narratives are filled with ominous images, it is well to take them as a sign of rather worrisome perceptions of the potential psychotherapist. In general, the more negative your ratings, the more negative your images. One should bear out the other. And if you decide to proceed with the consultation session, you will soon have a great deal more to dream about and rate.

Table 2: The First Contact

This is how the first contact happened:

Sound Answers
- I made the contact by telephone.
- The therapist answered the phone directly.
- The therapist had an answering machine/service and returned my call the same day.
- The contact was brief and to the point, handled professionally, and by the therapist alone.
- A definitive appointment was made—to occur within a few days of the call.
- The therapist gave me directions to his/her office.

Questionable-to-Unsound Answers: Reconsider Your Choice of Therapist
- Someone made the appointment for me (not an emergency situation).
- I met the therapist in person at a walk-in clinic or in a hospital emergency room.
- I called and left a message, but the therapist didn't get back to me for a day or so.
- The therapist was booked up—he/she couldn't see me for weeks.
- I made the appointment with a secretary.
- I had a long talk with the therapist when I called him/her—he/she asked lots of questions about my symptoms and history.
- I conveyed a sense of emergency, but the therapist didn't seem to take me seriously.
- I got off the phone and realized I didn't know how to get to the therapist's office.
- The therapist didn't seem to want to end the conversation, even though we had covered all the essential information.

Dangerous Answers: Beware of This Therapist

- Someone made the appointment for me so that I'd feel obliged to go.
- The therapist had his/her spouse call me back and make the appointment.
- The therapist didn't get back to me, and when I called again, I found out that he/she had forgotten.
- I told the therapist that it was an emergency, but he/she was completely insensitive to my situation and told me to make an appointment for later in the week.
- The therapist told me all about himself on the phone—where he/she went to school, what he/she believes about therapeutic technique, what his/her spouse does for a living, etc.
- Having ascertained my problems, the therapist prescribed medication over the phone.

·7·

The Setting

Just as most people dismiss the first telephone contact with a psychotherapist as inconsequential, the location, setting, and structure of a therapist's office seems, at first glance, to be of minor import. After all, you might say, it's the relationship between therapist and patient that's important—not the doors and rugs and furniture that constitute the therapist's "space." But this is true only for the conscious mind. Deep inside, you do not distinguish formally between the therapist and his or her environment—possessions, intermediaries, and even other patients that you know or relate to in the waiting room. Everything that you are aware of about your therapist becomes part of your therapy experience; there are no exceptions.

If the idea that the therapist's office building and waiting room can affect the course of your therapy seems farfetched, consider the fact that therapy exists in the first place because Sigmund Freud found that all manner of unconscious experiences can affect behavior. We routinely distinguish people on the basis of where they come from, and we consciously expect a person who was raised in an apartment in Brooklyn to have a way of seeing the world that is different from that of a person who grew up on a farm in Sheboygan, Wisconsin. Newscasters employ marketing experts who advise them on what to wear and how to arrange the news set so as to attract the largest possible audience. We may not even notice that Dan Rather is wearing a comfortable sweater vest or that a busy-looking news staff is constantly in motion behind Peter Jennings, but these factors have a psychological effect that can be measured to predict ratings.

Why, then, is it so difficult to believe that a far more intimate relationship with a therapist will be affected by the nature of his or her surroundings? A therapeutic relationship that is developed in a professional building will unfold differently and around different concerns than one that takes place in a clinic or a hospital, a home-office, or an office shared by other therapists. There are other considerations as well. What about a twice-weekly therapy that takes place in two different offices? What about a session somewhere other than the therapist's office? What if the waiting room is actually the therapist's parlor in a home-office setup? Is there a bathroom available off the waiting room—or is it in the hallway of an office building or off the therapist's consultation room?

Does the therapist have a secretary or receptionist? If the therapist sees patients from a home-office, is the door answered by a spouse or family member? If the home-office is otherwise private and soundproof, does it matter that other members of the therapist's family are present in the house or apartment?

We already know that the deep unconscious system scrutinizes every issue that impinges on therapy. Ideal conditions, as supported unconsciously by patients with absolute consistency, are as follows: a private office in a professional building, preferably one devoted mainly to health-care services; an innocuously but tastefully appointed waiting room counterbalanced by a separate exit from the therapist's consultation room for patients who have already been seen; window shades or blinds, providing a sense of comfortable enclosure; a soundproof office, so that what is said cannot be heard in the waiting-room area; and a bathroom accessible from the waiting room without intruding on the consultation space. As for ancillary personnel, psychotherapy is perceived by the deep unconscious system as the concern of patient and therapist alone; third parties of any kind are detrimental to the process and its results.

I will provide an illustration of the ideal therapeutic contact and locale—along with the sorts of unconscious perceptions communicated under such circumstances. Mr. Kipling is a young man in his late twenties who sought psychotherapy with Dr. Merrick for episodes of depression and worries that his career wasn't progressing. He had consulted with Dr. Sugalski, his internist, who recommended Dr. Merrick and gave Mr. Kipling the therapist's telephone number. The following morning Mr. Kipling called Dr. Merrick, who answered the phone himself. Mr. Kipling immediately identified himself and said that he'd been given Dr. Merrick's name by Dr. Sugalski. He explained that he had been feeling depressed of late and wanted to arrange a consultation.

Dr. Merrick responded by asking how severe the depression was. Mr. Kipling said that it was like a long-standing dull ache—not an emergency situation where he felt suicidal. Dr. Merrick then asked if Mr. Kipling could make use of a morning hour, and the patient responded that he could, if it were early enough. The therapist suggested an 8:15 A.M. session the following morning. Mr. Kipling said that that would be fine. Dr. Merrick then asked if Mr. Kipling had his address, and when the patient said no, Dr. Merrick provided the information. Mr. Kipling knew the office location, so he simply thanked his new therapist for the information and said good-bye. Dr. Merrick reiterated that their session would be the following morning at 8:15 A.M., and said good-bye as well.

I realize that this somewhat detailed description of an ideal transaction seems, consciously at least, like an amalgamation of trivial and pedestrian exchanges. For Mr. Kipling's deep unconscious system, however, the communications promised an ideal set of conditions for his psychotherapy—a secure frame, as I have called it (see chapter 9 for further discussion). A brief look at part of the opening minutes of his consultation with Dr. Merrick will tell us much about how this patient's deep unconscious system experienced the professionalism, concern, and brevity of his therapist's efforts.

During the session on the morning following the call, Mr. Kipling spent some time describing his sense of depression and his job difficulties. He then went on to say that some people thought he might be depressed because he was unmarried and living alone. To the contrary, the patient objected, "I like living alone and having my own space. I guess I have a problem trusting people to really care about me. Actually, the only person I ever fully trusted was my father's father, my grandfather. When I was six and seven and eight, he'd take to telephoning me every now and then in the evening. And though the calls were short, they were very special. He was always deeply concerned, genuinely supportive, and somehow always there if I needed a friend. It's not that my parents were all that bad, but my grandfather was really special."

Clearly, the trigger for these communications was Dr. Merrick's handling of the first telephone call. The allusion to the telephone call in the patient's story is what we call a *bridge* that links the surface story about Grandfather Kipling to the unconscious story related to the psychotherapist. Indeed, Mr. Kipling seems to be indicating that Dr. Merrick's responses on the phone were comparable to the responses of his grandfather when he was a boy. This is a highly positive characterization of Dr. Merrick's efforts. Notice, again, that the deep unconscious system is not concerned with declarations of affection; it is concerned with the supportive and reliable qualities of *behavior*. Notice also that this way of handling the first contact promises a secure frame—a private space—within which the patient expects to feel "held" and supported. Positive images of this kind in most instances speak for strong support from the deep unconscious system for the therapist's words and actions.

When Mr. Kipling arrived at Dr. Merrick's office, his unconscious anticipation of a secure frame was borne out. Dr. Merrick was a psychologist who practiced in a professional building. This building housed, for the most part, other psychologists, mental-health professionals, physicians, and dentists. His own office was on the third floor. It had its own entrance and waiting room, which was not shared with any other therapist. The waiting room was simply but tastefully decorated, and contained three comfortable chairs. There was no evident leakage of sound from the consultation room to this waiting-room area, and there was a bathroom available for use just off the waiting room.

Mr. Kipling wondered briefly whether he should in some way acknowledge the patient who had preceded him when he or she came out of the therapist's office; but, to his surprise, he never saw that patient. He realized later that the consultation room had a door from which one could exit directly into the hall. At 8:15, Dr. Merrick came into the waiting room, greeted Mr. Kipling by name, and introduced himself as Dr. Merrick. He motioned, and the patient understood that he was to proceed to the consultation room. Dr. Merrick followed behind, closing two evidently heavy, soundproof doors behind them. The consultation room itself was simply appointed, with a desk, a chair, a couch, and two comfortable chairs with a table between them. The desktop was bare except for a lamp. The window blinds were closed and there were no street sounds in the office. It was evidently well soundproofed all around. Mr. Kipling took the chair on the side of the table nearest the door; the chair on the other side had an ottoman and seemed more likely the therapist's. It was in this setting—one that will concern us further in the next chapter—that the material we have already considered unfolded.

During the next hour, Mr. Kipling said quite a bit about his relationship with his grandfather. He didn't know why, but he found himself suddenly remembering a long-ago weekend with his grandfather in a cabin in the mountains. The sensations surrounding this trip were quite vivid—Mr. Kipling remembered the interior of the cabin, meals cooked over a fire, a feeling of warmth and comfort. He also recalled being afraid at night because of the sound of animals outside, but this was combined with a sense of reassurance and safety because he knew his grandfather was nearby.

It seems clear that the cabin in the patient's recollections was a representation of the therapist's consultation room, so we may take this secure-frame setting as the trigger for Mr. Kipling's memories. These memories further elaborated Mr. Kipling's deep unconscious perceptions of his psychotherapist and his therapeutic setting. Clearly, the emphasis in the patient's story is on the sense of security he was experiencing unconsciously, even as he remained consciously somewhat apprehensive. Even his allusion to fear of animals is coupled with unconscious reassurance. One might speculate that this mention of fear is a reflection of Mr. Kipling's unconscious anxiety about the experience of communicating his deepest instinctual fears and wishes to the psychotherapist. The imagery is typical of patients who are experiencing ideal framework conditions, because unconscious meanings are liberated in such a situation, and the patient is unconsciously experiencing fear of entrapment. Even so, Mr. Kipling's images indicate the extent to which he expected to have the appropriate support of the therapist in dealing with his material and its attendant anxieties.

Let's take a look now at some of the most common departures from the ideals just described. By the standards of the deep unconscious system, an ideal therapeutic "hold" involves a sense of structure, containment, safety, and support. To put it very simply, these qualities are not fully available outside of a professional therapeutic location that ensures privacy and a one-to-one relationship between patient and therapist. Unquestionably, financial necessity often determines the setting to which a patient turns (and, often, that which a therapist creates); but the deep unconscious system will react nonetheless to the compromised aspects of a clinic or hospital-based office. All such settings, though they may well form the base for a helpful psychotherapy, have destructive and harmful qualities that must be resolved.

One patient, Mrs. Black, who was seen in a low-cost clinic because of her financial circumstances, reported a dream in her second session of being lost among animals in a zoo. The zookeepers were kindly, she said, but a sense of turmoil pervaded the dream nonetheless. As she thought more about the dream, she remembered, with some embarrassment, that she'd been describing the clinic to a friend of hers as "a zoo." The waiting room was terribly crowded, and the noise barely diminished once she was inside her therapist's office; in fact, Mrs. Black had often noticed that she was aware of patients in the various offices crying or raising their voices. Aside from patients, there were secretaries, bookkeepers, and other personnel, a group of whom were usually drinking coffee and laughing just off the waiting-room area. As she was realizing how much all of this had contributed to her dream, Mrs. Black found herself remembering her childhood home among eight siblings—the lack of privacy, the disorganization, the feeling of not getting enough attention from her parents. The chaos and deprivation of those early years were being repeated in the treatment setting.

Still, the concern and attention that Mrs. Black was able to obtain from her therapist did not go unnoticed by her deep unconscious system. The dream report makes reference to kindly zookeepers. This reference gives us reason to hope for a helpful therapeutic experience despite the detrimental aspects of the clinic setting. Indeed, the individual therapist can do much to minimize the extent to which patients are subjected to exposure, humiliation, and abuse—subtle or gross—in a clinic setting.

In the private therapy sector, the home-office is a consciously accepted setting for all types of psychotherapy—including insight-oriented psychoanalysis. Here, too, however, themes that indicate a departure from ideal conditions are unconsciously repeated over and over again by patients seen in this setting. Prominent among the unconscious perceptions provoked by this particular situation are images of a therapist who is unable to separate from his or her family, or who is unable to be alone with his or her patients. Other images portray a therapist who seeks self-exposure and the exposure of family members both sexually and aggressively, and who wishes to expose his or her patients to third-party intruders as well.

It should be noted that such departures from the ideal frame should be rated *Questionable* to *Dangerous/Beware*; they need not, however, preclude a paradoxical positive therapeutic outcome. I have mentioned this before. I am using the word "paradoxical" because the positive results are all too often produced by unhealthy underlying mechanisms. For example, the frame departure may be experienced unconsciously as punishment, which may temporarily relieve a patient's feelings of guilt. Or a therapist may be experienced unconsciously as in more need of help than the patient, which may help to relieve a patient's feelings of inadequacy and self-recrimination. Paradoxical cures of this kind feel good because they alleviate the troublesome symptoms that brought a patient into therapy. They all extract a price, however, which is generally ignored by patient and therapist alike. I don't mean to sound moralistic about this, because I'm not really saying that a dishonest cure will catch up with you sooner or later. I'm saying that an unhealthy cure takes care of the symptoms without taking care of their psychological source. The underlying problems are still problems, and they tend to show up in some other area of life in a new—and perhaps more tolerable—form. So we don't recognize them as residuals of a therapy that merely traded one set of symptoms for another.

Let's look now at unconscious perceptions of a home-office arrangement. Mr. Berry saw his insight-oriented psychotherapist, Dr. Salter, in the latter's home. Since Dr. Salter was seeing another patient before Mr. Berry, Dr. Salter's wife usually answered the door. Sometimes Mr. Berry heard her on the telephone or talking to the children. As it happens, Dr. Salter used his living room as the waiting room and a study off the central hall for his consultation room. Neither area was soundproofed. Keep in mind, however, that an entirely separate office entrance and suite attached to a therapist's home would not abrogate the effects of the home-office arrangement on the deep unconscious system. It would simply lessen some of the more powerful effects described in this particular situation.

Several dreams that Mr. Berry reported early in his psycho-therapy are almost transparent in their encoded unconscious perceptions of this setting and therapy. In one, Mr. Berry's deranged uncle is running around the house naked and out of control. In another, there is a house that is a combination of a residence and a barn. The setting is very shabby and people can be heard talking through the walls. Mr. Berry has the sense that someone is stalking him and will attack. Recall, in contrast, the safe, secure cabin that Mr. Kipling recalled from childhood camping trips spent with his beloved grandfather. Mr. Kipling's associations derived from his unconscious perceptions of his secure-frame, private treatment setting. Mr. Berry's images are strikingly different.

So too with Mrs. Sylvian, who had therapy in an office attached to her psychiatrist's home. Early in her psychotherapy, Mrs. Sylvian complained that her husband never left her alone. She meant this almost literally. Her husband was in the insurance business and he insisted that she come to the office with him every day to help out. "It's like he's afraid to be on his own," she said. "He clings like a baby. There's this friend of mine, too, who was having an affair with a married man. She finally left him because he was always making her go with him on his business calls. It's like he couldn't let go of her."

Mrs. Sylvian then went on to describe a recent sense of "paranoia." She said that she felt that strangers knew all about her, knew that she was in therapy, and knew that she had emotional problems. There was a look of malice in their eyes, as though her situation had been advertised on television. It was easy for her to see why some people stay at home all the time for fear of being watched or assaulted outside of their own safe space.

In this situation, the patient has selected for representation in her encoded images perceptions of her therapist as unable to separate from her family, as needing to expose her patient to other family members (experienced as malicious strangers who know all about her), and as reluctant to leave home for fear of attack and harm. Notice here that some of these images are not communicated through a dream or a story the patient tells, but through a new symptom. This, too, is nature: Patients often develop symptoms whose unconscious basis is the perception of departures from the ideal therapeutic frame. Because the process is so deeply unconscious, and so far from anything that the typical therapist would be willing to recognize and be responsible for, the true basis of the symptom usually goes unrealized. It is an unusual therapist who would see in Mrs. Sylvian's paranoia on the street an unconscious analogue to a therapy taking place in the therapist's home.

Sometimes it is not possible for a psychotherapist to have a private bathroom within the confines of his or her own office. Hall bathrooms are acceptable under such conditions, but the problem is the possibility of the patient running into the therapist in the bathroom setting. This may seem like a trivial concern at the conscious level. The deep unconscious system, however, reacts to this kind of incident in a powerful way. For example, a male patient ran into his therapist at the urinal just before his session; it was no coincidence that he began the session with a story about a male acquaintance who had unexpectedly come on to him. On the other hand, a therapist who maintains a bathroom inaccessible from the waiting room and available only through his or her consultation room is unconsciously perceived as unduly frustrating and as inviting intrusion into the consultation room space.

Inadequate soundproofing is always experienced as lack of privacy. Both privacy and confidentiality are fundamentally necessary for a psychotherapeutic experience during which a patient will inevitably, given the proper security, reveal his or her most painful secrets—the stuff of which madness is made. Again, the absence of privacy is also reflected in the presence of any third party to the treatment setting—spouse, secretary, other patients, etc. Under these conditions, patients invariably produce images of spies, intruders, rapists, newspaper reporters, and so forth. Apart from this, as I have said, the presence of third parties unconsciously suggests that the therapist is afraid to be alone with the patient, feels inadequate without assistance, and is incompetent or damaged in some way. Under such conditions, patients often opt for conceal-ment and long silences during therapy sessions. This reaction can be quite conscious. It would be natural for a patient to deliberately conceal information from his or her therapist for fear of exposure to others.

We live in a peculiar period of time, where millions of people are in some form of therapy, but the suggestion that a man may have consulted a psychiatrist over depression following a family tragedy is perceived as grounds for disqualification from candidacy for public office. The idea that any of a myriad of office personnel has access to potentially damaging information about patients is enough to keep many needy people from consulting a therapist. Worse still, it is not uncommon for patients to become involved socially and sexually with their therapists' ancillary personnel. As I've said before, the deep unconscious system does not distinguish between a therapist and his or her intermediaries; involvement with a therapist's secretary or other clinic personnel typically re-sults in dreams of incest and ménage à trois. Such gratifications can actually bring relief from emotional suffering for some patients, but, again, the experience unconsciously teaches a patient to seek out comparable relief in other areas of his or her life. Relief of this kind—if it does occur at all—is tantamount to trading the original set of symptoms—themselves failed attempts at relief from emo-tional suffering—for another, momentarily more successful, set.

While on the matter of setting, we should discuss one last issue: the ground rule that specifies a session should take place in the therapist's office/consultation room. I mentioned earlier a female therapist who injured her back and continued to see patients from her bed at home. I later interviewed one of her former patients, who said: "It was the weirdest feeling—like she was the patient lying on a couch and I was the therapist." This image captures the extent to which a therapist can use deviant practices to reverse roles with the patient—to be the person seeking help instead of the one providing it.

A rather common variation on the setting is the telephone session. Although the phone is rarely used for the first hour of a therapy, many therapists do offer to hold sessions by telephone if one party falls ill or cannot get to the therapist's office for one reason or another.

Even in cases of dire emergency, a telephone session should be as short as possible. Under all other circumstances, therapy sessions should be held in person. Telephone hours are invariably perceived by the deep unconscious system as highly defensive on the part of the therapist, and an indication of the therapist's fear of being with the patient—a dread of violence or intimacy. No matter how strongly rationalized the practice is ("My car was at the repair shop"; "I had a temperature of 102°"; "I couldn't get a baby-sitter"; "I live too far away to make that kind of trip"), the therapist who offers phone sessions is unconsciously seen as unable to separate from the patient; as needy, depressed, and clinging; and as overindulgent.

To illustrate: Mrs. Stuart was having problems getting to her sessions with Ms. Brody, a social worker, because she had three children to take care of, all under age eight. Ms. Brody therefore suggested that they conduct their sessions by telephone—either at the appointed time or at another convenient hour. Mrs. Stuart was grateful for Ms. Brody's understanding.

After their first phone session, however, Mrs. Stuart had a dream: She is in murky water and her body is coming apart. Nothing is there to hold her together. Her associations to the dream involved a time at the seashore as a young teenager, when, on a dare, she had had sex with her cousin and his best friend. Afterward, she had felt so humiliated and ashamed that she couldn't even look at her cousin; she didn't even want to be in the same room with him.

Notice again how the conscious system accepted the frame deviation and even felt grateful to the therapist. But the deep unconscious system had a different view. Unconsciously, the patient felt fragmented and without support, and she saw the therapist as requiring a defense against inappropriate (incestuous) contact with her. These encoded messages were communicated by the deep unconscious wisdom system. The deep unconscious memory system simultaneously advocated a behavioral response to these perceptions: When her husband did not come home one night, Mrs. Stuart abruptly decided to divorce him. He had called toward dawn, claiming business obligations, but she didn't believe him. The precipitous quality of the patient's decision—the absence of reasoned thinking or discussion—bespeaks the neurotic element in her action. She told Ms. Brody that she was particularly insulted by her husband's empty phone call, as though the telephone contact were going to make her feel better about what he did. If Ms. Brody had been listening for encoded communication, she would have seen that the reference to an empty telephone call linked Mrs. Stuart's reaction to her husband with the phone sessions. Indeed, Mrs. Stuart had made her sudden decision on the night of a phone conversation with Ms. Brody, even though the issue didn't even come up during the session.

We have seen, then, that much of significance takes place before a patient actually meets his or her therapist. Each and every transaction is loaded with conscious and unconscious meaning, and will have a profound influence on the course of the therapy and the life of the patient (and therapist as well). The nature of the referral, the handling of the initial contact, the structure of the setting, and the presence or absence of ancillary personnel—each of these evoke powerful unconscious images that remain deep within the patient and resonate with a wide range of early life experiences; all of this influences current adaptation—as well as adaptation in the future. There is, as a result, quite a bit to consider when rating your psychotherapist in these three areas. An accumulation of *Questionable* and *Dangerous/Beware* items should be a definitive cause for concern; the presence of one or more *Dangerous/Beware* items should lead to serious reconsideration as to whether you wish to continue with this particular therapy. For the moment, however, these ratings will become the backdrop for a new set of considerations: the manner in which the therapist handles the first consultation, and especially the ground rules of psychotherapy. All of this taken together will give you an extensive and sound basis for a comprehensive rating of your psychotherapist after the first hour.

Table 3: The Setting

This is how my therapist's office is set up:

Sound Answers
- He/she maintains a private office in a professional building.
- There is a bathroom readily accessible from the waiting room.
- There is a door in the therapist's office that allows me to leave without having to go back through the waiting room.
- The furnishings are tasteful but not obtrusive.
- The windows have shades or blinds that are closed.
- The office is soundproof.

Questionable-to-Unsound Answers: Reconsider Your Choice of Therapist
- He/she maintains a home-office separate from his/her living quarters.
- He/she shares the waiting room with other therapists, so I'm usually not alone there.
- He/she has an office in a clinic.
- The only bathroom is just off the therapist's consultation room.
- I always meet the next patient in the waiting room on my way out.

Dangerous Answers: Beware of This Therapist
- He/she uses his/her living quarters as an office.
- When I go to my therapist's home-office, I'm aware of his/her family.
- My therapist's office isn't soundproofed; you can hear what's being said inside—particularly if someone is shouting or crying.

·8·

The First Interaction

Mr. Kelly, a social worker, believes that the first session of therapy is an opportunity for detailed history taking. In his point of view, the first session is a blueprint for the therapy to follow, and his practice is to ask as many questions as possible to secure the therapy to a solid foundation of knowledge about the patient. This is not an unworthy theory—from the standpoint of the conscious system. Unconsciously, however, Mr. Kelly's approach elicits a very powerful reaction from his patients. And the tragedy is that Mr. Kelly is completely unaware of that reaction. He never notices that every patient he interviews winds up complaining about people who talk too much, parents who don't know how to listen, bosses who don't know how to play or be creative, teachers who ask inane questions. One might even consider these patients' remarks as indirect accusations as much as unconscious perceptions. But Mr. Kelly isn't listening to his patients' associations for unconscious messages, so it doesn't occur to him to connect his patient's stories with his own style of handling the therapy. Moreover, his method often elicits expressions of conscious appreciation from his patients.

You have read enough now to recognize that Mr. Kelly's patients may well feel consciously gratified by their therapist's apparent interest in them, even as the deep unconscious system is characterizing his therapeutic style as intrusive, disturbing, and preventing creative unconscious communication. In fact, many of Mr.

Kelly's patients talk about the hostility of his approach—telling stories about assaultive, attacking people. Yet this approach can provide relief, too—because it assures a patient that he or she will not be required to reveal painful secrets nor to take responsibility for the direction of the therapy.

Consider now a nearly ideal situation—from first contact to first session. I say nearly ideal because the therapist, Dr. Webb, would be highly rated in almost all respects but one. His failure to maintain a secure frame in that one particular respect was perceived unconsciously by his patient, Mr. Cole, as an obstacle to good therapy. Because Dr. Webb was listening to the patient's encoded communications, he became aware of Mr. Cole's unconscious perceptions and responded to them appropriately. This is why I am presenting the example. It is important to recognize the way in which a good therapist listens and responds to a patient's unconscious perceptions of the therapist's behavior.

Mr. Cole, a young man in his mid-twenties, was referred by his ophthalmologist to Dr. Webb. When he called the therapist's office, a secretary answered and took enough information so that Dr. Webb could call back later and make the first appointment. The office was located in a professional building and was private, with its own bathroom and waiting room; the secretary's office was through a side door and out of sight.

At the appointed time, Dr. Webb came out from the secretary's area, entered the waiting room, and greeted Mr. Cole. He opened the door to his consultation room, motioned for Mr. Cole to go in first, and followed the patient in, closing the door behind him.

Mr. Cole found himself in a room with a desk whose top was clear, two chairs with a table between them, a couch, and a few simple prints on the walls. He went to sit in the chair farther from the couch. Once they had both settled in, Dr. Webb said, "With what may I be of help?" Mr. Cole immediately told him that he was having problems with women. He had a girlfriend, Melinda, who was pressuring him to get married, and he was reluctant to make a commitment. Perhaps, he suggested, he really needed couples therapy. Would Dr. Webb see the two of them together? The therapist responded by suggesting that Mr. Cole continue to talk about whatever came to mind; Dr. Webb wanted to hear more before giving him an answer.

Mr. Cole went on: Although he had become deeply involved with Melinda—to the point where she might validly expect him to marry her, he had recently formed a romantic attachment to Nancy, a fellow architect in his office. There had always been some chemistry between them, but he had never intended to do anything about it. He didn't really understand his own feelings anymore. His friends felt that he was sabotaging the relationship with Melinda and advised him to stop seeing Nancy, but he found that he didn't want to do that. "There's something about her," Mr. Cole explained, rather lamely, "like—I mean, even her voice: She has the same kind of inflection that your secretary does—or whoever it was that answered your phone when I called. You know what I mean? She has this way of talking that's both sensual and innocent, and it's a real turn-on."

Mr. Cole spoke for quite a while after this. There were a few long pauses, but for the most part, Mr. Cole spoke easily and rapidly. Dr. Webb listened, looking at his patient directly most of the time. Mr. Cole's associations wandered about. He went from the question of breaking up with Nancy to the difficulty of having an office romance without everyone else in the department becoming aware of one's private life. In fact, he had recently been forced to share his office with another coworker, and he deeply resented the man's presence. Mr. Cole felt a real need to be alone; his work required it, he said. He couldn't concentrate unless he had peace and quiet and a space of his own. Still and all, he concluded, the main problem was his relationship with Melinda. He didn't feel that he had any perspective anymore—was he avoiding marriage because he was afraid of commitment or because he had valid reservations about Melinda? Even her jealousy: God knows, Melinda currently had good cause to be suspicious of an involvement elsewhere, but her alternating insecurity and possessiveness were irritating all the same. Now that he was thinking this out, he was sure that it would be helpful for Dr. Webb to see how he and Melinda interacted. Perhaps he could set up an appointment for the two of them next week?

Dr. Webb intervened actively for the first time—it was now halfway into the consultation hour. He pointed out that Mr. Cole had mentioned his secretary, the woman who had answered his telephone call. He was now asking to bring his girlfriend Melinda with him to his next session. There seemed to be a connection: Dr. Webb, as it were, brought a woman into the office; Mr. Cole wanted an equivalent situation. But indirectly Mr. Cole was saying that neither woman belonged in his therapy. Directly, of course, he was asking Dr. Webb to accept Melinda's presence. But the stories he was telling communicated an indirect message; these stories were relevant to the therapy even though they were superficially about other matters. By way of these stories, Mr. Cole had stated quite firmly that he needed a private space if he was going to get any work done in therapy. The secretary was like the intruder with whom Mr. Cole was reluctantly sharing his office, and Melinda's presence would only compound the lack of privacy. His references to Nancy and his sense of the impropriety of their affair in a professional setting reflected his unconscious sense that including Melinda in his therapy was inappropriate. Indirectly, then, Mr. Cole was supplying the answer to his own request: If therapy is to proceed, there can be no intruders. In fact, Mr. Cole had even provided Dr. Webb with unconscious advice through his reference to the advice of his friends: Involving a third party will sabotage the primary relationship. Dr. Webb said that he understood this advice on two levels: He would not see Melinda, and he would rethink his position on maintaining a secretary.

Mr. Cole was silent for a while. Then he told Dr. Webb that he had been orphaned as a child. Although he had been adopted, he felt that he never knew what it was like to have parents of his own—a mother whose love was first his, whose love had been his from the very first moment of his life.

More followed: further associations from Mr. Cole; more interpretations from Dr. Webb; the offer of a course of therapy and a
set of ground rules; and a final volley of associations. But for our
purposes, we have a model first session and, with one main exception, a generally high-rated psychotherapist.

Dr. Webb scores high for making the appointment with Mr. Cole
himself; for the private and professional setting in which he practices; for his way of greeting Mr. Cole and his way of escorting
him into the consultation room; for his opening question; for his
initial silent listening; and for not answering his patient's question,
but instead inviting free associations. He also rates highly for his
intervention, which is an interpretation in light of a therapist-
created trigger: The presence of the secretary is used to clarify Mr.
Cole's *unconscious* reasons for wanting Dr. Webb to see his girlfriend. The intervention also secures the frame of the therapy (it
maintains the privacy and confidentiality of the therapeutic relationship) by attending to the patient's disguised advice to do so.
Much of this will be covered in subsequent chapters. For the moment, I would like to stress mainly that Dr. Webb's initial silence,
which permitted Mr. Cole to free-associate, and his restriction of
intervention to explanation and frame-management responses are
highly rated. Indeed, the interpretation is followed by disguised
confirmation in the fresh and illuminating story of Mr. Cole's adop-
tion and hunger for a devoted source of love. Dr. Webb could not
offer Mr. Cole this kind of one-to-one acceptance in the presence
of a third party to therapy.

Dr. Webb also rated highly in a dimension of therapy I have not
as yet considered: how the therapist dresses. He wore a business
suit and a shirt and tie, thereby conveying one aspect of his professionalism.

The deep unconscious wisdom system confirms businesslike
dress in a therapist, such as a suit, or for a woman, a dress. Less
formal garb is unconsciously perceived as overly casual and seductive, suggesting the offer of a social relationship rather than
one of a concerned psychotherapist. Just how much an exceedingly

warm climate justifies a departure from this ideal is an issue I have not as yet explored. Although a seemingly minor issue, therapists who are lax with their dress tend to be lax with other aspects of the frame.

We are considering in this chapter and in the two that follow the way in which a therapist handles the first session—from the initial greeting to the final parting comment. Although the next two chapters deal with the most critical aspect of the therapist's interventions in the first session—his or her handling of the ground rules, boundaries, or framework of the treatment (the basic contract)—the division of topics is somewhat artificial. All departures from the ideal approach to a first hour will impinge to some extent on the framework of the treatment. Still, it will be helpful to look at some of the issues outside of the ground rules that arise in the first session and to rate them in a general, global way.

We are now entering an arena where therapists sharply disagree and different schools advise strikingly different techniques. Perhaps it is clear to you at this point that most psychotherapeutic techniques have been developed on the basis of direct communications from patients, to which therapists have responded superficially and naïvely—largely because of certain anxious and unrecognized inner needs in both parties to therapy. These needs stem from the deep unconscious memory systems of each.

The conscious system, as we saw in chapters 3 and 4, is an extremely unreliable guide for the shaping of a psychotherapy. Conscious needs in patients vary tremendously, as do the conscious needs of psychotherapists. And all such pressures are under the strong influence of unconscious forces that go entirely unrecognized. The result is a hodgepodge of claims, counterclaims, and contradictory recommendations, and is a field without clear standards.

The situation is quite different in the deep unconscious system. There the view of the world and of psychotherapy is consistent and evenhanded. The capacity of the deep unconscious system to process information soundly and to generate encoded recommendations for the process of psychotherapy is consistent across Western culture (I have studied case material throughout much of the United States and Europe), and the advice is invariably worth heeding. Consciously basing one's standards on deep unconscious intelligence results in the best possible therapeutic experience.

It should be noted, in terms of departures from the ideal frame, that the conscious system likes to be asked questions, because questions promote intellectualization and loss of deep meaning. They preclude the expression of emotionally painful material that is vital to the structure and sound resolution of emotional disorder.

This is particularly true of patients who have been highly traumatized in early childhood and later life. Such patients have been prematurely and overintensely exposed to death anxiety issues and unconsciously dread unconscious meaning. They will consciously prefer and rationalize their need for an active, questioning, and gratuitously commenting psychotherapist.

Therefore, an actively probing psychotherapist must be rated relatively low. Some patients may find it hard to tolerate and accept the relative silence of a therapist and the interpretation of unconscious meaning, but this sort of psychotherapist deserves a high rating.

Of course, there is no guarantee that a therapist who is silent throughout a first session has made the ideal intervention. Indeed, silence does not necessarily reflect a position of sound holding and good frame management; it could reflect instead a missed intervention—a failure to speak up in the face of material that calls for comment. Nevertheless, the silent therapist, at the very least, provides a general opportunity for deep communication, and therefore for an effective type of exploratory psychotherapy. Barring undue or inappropriate extensions of silence, the therapist who is a relatively silent listener in the first hour is to be rated as ideal or acceptable—with one proviso: Mounting frustration with a therapist's silence should lead you to pay more attention to your dreams and stories for unconscious perceptions. The silence may well be in error; your therapist may have missed important opportunities to intervene helpfully. It is also wise at such times to review the therapist's other ratings for signs of difficulty; low ratings tend to cluster.

In this context, I must state again the importance of examining the dreams and narratives that you bring up during your sessions with your psychotherapist, as well as those that come to you outside of the hour. Although this book compiles the accumulated experience of thousands of patients, none of these patients has had your particular experience with your particular therapist. This is why I encouraged you in part I of this book to learn how to interpret your own encoded communications. My general ratings are only a start; they should be supplemented with your own personal unconscious ratings of your psychotherapist. Decoding your own dreams and narratives is really the only way that you will be able to detect an unconscious perception that your therapist has remained silent even though you have offered material that warrants comment and interpretation.

What I mean by this is that the ideal therapist should be helping you to understand those aspects of what you are saying that are outside of your awareness and pertain to the underlying structure of the problems that brought you to therapy. If he or she isn't doing that, your deep unconscious system will perceive the absence of an intervention quite negatively, crediting the therapist with fear of unconscious material or with hostility. These negative perceptions will be reflected in your stories and dream reports, whether or not you bring them into therapy. (I will have more to say on silence and other therapist interventions in chapter 11.)

Remember: Your therapy is unique; the issues that will arise for you may be different from the issues that I am illustrating in this book. One might even paraphrase Tolstoy here and suggest that ideal interventions are very much the same, but every therapy deviates in its own particular way. There are infinite variations on misuse and abuse of the ideals, and the character of a flawed intervention can be suggested only very broadly.

Ideally, then, at the time of your first session, your therapist will greet you in the waiting room by your surname and introduce himself or herself by first and last name, or surname alone. If the waiting room is shared, the therapist should identify only himself or herself and not compromise your privacy by using your name. A handshake should accompany this greeting, after which the therapist should motion to you to enter the consultation room. He or she should follow behind, closing the necessary doors and securing the consultation room space.

As a rule, the chair on which you should sit should be self-evident. At times, the therapist's chair will have an ottoman, because the therapist sits for such long periods of time and needs the support, or the chair will be located so that a patient can be heard from either the couch or the other chair. If you are uncertain as to which chair to use, you might ask a question and expect a direct response. Once the two of you have settled in, the therapist should ask a question such as, "With what may I be of help?" After that, it's up to you, given the general goals of a first session, to describe the nature of your emotional difficulties, something of their history and background, something about yourself past and present, and anything else that happens to come to mind.

The therapist should already be listening carefully to both the surface of your communications and the depths in order to decode your unconscious perceptions of your first contact with him or her, your referral source, mediators, and so forth. The therapist should also be deciding on recommendations with regard to the frequency and type of therapy warranted. Undoubtedly, the therapist will be assessing the nature of your problems, your character structure, your strengths and weaknesses, your style of communicating, your capacity to relate, your commitment to the treatment, and the existence of factors that will either facilitate or pose obstacles to the therapeutic process.

Indeed, the first session is especially significant and complex. The therapist should be listening for much of the session, and ideally will make one or two interpretive comments regarding issues of which you are not aware. As we will see in chapter 11, these issues should be connected to the trigger situations involving the conditions of the treatment and the therapist's own prior interventions, and they should define your unconscious reactions to those situations. It can be shown that *unconsciously* these are the main issues for the patient, as they relate to his or her emotional problems. These interpretations should be explanatory in tone—they should not be accusing or advice-giving.

Again, I am describing the *ideal* first session. I realize that the vast majority of therapists do not use this approach. But this is one situation in which the majority does not rule—at least not in the deep unconscious system. To continue, about half to two-thirds of the way into the first hour, the ideal therapist should indicate that he or she can help you with your emotional difficulties. Nothing more about the nature of your problem or the ways in which the help will be offered should be stated. Once the therapist has indicated the ability and willingness to be of help, he or she should present the ground rules of the therapy (see chapters 9 and 10). There should be enough time for you to react both directly (consciously) and indirectly (unconsciously) to the therapeutic structure that you have been offered—or to the absence of structure. Here, too, the therapist may address aspects of your reaction outside of your awareness.

With the time of future sessions arranged, the therapist need do nothing when the session is over except to indicate that the time is up and wish you good-bye. Ideally, the first hour is concluded with a handshake, but the therapist should make no physical contact again until the termination of treatment, which is also concluded with a handshake. You should be responsible for finding your own way out. The therapist need not accompany you to the door or walk you back into the waiting room. In this way, the transition from the charged emotional space of the psychotherapeutic consultation room to the outside world will have begun with a vote of confidence for your ability to function and with full respect for your autonomy.

I have little doubt that the foregoing outline of an ideal first session will strike some readers as rigid and cold. I can state with full confidence, however, that this particular way of conducting the first hour is unconsciously perceived as warm, concerned, helpful, safe, and constructive. These positive perceptions are, as already noted, usually accompanied as well by signs of anxiety regarding the unconscious meanings that you will reveal under these conditions. Nonetheless, this mix of security and anxiety will give you the best possible therapy, under the best possible conditions, with a therapist who is using the best possible techniques.

Let us turn now to some of the more common departures from this ideal. In the waiting room, the therapist may blurt out your name in the presence of another patient or other therapists, if the waiting room is shared. This may sound quite trivial, but the fact is that any violation of privacy and confidentiality is *Questionable*. The same is true of any extraneous comments the therapist makes to you in the consultation room. Remarks about your hairstyle or weight, the extension of sympathy for a trip made in the rain or snow, comments about the referral source or a common acquaintance—any attempt to engage you in small talk or personal conversation should give you pause. These departures may seem friendly and innocuous on the surface, but they suggest a therapist who has little regard for proper boundaries and little capacity to handle his or her own anxiety or need to be contained. From the very first moment, from the very first contact, a psychotherapy belongs to the patient. The revelation of feelings, opinions, observations, and wishes should be his or hers entirely.

The therapist who is self-revealing or who makes extraneous comments (which are inevitably self-revealing as well) is a therapist who wishes unconsciously to reverse roles with you. A therapist who needs to place himself or herself at the center of the psychotherapy is a therapist with serious unresolved personal problems—problems that would become your burden as his or her patient. The most insidious aspect of this kind of role reversal is the fact that it can alleviate symptoms for all the wrong reasons. The unconscious knowledge that you are trying to cure your own therapist can make you feel somewhat less emotionally disturbed yourself, but this is far from the ideal way of obtaining relief.

Should any physical contact beyond the initial handshake take place at any time during the course of therapy, you should consider yourself in a dangerous situation. I realize that there is a certain breed of therapist who extols the virtues of a friendly hug or other physical signs of affection, acceptance, and support. I am not implying that every therapist who throws an arm across your shoulders as you leave the office has a conscious ulterior motive. My concern here is with unconscious needs for boundaries. All physical contact in the psychotherapeutic domain is viewed unconsciously as a violation of individual integrity and autonomy, and is typically experienced as aggressive, seductive, and malevolent. A therapist who feels the need to make physical contact with a patient as early as the first session is a therapist who is seeking gratification of his or her own unconscious needs at the patient's expense. This does not bode well for a therapeutic relationship.

Once you have settled in your chair, the therapist should say little beyond an inquiry as to the nature of your difficulties. Should he or she choose to speak first, to go into explanations of any kind, or to find any other reason to speak at length before you do, the rating should be *Questionable* to *Dangerous/Beware*. I cannot stress enough the fact that the therapeutic space should be occupied by your problems and considerations, not your therapist's. Except for the therapist's initial question in the first consultation hour, it is your prerogative to speak first in every session. It is also your prerogative and privilege to continue to speak and to free-associate in the first hour. Indeed, this is the only way that a therapist can make a full appraisal of your conscious and unconscious communications. All interruptions must call into question the rating of your new psychotherapist.

We will look more carefully at the specific interventions of a therapist in chapter 11, confining ourselves here to issues of intervening that can arise in the first session. I have already indicated that the only verbal interventions appropriate to therapy are interpretive (designed to explain aspects of your communications that lie outside your own awareness). In the first session, such an intervention may clarify a problem with a referral source or the first contact (as we saw in the case of Dr. Webb's recognizing Mr. Cole's unconscious perceptions of his secretary's presence); or it may indicate something about your emotional difficulty that already lends itself to interpretation. Most often, perhaps, such an intervention will address an unconscious component of reluctance or skepticism on your part regarding therapy—an early sign of what is called *resistance*, or an obstacle to the unfolding of the psychotherapy.

In summary, in the ideal first session, the therapist asks no questions, makes no extraneous remarks, offers no personal opinions or self-revelations, and is otherwise concerned almost entirely with an occasional interpretive remark and with establishing the therapeutic contract. The deep unconscious system, through encoded messages, asks for adherence to these principles with great clarity. Realistically speaking, however, there are very few therapists who practice this way. My suggestion to you, therefore, is to pay attention to the kinds of questions that your therapist is asking, the kinds of comments that your therapist is making. The least objectionable questions will function as attempts to clarify and to understand what you have said; the least objectionable comments will function as attempts to structure the treatment. The more your therapist's remarks depart from efforts to clarify and to structure treatment, the less acceptable they are. If they shade off into attempts to change the subject, interruptions, expressions of sympathy or impatience, advice, anecdotes, and the like, you should rate the therapist's behavior as *Questionable* to *Dangerous/Beware*.

The same kind of ratings apply to the recommendations your therapist makes in the second half of the session. They should be simple, brief, empathic, tactful, and made without technical language, elaboration, or speculation. It is enough to confirm that you are suffering emotionally and that he or she, as therapist, can be of help. If something has already been clarified in regard to the unconscious basis of your difficulties, this, too, can be reiterated. Virtually nothing else is needed. The more a therapist departs from this ideal, the lower the rating. This applies particularly to those therapists who give minilectures, so to speak, on the nature of your problems, or who offer personal opinions on your behavior and associations, and to those who offer directives, suggestions, reassurances, and so forth.

If you have indicated that you do not intend to continue therapy, your therapist might help you to understand some unconscious factors in this decision as evoked by triggers related to his or her own prior interventions. Signs of anger, accusatory attitudes, seductive efforts to keep you in treatment—all of these deserve *Questionable*–to–*Danger/Beware* ratings. Your reluctance should be interpreted and respected, and you should have a fair and open chance to evaluate your therapist just as your therapist is attempting constructively to evaluate you. Poor therapists, low-rated therapists, actively harmful therapists—all of these do exist. To remain with such a therapist is a serious sign of emotional disturbance; because of this, each decision to quit a psychotherapy must be examined on its own terms. This, too, will be discussed later on, mainly in chapter 12.

As I have already indicated, once the therapist has said that the time is up, no more need be said beyond good-bye, followed by a final handshake. Endings and separations, no matter what their nature, are always difficult for human beings (unconsciously, they remind us of death). Many therapists with unresolved separation and death anxieties will make a variety of extraneous and unnecessary comments toward the end of the session. Some will indicate that time is up and then offer a variety of comments beyond that point. Still others will arrange a consultation of indefinite length, or of a time longer than the usual session. All such practices are deviant and inappropriate, and deserve *Questionable*–to–*Dangerous/Beware* ratings. Once the hour is at an end, it is good to know that the hour is at an end and that therapy has a finite definition with clear temporal boundaries. Extensions beyond these boundaries can sometimes be enormously gratifying, but their unconscious ramifications are invariably destructive.

The entire first session should take place face-to-face. Ideally, your therapist should recommend the couch to you as part of the structure of treatment, and the shift from chair to couch should begin with the second session. A therapist who asks you to lie on the couch for the first session should receive a *Questionable*–to–*Dangerous/Beware* rating.

Mr. Landauer saw Dr. Koch in consultation. He had never been entirely faithful to his wife, Mr. Landauer said, but lately he had been initiating affairs with so many women that he didn't understand his own motivations. He felt compulsively led to become involved with almost any woman who seemed available to him. During much of the first hour, Dr. Koch asked many questions: "How many women have you slept with in the last month?" "Does your wife suspect?" "Do you and your wife still have an active sex life?" These questions seemed reasonable to Mr. Landauer, but some of the therapist's comments made him feel that he wasn't being taken seriously—"Don't you think that most men are unfaithful to their wives?" and "Perhaps the problem is not your affairs, but the fact that you feel so guilty about them," and "A lot of us, when we hit middle age, need a shot in the sexual ego." Mr. Landauer also noticed that Dr. Koch let the session go on for an hour, even though he had said that he worked for fifty minutes.

Still and all, Mr. Landauer felt better after this consultation, and he considered some of what Dr. Koch had said about his affairs reflecting a need to prove himself and to boost his self-esteem. That seemed like a possibility worth thinking about. Maybe he required some emotional something that his wife had never been able to provide. Maybe the marriage was the problem.

Mr. Landauer began the next session by exploring some of these ideas. At Dr. Koch's suggestion, he tried to remember how he and his wife had first met, and whether he felt at that point some reluctance to sexual or marital commitment. As he spoke, he found himself remembering a class that he and his wife had shared during college before they were married; then his thoughts turned to a young man who had also been in that class—Jerry Cansfield. Mr. Landauer had enjoyed Jerry's wit and banter, and during the course of the semester, they became what you might call classroom friends. During final exam period, Jerry invited Mr. Landauer to come over to his apartment for a study session together.

To Mr. Landauer's surprise, on his home turf, Jerry was an incessant talker. More disturbing was the fact that Jerry had misinterpreted his classmate's interest in him. Jerry was a homosexual, and he had become convinced over the course of the semester that Mr. Landauer was latently gay and hadn't yet realized their mutual attraction. Mr. Landauer found himself unable to hide his feelings of dismay and embarrassment, which Jerry interpreted as a conventional sense of morality. "There are lots of us," he said. "It's society that makes us feel guilty and abnormal." As Mr. Landauer attempted to politely extricate himself from the situation and go home, he realized that Jerry was becoming unreasonably angry with him, and it struck him that what he had taken for a live-wire wit was something closer to emotional instability. He figured that his best bet was to get out fast, but when he got to the door he found it dead-bolted. He felt a wave of real terror go through him, anticipating that he would turn to find Jerry poised to attack him.

On the conscious level, Mr. Landauer appreciated Dr. Koch's suggestions and the extra time at the end of their first session. He thought of it as a "gift" and saw it as a sign of the therapist's concern and devotion to his work. And yet it is clear that the deep unconscious system had a far different view: In the place of devoted concern is an image of homosexual entrapment and violence. Images of this kind are typical unconscious responses to noninterpretative therapist comments and to alterations of the ground rules of treatment. It is for reasons of this kind that extensions of the first session beyond the usual length of a therapy hour must be rated as *Questionable* or *Dangerous/Beware*. One can also hear in

Mr. Landauer's story his unconscious perceptions of Dr. Koch's style of conducting therapy—his "incessant talking," the clichéd rationalizations he had provided for the behavior that Mr. Landauer felt guilty about.

The first session is a bellwether session; it portends much of the future of the psychotherapy. Every detail, every nuance, every aspect is taken in by the deep unconscious system and processed and understood, though, as a rule, only a small portion is worked over consciously and brought into direct awareness. It bears repeating that all of these unconscious perceptions will have an influence and affect both your life and your therapy. In a way, it is not possible to do justice to the exquisite perceptiveness of the deep unconscious system. No matter how much we know consciously about the many details and variations on how a therapist may work, and no matter how many implications we recognize in these efforts, the deep unconscious system sees more and knows more. At best, through these broad strokes, we can get a sense of the picture.

With these global ratings and your own dreams and narratives as a guide, you can be in a position to make an extensive and critical appraisal of the therapist you have chosen. An accumulation of low ratings should be fair warning to think long and hard about whether to enter therapy with this particular therapist. Still, in order to appreciate fully this basic constellation of ratings, we must turn to the central issue in all psychotherapeutic systems: the ground rules of psychotherapy, their management by the therapist, and your reactions to them as a patient.

Table 4: The First Interaction

This is how my therapist handled the first interaction:

Sound Answers
- He/she seemed to be concerned and listening.
- He/she said very little—restricting comments to attempts to help me understand myself better.
- He/she asked no questions—except to clarify something I said.
- He/she answered no questions, but sought more exploration from me.
- He/she said nothing of a personal nature.
- Except for an initial and concluding handshake, there was no physical contact between us.
- In the second half of the session, the therapist briefly stated that he/she could help me and then proposed a set of ground rules for treatment.

Questionable-to-Unsound Answers: Reconsider Your Choice of Therapist
- He/she was angry.
- He/she was indifferent.
- He/she was seductive.
- He/she talked almost as much or more than I did.
- He/she asked a lot of questions, which broke my train of thought.
- He/she kept giving me his/her personal opinions and told me about his/her private life.
- He/she gave me specific advice on how to handle my problems.
- He/she asked me to lie down on the couch for the consultation hour.
- He/she tended toward nonsexual physical contact—such as giving my hand a reassuring pat when I was nervous and upset, etc.

- He/she didn't say anything about whether he/she could help me or what the ground rules of therapy would be.

Dangerous Answers: Beware of This Therapist
- He/she was very demonstrative physically—hugging me, touching my arm or shoulder when talking to me, etc.
- He/she came on to me sexually.
- He/she was verbally/physically assaultive.
- He/she was downright unprofessional—very personal in his/her responses and self-revealing.
- He/she talked far more than I did, constantly interrupting me to ask questions, to offer opinions and advice, and to talk about himself/herself.
- He/she was exceedingly manipulative.

·9·

The Fee and Temporal Frame

In countless ways, we have already established the primacy of the ground rules or framework of a psychotherapy as the single most important dimension of treatment (see especially chapter 4). It follows, then, that the ways in which the therapist presents these ground rules in the first hour—or fails to do so—will determine the basic nature of your psychotherapeutic experience. And the means by which a therapist articulates the ground rules will usually predict his or her frame-management behavior throughout the treatment. Indeed, these issues remain the overriding concern of the deep unconscious system from the first moment to the very end of a psychotherapy. In focusing on the delineation of the ground rules in the first hour, then, we are actually addressing, by extension, their management throughout the psychotherapy.

The secure and sound frame is so appreciated by the deep unconscious system that for many patients, it can carry the work of cure with only occasional interpretive work by the psychotherapist. Other patients experience a great deal of anxiety in response to the secure frame and will find many reasons to propose or engage in alterations of the frame. On the unconscious level, these alterations constitute in part a powerful request for understanding—for interpretive interventions. As a rule, the material from the patient will permit and even require such interpretations. These patients obtain cure in two ways: by experiencing the security of the therapist's holding to the frame, despite pressures that may arise to deviate, and from the therapist's capacity to interpret the patient's material in light of the ground-rule issues at hand.

I remind you again that most of what is described in this section is experienced in the deep unconscious system and communicated indirectly, through disguised and encoded images. Consciously, most patients merely ask the therapist as a matter of course to reschedule a session or to sign an insurance form; or they will accept without question a shared waiting room, a cash-on-delivery arrangement, or the presence of a secretary. Of course, some deviations do strike a patient consciously as inconsiderate or annoying—for example, a therapist who answers the phone during sessions or cancels sessions indiscriminately. But most deviations seem perfectly acceptable to the conscious system.

Yet the secure frame has many aspects that can be appreciated consciously. Apart from its power to contain, the secure frame defines the roles of both participants to therapy. It makes clear the absence of physical and sexual contact, of direct battle, and of the satisfaction of needs inappropriate to a psychotherapeutic experience. Instead, this frame promises a focus on holding and understanding. This is why the therapist who can establish and maintain a secure frame is seen unconsciously as healthy, sane, strong, and devoted to the cure of his or her patient. Ultimately, a patient comes to identify with this unconscious image, which facilitates a healthy cure.

With this in mind, we will make our ratings of how the therapist establishes and manages the ground rules in the first hour—and throughout the therapy.

It is helpful to think of the treatment frame as grounded in a few relatively basic components, to which several essential, but somewhat more "fluid," elements are added. The more concrete ground rules, which form the bedrock of the therapeutic relationship, include the location of the therapy, the fee, the time of the session, and its length. The remaining aspects of the frame include such diverse aspects as the therapist's relative anonymity; the total privacy of the treatment, including the one-to-one relationship; the physical position of both patient and therapist; the fundamental rule of free-associating for the patient; and the use of neutral interventions by the therapist. In addition to these particular ground rules which, ideally, are explicitly stated or implicitly conveyed by the therapist in the first hour, there are a number of other unstated ground rules: the absence of physical contact except for an initial and final handshake, as discussed in the previous chapter; the absence of sexual interplay; and a mutual commitment to the patient's cure.

Some may argue, as I have suggested, that the secure frame is rigid, uncompromising, and precludes spontaneity. I must emphasize again that these are conscious assessments. If you were having a surgical operation, you would expect as a matter of course the maintenance of particular circumstances in the operating room; you wouldn't complain that sterilization procedures and heart monitors and anesthesia destroyed the potential for spontaneous behavior. In the same way, the ideals maintained in the deep unconscious system for therapy are part of the human healing process. They do not preclude spontaneity; they are designed for the safety and support of the psyche "under repair." Moreover, the therapist who is endeavoring to maintain a secure frame is not arbitrarily imposing rules from without; he or she is obliged to manage the frame at the behest of the patient's own unconscious perceptions and directives. A therapist who genuinely has no option but to operate in a somewhat deviant frame must contend with the patient's unconscious responses to the deviations. The goal is always to keep deviations to a minimum, to explore their unconscious meanings, and to deal with their actual ramifications in the therapy.

This leads us to some introductory comments about how the ground rules and boundaries of the therapeutic relationship are to be established. What needs to be stated by the therapist? What is conveyed by his or her behavior? And is there a place for a written as well as a verbal contract?

In general, the highest ratings would go to a therapist who specifically states and defines the fixed components of the frame about twenty to twenty-five minutes into a forty-five- to fifty-minute first session. The locale of the office speaks for itself, as discussed in the previous chapter. The therapist's relative anonymity is seldom directly addressed. It is conveyed in what the therapist says and does. Ideally, the patient will have no personal knowledge of the therapist's family or social or professional life, and the therapist will refrain from expressing personal opinions and self-serving responses to the patient's communications. The privacy of the therapy is also implicit, unless the patient wishes to modify the one-to-one relationship by bringing a friend or family member into the therapy, by introducing insurance coverage (and through it a multiplicity of third parties), or some other similar request. In such instances, the therapist is forced eventually to take a position one way or the other.

Similar principles apply to total confidentiality, which is an unannounced "given" unless an issue is raised in this area—for example, a request to release information to any third party, or to tape-record sessions (which are likely to then be heard by others), etc. Both the positioning of the patient and need for free association are usually made explicit by the therapist, and the neutrality of his or her interventions is inherent in the therapist's way of working.

It follows, then, that in the first session the ideal therapist defines those ground rules that need stating and maintains in action and deed those ground rules that are essential to his or her behavior. Some therapists have recently advocated the practice of creating an actual written contract, signed by both parties to the therapy. Often the patient is asked to read a document that lists the risks and dangers of psychotherapy, and releases the therapist from responsibility for untoward side effects. The patient may be asked to guarantee that he or she will remain in therapy for a certain number of sessions, or to accept penalties for failure to adhere to various aspects of the written contract. This practice is rationalized with the idea that it follows the medical model and uses forms comparable to those adopted for surgical and other invasive medical procedures in which the patient's right to know the risk is respected.

Notwithstanding this reasoning, the unconscious system is offended and repulsed by this type of transaction. Today's therapy-related legal procedures have been developed and stated with little if any regard for the deep unconscious needs of psychotherapy patients. On the other hand, if the law in your state requires that you sign such a contract, you have no choice but to comply. Be alert, however, for adverse unconscious reactions.

To illustrate: Dr. Peer, a male psychologist, saw Ms. Cabot in consultation. Halfway into the first session, he took a two-page document from his desk drawer and handed it to her. He said that he wanted Ms. Cabot to be clearly informed of the risks of psychotherapy and of his liabilities in her case. He asked her to read the document, and to date and sign it on the second page. The document spoke of major adverse effects such as suicide and homicide, along with an increase in symptoms, disturbances in marital and other relationships, and inadvertent tendencies to criticize the therapist's work. It also outlined the limits of the therapist's responsibility for the outcome of treatment, emphasizing the contribution of the patient's pathology to poor results.

Having signed the document with the conscious feeling that it was a good idea to have this information, Ms. Cabot returned the following week with a brief dream: Her father and a strange-looking man are pushing her mother down a flight of stairs. In associating to the dream, Ms. Cabot connected the stranger to her father's attorney, the man who had handled the father's part of a bitter and ugly divorce from the patient's mother. This attorney had in fact colluded with the father to produce a divorce agreement that brutalized the mother and deprived her of many of her rights; ultimately, however, she had signed the agreement because she was in dire need of money. Ms. Cabot felt that it was weakness on the part of both her mother and her mother's attorney that had led her to participate in that legal atrocity.

This is another very clear encoded message. The deep unconscious system regards informed-consent documents for psychotherapy as a way of doing violence to the patient and in some sense disrupting or ending effective psychotherapy before it even begins. The practice can lend itself to an unconscious need for punishment or victimization on the part of the patient.

On the other hand, it is possible that a signed contract will emerge as the only major deviation in an otherwise secure-frame psychotherapy. I say it is possible; but unfortunately, in most instances, therapists who ask their patients to sign informed-consent documents tend to be relatively insensitive to ground-rule issues and unmindful of a patient's deep unconscious need for a relatively secure frame. Assault along one dimension of psychotherapy is often accompanied by assault along other dimensions. The use of such documents, then, is not a hopeful sign, but must be considered in the context of other ratings obtained by the psychotherapist in question.

Turning now to specific ground rules for psychotherapy, let's begin with the fixed frame. This frame involves a single, reasonable, and appropriate *fee* that is maintained throughout the psychotherapy. This fee implies that both patient and therapist accept responsibility for being present at all sessions. That is, the patient accepts responsibility for the fee for all scheduled sessions at which the therapist is present; and the therapist does not receive payment for hours that he or she cancels for vacations or emergencies. If the patient cancels a session, responsibility for the fee remains intact. It should be understood that missed sessions, for any reason, even vacation, always have unconscious ramifications, but they do lend themselves to analysis and diminution through insight when properly interpreted.

The session itself is defined as either forty-five or fifty minutes in duration, and the specific time and frequency of the sessions are stated explicitly in the first hour—usually as part of defining the basic ground rules. At times a therapist may recommend a greater frequency than the patient can afford or accept; a lesser frequency is then established, and it, too, should be maintained for the rest of the therapy. Accomplished in this way, there is essentially no damaging residual.

The agreed-upon schedule is sustained throughout the psychotherapy in the same locale in which the patient is seen for the consultation hour. Although a therapist does sometimes move into a different building or change his or her office location for some unavoidable reason, this type of event is always traumatic. The rare move does not deserve a *Questionable* rating, but full analysis is required to diminish the hurtful effects.

This definition of the basic elements of the frame—a set fee, full responsibility for sessions, a fixed time and place, and fixed length and frequency of sessions—may, as I have said, strike many readers, patients and therapists alike, as rigid, impersonal, and insensitive. Perhaps they seem to favor the therapist, especially his or her financial needs, and to exploit the patient. Perhaps they seem too psychoanalytic and out of step with reality.

I can state unequivocally, however, that it is only when a therapist *departs* from these ground rules that an unconscious view emerges of someone who is abandoning, insensitive, and exploitative. At the very moment that a patient consciously thanks a therapist for understanding his financial situation and reducing the fee, an image will emerge of a prostitute or a hustler who will accept any client on any terms at any time. At the very moment that a patient thanks her therapist for changing an hour, an image appears of a boss who exploits employees by making excessive demands on their time schedules. Just as a tearful patient is telling her therapist how much she appreciates a concerned extension of time, she is remembering that she was once punished by being locked in her bedroom, unable to escape. Without fail, all departures from the conditions under which an insightful cure can occur, no matter how welcome directly and consciously, are experienced unconsciously as detrimental.

If you, as patient, request a departure from the ideal frame, the highest ratings go to a therapist who asks you to continue to say what comes to mind (to free-associate), and then makes use of the *encoded* or *unconscious communications* in the associations that follow to handle the request. What this means, as a rule, is that the therapist will show the patient that his or her unconscious communications have directed adherence to, rather than deviation from, the particular ground rule at issue.

To offer a brief example, Mr. Scofield explained to his therapist, Dr. Russo, that he would need to cancel one session a month because of travel responsibilities in connection with his job. Dr. Russo directed Mr. Scofield to go on—to continue to say whatever came to mind. Mr. Scofield's thoughts gradually went to negotiations on a contract with a new customer. Mr. Scofield was irritated with this customer, because their representative had asked him to include a clause in the contract that would exclude payment for goods received under certain conditions. Since the goods involved were subject to decay over a short period of time, the customer's request struck Mr. Scofield as patently unfair and exploitative. "A contract is a contract," he said. "Unwarranted exceptions destroy the whole thing. It's like they were trying to take advantage of me. I realized I couldn't trust them."

These associations are very clearly shaped as an encoded recommendation to Dr. Russo, advising him to hold to a standard contract, and to make no exceptions. Dr. Russo had no problem showing Mr. Scofield that he had unconsciously warned the therapist that acquiescence would destroy the therapeutic contract and permit Mr. Scofield to exploit him. Again: Throughout a psychotherapy, whenever an issue related to a ground rule arises, the highest ratings go to the therapist who uses the patient's encoded material as a basis for deciding how the issue should be handled. Therapists who respond precipitously, directly, use only a patient's manifest thoughts and associations, and act without exploration of the issues involved deserve *Questionable*–to–*Dangerous/Beware* ratings. And if the therapist's decision is to deviate rather than to adhere to the ground rule in question, the *Dangerous/Beware* rating applies.

◆ ◆ ◆

Money issues are one source of considerable trouble between patients and therapists. We entertain so many irrational attitudes toward the payment of psychotherapy fees that a great number of peculiar deviations in this area not only exist, but flourish.

Some deviations are probably not regarded as problematic, but they deserve *Unsound/Reconsider Your Choice*–to–*Dangerous/Beware* ratings—for example, the use of a credit card to pay the therapist. This practice renders psychotherapy as an insensitive business proposition and brings third parties into the encounter. Another common practice is the fee range. The problem here is that a therapist who cites a fee range inevitably must select either the high or low end for the patient, and either will have unconscious detrimental consequences. The ostensibly humane practice of reducing a fee for a patient in need or the seemingly fair idea of increasing a fee for a patient whose income improves or because the therapist feels entitled to a cost-of-living increase can have far-ranging ill effects in the deep unconscious system.

Some fee deviations border on dishonesty; some are downright corrupt. There are therapists who will negotiate a reduced fee for a promise of cash payment, which permits the therapist to report less income than he or she actually receives. Some therapists allow patients to accumulate large unpaid balances, to be paid later, with or without interest. Others ask to be paid in advance—or at the end of each session. The ideal is a single payment made at the beginning of each new month for the previous month's sessions.

One of the most common modifications of a private fee arrangement is, of course, the use of insurance coverage and, with it, the introduction of third-party payers to the psychotherapy. Now, it is certainly true that insurance makes private psychotherapy possible for patients who might not be able to afford it otherwise. Indeed, it is this massive social need—and the financial needs of therapists—that generate powerful wishes not to know how third-party involvement contaminates a therapy.

Ms. Hines was in psychotherapy with Dr. Bartley—a male therapist—because of recurrent bouts of depression and an inability to endure intimacy with a man. Her mother had died when she was six months of age. In her consultation session, Ms. Hines insisted that Dr. Bartley complete an insurance form, which would allow 80 percent coverage of her fee. When Dr. Bartley asked the patient to continue to say whatever came to mind, she spoke of a girlfriend whose husband had hired a private detective to follow her. The wife was so incensed when she found out, that she stopped talking to her husband. "My father's like that," she went on, "he's always horning in on my private life. He pushed himself right into my relationship with my last boyfriend and drove him away. He can't seem to stick with any relationship of his own."

Dr. Bartley intervened and said that unconsciously Ms. Hines felt that his signing the insurance form would be asking a third party to horn in on their therapeutic relationship—to spy on them, really. Her reaction to this intrusion would be to stop telling him anything meaningful, the way her girlfriend stopped talking to her husband. Ms. Hines nodded. She said she remembered a dream about a warm and friendly man who wanted to get close to her, but she was afraid of him—afraid of being trapped.

Though these last images seem to validate Dr. Bartley's intervention (there is a positive figure and an expression of anxiety about entrapment by the secure frame), at the end of the hour, Ms. Hines said that she could not afford the therapist's fee without help from her insurance company. Either Dr. Bartley signed the insurance form or she would not return. Reluctantly, and with a comment that they would have to explore the situation further in the next hour, Dr. Bartley completed, signed, and returned the form to his patient.

Ms. Hines began the next hour by speaking of the sudden death of her mother, who had been pressured by friends to go swimming in rough waters against her better judgment. Three months later, Ms. Hines left therapy. She had said little of consequence, was silent much of the time, and felt that she couldn't really trust Dr. Bartley or feel comfortable telling him anything.

The therapist's signature on the form was a kind of death sentence as far as the deep unconscious system was concerned. Dr. Bartley had become the mother lost to Ms. Hines since childhood; and he was the reckless friend encouraging her to swim in rough waters to her own death. She couldn't trust him. Like the husband who hired a private detective to follow his wife, he didn't trust her either. Why even talk to him? No matter how necessary in terms of financial need, bringing a third-party payer into therapy always has serious consequences.

Another patient, Mr. Templeton, entered psychotherapy under financial pressure. The therapist insisted that Mr. Templeton obtain insurance and helped him to contact an insurance agent. The patient made arrangements for a policy that would pay part of the therapist's fee. Following this incident, the patient spoke about getting into relationships destined to go nowhere. This brought to mind a man at work who seemed to be infatuated with him and to want a relationship with him. The following week, Mr. Templeton reported a dream in which a stranger is observing two men making love to each other. His immediate association was to an early childhood memory: his mother watching as a doctor examined his genitals.

The unconscious perceptions of the third party to therapy who would modify the patient's privacy and confidentiality are readily decoded. Again, third-party payment is questionable at best, and dangerous at worst. The main way to salvage an insightful and meaningful psychotherapeutic experience under such conditions is for the therapist to consistently analyze the patient's unconscious perceptions of this particular departure from the ideal ground rules of psychotherapy.

I realize that these deep unconscious ratings of deviant fee arrangements are difficult to accept. They ignore the nature of the patient's financial situation, and the images generated are destructive and unpleasant. Nonetheless, the definition of the therapist's fee stands as perhaps the most critical component of the fixed frame, and the fundamental outcome of a psychotherapeutic experience may be fatefully influenced in the very first hour when the fee arrangements are made.

Ignoring or failing to recognize the consequences of fee alterations does not eradicate their actual existence. Remember, the deep unconscious system perceives without desire or greed; what it reflects back to us via encoded messages is worth considering for its integrity and honesty. The ideal therapist is committed to a single appropriate fee. And the patient accepts with satisfaction the frame-securing and interpretive interventions of the therapist and the ultimate achievement of emotional cure.

Notwithstanding economic reality, it is simply a fact that a patient will not reveal his or her emotional history and deepest and most painful secrets in the presence of third-party observers. Some other mode of relief, if any, must be fashioned under such circumstances. The blind use of third-party payment has prevailed because psychotherapists are not paying attention to the unconscious ramifications of this practice, and because patients have naïvely accepted their conscious rationalizations without knowing how to explore their own encoded material. Ultimately, the practice meets the need of both patients and therapists to create treatment situations in which unconscious meaning is greatly diminished or absent.

Overall, then, the use of third-party payers must receive a *Questionable*–to–*Dangerous/Beware* rating. It is important to understand that the insurance component becomes part of a much larger deviant frame in which clichés and intellectualizations can and will prevail. Under such circumstances, genuine insight into the unconscious issues that underlie a particular patient's emotional problems is simply not a factor. At best, those patients who find it necessary to utilize insurance are well advised to find a therapist who can interpret the unconscious meanings of this deviation in light of the material that emerges in the psychotherapy. Indeed, if a therapist is insensitive to such communications, the patient should engage in his or her own decoding. When you have dreams or hear yourself telling stories in therapy, remember the narratives and think about their meaning in light of using insurance to pay the therapist.

Not infrequently, the use of insurance leads to outright fraud. I know of a case where a family had two insurance policies, and the therapist actually agreed to send them two bills. Essentially, the treatment of the adolescent boy in this family provided them with $300 a month, tax-free, in insurance benefits. Apart from the destructive unconscious effects of this practice, the parents could hardly afford to allow their son to get well; and the son himself did not want to deprive his parents of much-needed income, even though the money depended on his continued illness.

In certain professional organizations it is accepted practice for a therapist to charge a higher fee to patients with insurance than to patients without it. As a result, some therapists assist their patients in obtaining coverage for their therapy, knowing that it will enhance their own income. Of course, such practices are usually rationalized as a way of helping the patient to reduce his or her costs for treatment.

Certain psychoanalysts will charge a high fee for once- or twice-weekly psychotherapy, but a much lower fee for four- and five-times-a-week psychoanalysis. This generally occurs because psychoanalysts prefer to do the latter kind of work—or need cases for accreditation. Some therapists charge one fee for a first session, and another for a second; some charge more—or nothing at all— for the initial consultation. Others are willing to barter for their psychotherapy services, exchanging their fee for the services or goods of the patient—a practice that may be utilized in order to avoid paying legitimate taxes. Barter arrangements border on the exchange of gifts, another widely practiced deviation that has profound detrimental consequences.

The exchange of gifts between patient and therapist is unconsciously viewed as pathological, exploitative, and seductive. It blurs the boundaries between patient and therapist, and ultimately deprives the patient of what is needed from the psychotherapist. At the very moment that a therapist gives a patient a gift, the deep unconscious system experiences a dramatic sense of deprivation, loss, and harm.

I recognize that it is not uncommon for patients to give gifts to their therapists, especially during the Christmas season. And a fair number of therapists give their patients gifts in return. Just recently I saw an advice column written by a psychiatrist who recommended that therapists give their patients copies of a certain book that she had found helpful herself. Believe me, I'm no Scrooge. I like presents. I like to give people books I think they'd enjoy. But none of this is the point.

My recommendation against exchanging gifts in therapy is not a matter of opinion; it has been determined entirely by patients' consistent unconscious reactions to the practice. Here is a typical example: After exchanging gifts with her therapist, Mrs. Shannon found herself remembering a time when the therapist had slept through one of her sessions, totally unaware of her presence in the waiting room. Then she began to talk about a man who had burglarized her apartment: The intruder had left a token gift behind as something of a trademark. The deep unconscious system invariably portrays gift giving not only as a lack of engagement but as a form of dishonesty—a robbery masquerading as the act of giving.

It doesn't matter which side of the exchange you are on: giver or receiver, the unconscious reading of the situation is always the same—that the act of giving has taken something away. In one situation, a female therapist accepted a scarf from a male patient at Christmas time. Though consciously pleased with his therapist's reaction to the gift, the patient went on to talk about a time when someone had offered him a bribe to forge certain papers as a consultant. The patient still remembered the incident with a feeling of outrage, and had responded at the time by withdrawing his services from that account.

Notice here that the patient's deep unconscious system not only conveyed its view of the therapist's behavior (accepting the gift) as dishonest; it also provided a *model of rectification*: a directive to the therapist to manage the ground rules correctly and to maintain a secure frame for the therapy.

Ideally, a therapist never offers a gift to a patient. If a patient brings a gift to a session, the highly rated therapist will politely refuse the gift—suggest that the patient hold on to it so that the incident can be explored. Almost without exception, the patient's associations in the session will reveal important and inappropriate unconscious motives and perceptions of the therapist behind the consciously well-meaning gesture. The material will also support the rectifying decision that the gift should not be accepted by the therapist. This is a situation in which the frequent split—the difference in basic attitude and need—between the conscious and deep unconscious systems is glaringly evident.

In one situation, when a therapist asked her patient to hold on to her gift and continue to free-associate, the patient spoke about her parents using gifts as bribes to manipulate their children. "If they had been sincere," she said, "they would have given love rather than things." We can always rely on the encoded messages from the deep unconscious system—as long as we give it room to speak.

Finally, failure to keep to these principles came up in a different therapy at the time of termination. Gift giving is common as a therapy nears its end—for reasons that I will get to shortly. Mrs. Weaver had been treated in a clinic by Mr. Banks, a social worker, for a year because of episodes of depression; she seemed much improved in the course of the treatment. At the end of the year, Mr. Banks informed her that he would be leaving the clinic and moving to another city. The patient expressed some resentment, and over the next several weeks began to report having quarrels with her husband. Little comment was made by Mr. Banks.

For her final hour, Mrs. Weaver brought a photograph that she had taken of her mother holding an infant. Mr. Banks accepted the photo, but suggested that his patient explore the meanings of the gift. Mrs. Weaver seemed irritated and said that it was merely an expression of gratitude. However, she went on to recall an affair that she'd had with an executive at the hospital where both had worked. Because of the affair, this man had given her special favors. She also recalled a married couple who worked at the hospital; it was almost as though they needed to work at the same place, she said, because neither was able to let the other out of his or her sight.

Through these encoded images, the inappropriate sexual and merging aspects of the therapist's acceptance of her gift were conveyed. Gift giving is especially common in psychotherapies in which separation issues and related death anxieties have not been resolved. Failing such resolution, the patient attempts to leave part of himself or herself with the therapist, thereby creating an everlasting merger used unconsciously to deny the patient's—and therapist's—sense of loss and finality. Whatever the gratification, these defenses are costly in the long run.

Overall, then, the trend is clear: There is no substitute in the deep unconscious system for a consistent and appropriate fee, privately and individually paid by the patient. In principle, when a deviation is unavoidable, the effects can be minimized—though never entirely eliminated—by suitable interpretation and by keeping the alteration in the ground rule to the absolute minimum. Although these issues are complicated, the basic guideline is clear: Ideal management of the fee should receive the highest ratings, with the lowest ratings reserved for basically dishonest fee arrangements, which unconsciously reinforce the corrupt aspect of a patient's character and emotional disturbance. In between exist all gradations of deviation. If a deviant fee arrangement is essentially honest but unnecessary, the therapist should receive a rating of *Questionable* or *Unsound/Reconsider Your Choice*. However, if a therapist is incapable of or not open to exploration and interpretation of the issues involved in the fee deviation, he or she deserves a far lower rating than the therapist who participates in the deviation but is able to interpret the patient's unconscious perceptions of its implications and ramifications.

To illustrate, consider Tammy, a twenty-seven-year-old woman tied to a manipulative and blatantly destructive mother. The mother kept her daughter knotted in the relationship by plying her with gifts of money. Tammy hoped that psychotherapy would help her to free herself from this entanglement. Toward the end of the consultation hour, Dr. Kirk asked Tammy how much she could afford to pay for her psychotherapy. (This in itself is an inappropriate question; it is the therapist's responsibility to state a fair and equitable fee without assistance from the patient.) Tammy, understandably, responded by asking his standard price, and Dr. Kirk told her that his usual fee was $80 for a forty-five minute session. Tearfully, Tammy said she could not afford a fee like that—all she could scrounge up for psychotherapy, even with her mother's help, was about $100 a month. Dr. Kirk agreed immediately to set a fee of $25 per session and, consciously, Tammy was both relieved and grateful.

Soon after this interchange, Tammy returned to the subject of her mother's attempts to manipulate and control her with gifts of money. "And it's not just her," Tammy said. "It's my aunt, too; she's always butting into my life, giving me money and gifts, and I just keep on taking them. I know I shouldn't be playing this money-gift game; I'll never be my own person as long as I go along with them. But I just keep on doing it."

These stories are, of course, displaced and encoded unconscious perceptions of Dr. Kirk's agreement to reduce her fee. Despite Tammy's conscious relief and acceptance, she unconsciously saw the reduced fee as a form of seduction, manipulation, and a way of binding her to the therapist. It may be argued that Tammy was complaining about her mother before Dr. Kirk agreed to reduce her fee; how can one prove that these images were now reflecting her unconscious perceptions of the therapist? Clinical experience is absolutely consistent on this point: Had Dr. Kirk handled the fee arrangement in an ideal way—by stating an equitable amount of money, or had he held the frame by refusing to lower his fee, Tammy's subsequent associations would have been different. Notice that following Dr. Kirk's reduction of the fee, Tammy not only continued to complain about her mother, she introduced a second person whose behavior is the same as her mother's. This is a clear encoded description of Dr. Kirk. Had Dr. Kirk maintained a secure frame, Tammy would have introduced a different sort of figure— perhaps a boyfriend who had refused to encourage her dependence on him.

In Tammy's therapy, as is so often the case, the fee arrangement replicated precisely the kind of pathological relationship for which Tammy had sought help. Repetitions of this kind are remarkably common. I have already pointed out that relief from emotional disturbance can be obtained very quickly by securing a therapist whose destructive or sick behavior unconsciously justifies one's own. It is possible, of course, to enter a psychotherapy that duplicates a destructive outside relationship for the purpose, however unconscious, of learning to handle the situation more constructively. When faced with emotional problems in both parties to therapy, a patient can sometimes mobilize his or her resources both as a model of health for all concerned and as a way of finally resolving the sick relationship. These results are by no means assured, however; and the deep unconscious system always reflects highly negative perceptions of the therapist involved.

When Mr. Kittner was offered a low fee for psychotherapy by his social-worker therapist, he immediately remembered two dreams: In the first, a dog is biting at him, and in the second, a man is trying to seduce him sexually. Here the fee reduction is unconsciously experienced as both an assault and a seduction, qualities that lead this therapist to deserve a *Dangerous/Beware* rating. Again and again, frame deviations that are consciously experienced as gratifying are experienced in the deep unconscious system as destructive in a variety of ways.

Another example: Dr. Hawkins assured her patient, Mr. Shane, that it was all right for him to accumulate a large bill—just as long as he paid her eventually. Directly after this assurance, Mr. Shane spoke about his mother, who had overindulged him, he said, to the point where he felt little need to function at all. He then spoke about a business colleague who came on to every woman he met. He was deeply critical of these people—a reflection of the way he saw his therapist unconsciously. Ideally, Dr. Hawkins should have terminated the treatment until Mr. Shane could pay her what he owed.

As the months passed, Mr. Shane began to worry consciously about his mounting indebtedness. He told Dr. Hawkins that he was feeling trapped and guilty. Dr. Hawkins, knowing that Mr. Shane had an excellent reputation as an advertising writer, proposed a barter arrangement. If Mr. Shane would write the essay required by an advanced psychotherapy training program that she was taking, she would forgive Mr. Shane's fee. Mr. Shane agreed, and was elated when his paper received an excellent appraisal from the program board. Neither patient nor therapist noticed the extent to which Mr. Shane's subsequent associations had turned to the subject of buying term papers in college. Mr. Shane said that he abhorred this practice as dishonest not only in form but in spirit—because it robbed the student of an opportunity to learn and to grow.

Clearly, this patient's perception of the barter agreement is split between the conscious and unconscious systems, at entirely opposite poles. Although Mr. Shane was consciously relieved by the opportunity to clear the books on his unpaid bills, he unconsciously rated the therapist's proposal as *Unsound/Reconsider Your Choice* to *Dangerous/Beware*. During this same period of time, Mr. Shane dreamed that a hand reached up through a hole in the ground and tried to pull him in. This imagery reflects the smothering and trapping qualities of the barter arrangement. Even though Mr. Shane took an active, creative role in the situation, he unconsciously felt pulled in over his head.

Contrast the imagery here with the associations of Ms. White, a computer sales representative, who was also having trouble paying her therapist's fee. She proposed an exchange of services: She would provide the therapist with a computer and a variety of graphics cards and software packages, and he would provide her with a year of therapy. Dr. Kelsey suggested that Ms. White simply continue to say whatever came to mind. Ms. White spoke for a while about her work, and then recalled a married man whom she had met through the business. They had had an affair, and during that period of time Ms. White had pirated several programs for use on his home computer. In retrospect, Ms. White felt that she had in some sense lost sight of her own standards; she really didn't believe in seeing married men, and she now regretted the sort of roller-coaster emotions that had led her to steal for this man as well.

On the basis of this material, Dr. Kelsey was able to interpret the patient's unconscious view of the barter arrangement she had proposed to him. Ms. White unconsciously felt that the exchange would be tantamount to creating an illicit and dishonest relationship. The patient did not respond directly to this interpretation, but her associations turned to another man she knew: someone she had been dating, who struck her as absolutely incorruptible. She greatly admired him and wished to see him again.

Here Ms. White's negative unconscious perceptions of the therapist anticipated his agreeing to her proposed exchange, which would have obtained an *Unsound/Reconsider Your Choice*–to–*Dangerous/Beware* rating. When the therapist held the frame and eventually interpreted the patient's unconscious directive to him, a highly positive and constructive image emerged—a displaced and unconscious perception that spoke for the ideal qualities of this way of handling the situation.

The consistency of the deep unconscious system always amazes me. Countless fee arrangements exist, consciously acceptable to all concerned; yet the deep unconscious system (of both patient and therapist) reviews them as plainly destructive and advises against them. And despite its necessity and its legality, the use of insurance prompts the same kind of negative unconscious reading.

Consider Mr. Stevenson: In his first consultation session, he insisted that his therapist, Mr. Garrett, a social worker, sign insurance forms so that he could recover 50 percent of the therapist's fee. Mr. Garrett was reluctant, but the patient was so insistent that he finally agreed. Once the forms were signed, the patient recalled a burglar who had come into his office in broad daylight; he was brandishing a gun and threatened to shoot Mr. Stevenson unless he handed over all of his money. The patient moved then from the image of a burglar in his office to the image of his boss. He didn't trust his boss, he said; he suspected that the man was giving kickbacks to customers. (Images of this kind are repeated again and again at the juncture where a therapist agrees to include a third-party payer in a psychotherapy.)

Soon after producing these images, Mr. Stevenson said that he had nothing more to say. He was silent for the next fifteen minutes, even though this was his first consultation with this therapist. When he finally spoke again, he went back to his boss's lack of integrity; he said that he found the man so untrustworthy that he had stopped telling him anything important.

I will conclude this discussion of fee issues with a final vignette. It shows rather clearly how adhering to the ground rule regarding responsibility for the fee for all sessions, though consciously both bothersome and burdensome, is well appreciated by the deep unconscious system and can also have very positive effects on the life of a patient. Mr. Criswell, a married man in his early forties, was in therapy with Dr. Koyama, a male psychologist. Mr. Criswell had a history of frequenting pornography shops and engaging in occasional one-night stands. He finally realized that he was losing control when he exposed himself to the young woman who took care of the children when he and his wife were out.

Early in his once-weekly psychotherapy, he had to miss a session because of a meeting related to his job. His conscious feeling, despite his initial agreement to the ground rule that he would pay for missed sessions, was that a business meeting was an exception. It wasn't his fault that he had to attend; it wasn't as if he had canceled the session frivolously. These rationalizations were invariably followed by images that indicated Mr. Criswell's own deep unconscious directive to pay for the missed session: for example, he spoke about delinquent payments in business—how people shouldn't be allowed to cheat other people out of money owed to them. The therapist interpreted these unconscious directives to him, but Mr. Criswell still refused to pay for the missed session.

One afternoon, some months later, Mr. Criswell missed another session. He began the following hour by explaining that he had taken a cab to Dr. Koyama's office and been involved in an accident. He was sufficiently shaken by the incident, he said, that he couldn't make his therapy appointment. In fact, he had gone to a doctor, but examination revealed no notable injury.

Mr. Criswell went on to talk about management changes at work. "Suddenly I've got responsibility for the petty-cash fund. I'm supposed to keep a log of all the money taken out, but my new boss doesn't want me to do it. It's pretty clear that he's had his hand in the till with small amounts and doesn't want to get caught. I told him that I'd either keep a complete log or I'd quit the job; there's no way I want to support that kind of petty dishonesty."

Then he said: "What bothers me most about the accident is that I'm going to have to pay for the session I missed. Oh—I had a dream. I corner a woman and make her do what I want her to do sexually. She reminds me of that sitter I flashed last year. I don't know. Maybe it's all related to my mother and how she treated me when I was a kid. Actually, I *don't* feel bad about paying for last week's session; I feel sort of good about it—like I'm taking some responsibility for a change. In fact, lately things have been really good with my wife. I mean, you know how aggravated I've been with her—it's like we spend all our time fighting until I just walk out. Well, last night, she started complaining about the kids and everything, and instead of getting into a fight with her, I really tried to understand how she was feeling. I figured, okay, if it's the kids she's bothered with, I'll take care of the kids for a change. I mean, usually, I get out and go to a porn shop or something. But this felt good—like I was there for her. You forget sometimes how it can be to feel close to your wife and to treat her the way she should be treated. Anyway, I know you expect me to pay for that missed hour; don't worry, I'm gonna do it."

The central organizing trigger for this session was Dr. Koyama's expectation that Mr. Criswell would accept his responsibility for the fee for the hour that he missed. Mr. Criswell beautifully portrayed his own unconscious appreciation of the need to maintain the ground rule regarding the fee by telling a story about keeping a complete record of petty-cash outlays at work. Unconsciously, he recognized that he needed to be responsible for all his sessions or leave.

Mr. Criswell in fact followed that story with an attempt to secure the frame of his treatment: He said that he felt good about taking responsibility for the missed session. Indeed, the dream images that Mr. Criswell described—his cornering a woman and abusing her sexually—typically follow attempts to secure a treatment frame. Mr. Criswell was experiencing a conscious sense of satisfaction in maintaining the frame; but unconsciously, he was experiencing secure-frame anxiety—the sense of being trapped and in danger. This kind of anxiety is health-promoting; it is likely to enable Mr. Criswell to get to forgotten or repressed experiences that are a factor in his exhibitionism.

Notice that these images were followed immediately by a positive description of a secured marital frame. Mr. Criswell's decision to keep the therapeutic frame secure was paralleled by a positive turn in his relationship with his wife. Mr. Criswell's refusal to take responsibility for the therapeutic frame had been paralleled in the past by violations in his marital contract. There is a genuine relationship between boundaries within and outside of therapy. Mr. Criswell's motivation to secure the therapeutic frame had an immediate and salutary effect not only in his marriage but at his job, where he also took a stand on maintaining boundaries and a sense of honesty and commitment to his responsibilities.

Decisions made around the framework of therapy have unconscious effects that are lived out behaviorally in extratherapeutic situations. In other words, the interventions of highly rated psychotherapists, especially when they relate to the ground rules of treatment, have real-life consequences for a patient. Whatever the attendant anxieties, the secure frame is a constructive therapeutic experience that almost always produces constructive life experiences. In the same way, alterations in the ground rules almost always lead to destructive life experiences—whose source and meaning go unrecognized by both patient and therapist.

We turn now to the various issues related to the time and duration of sessions.

There are many pressures, professional and personal, that may lead either party to therapy to propose temporary or permanent shifts in the time of a session or the frequency with which a patient is seen. There are also instances where patients are seen for medication or so-called supportive therapy without a scheduled time for the therapy hour. In these instances, the patient or therapist telephones the other and arranges a session as needed. Whatever the necessity of such arrangements, in the deep unconscious system they are poorly rated and seen as a sign of the therapist's instability, uncertainty, and manipulative tendencies. Ideally, as I have said, both the time and frequency of sessions is set for the entire course of the therapy.

Although changes are sometimes necessary—perhaps because of a new professional commitment on the part of the therapist or a permanent change in your own time commitments—the shift should be permanent and its unconscious meanings explored. No matter how necessary the change in hour may be, the patient unconsciously experiences overgratification, merger or fusion with the therapist, a lack of certainty, and the like. The same principle applies to shifts in the frequency of sessions, particularly the use of an extra hour in situations of seeming or evident urgent need. Although such sessions are indeed sometimes necessary in the presence of suicidal and homicidal impulses, and other extremes of psychological and emotional distress, the deep unconscious mind still registers a perception of the therapist who makes such a move as destructive. The same applies to increasing or decreasing the frequency of sessions, the latter often proving to be a harbinger of the termination of a therapy.

The highest rating goes to therapists who create a set time and frequency of sessions for the entire therapy, and who do not engage in such practices as reducing the frequency of sessions as treatment winds down. The sensitivity of the deep unconscious system to these issues is so great that the least variation is fraught with detrimental consequences regardless of the conscious experience. Nonetheless, when psychotherapeutic emergencies do occur, the direct and conscious need must be addressed, considered, and at times gratified, and the unconscious ramifications can then be explored, interpreted, and corrected to the greatest extent possible.

Ms. Brandon, a chronically depressed woman in her early thirties, telephoned Dr. Mihalik asking for an additional session because she was feeling particularly depressed. During the extra hour that Dr. Mihalik arranged, the patient had a great deal of difficulty talking. She spoke of an error she had made in setting her watch, so that she had shown up at the wrong time for an appointment. Her mother was all screwed up about appointments and never kept them straight. "Like mother, like daughter," she said. "My mother is a mess and so am I."

All of these negative images indicate that the patient's deep unconscious system perceived Dr. Mihalik's offer of the additional hour as an error: He should have kept to the correct hour; they were meeting at the wrong time; he "screwed things up"; he wasn't any better than she was about keeping things straight. When these images went unrecognized and uninterpreted by Dr. Mihalik, Ms. Brandon became even more depressed and began to cry about how poorly her mother understood her needs and what she had to say. Again the images indicate her perception of the therapist—as unavailable to her and unable to understand the meaning of her words. This material was followed by a long silence; and as if to set the matter straight in her own particular way, Ms. Brandon missed the following session.

Similar themes appeared in the displaced and disguised images of another patient, Mrs. Barglow, in therapy with a female psychiatrist, Dr. Colagrande. Toward the end of one session, the patient asked to have her hour changed because it coincided with her daughter's performance in the annual school play. Suitable arrangements for an alternative session were made, but the patient called at the last minute to cancel the hour because she felt physically ill (this is a relatively common response to an altered framework and to the weakened unconscious support reflected in unnecessary deviations). I recognize the basis of the patient's request as love and pride; one would regard as unfeeling the absence of desire to see a daughter in a school play. When I say "unnecessary" deviation, I am reflecting the view of the deep unconscious system. One may quarrel with this point of view; but it is there and it has consequences that must be dealt with in a therapy.

Witness the fact that Mrs. Barglow began her next regular session by saying that she had felt confused about the time of her appointment. She mentioned again that she'd been feeling ill, and then remembered an incident of physical assault and sexual abuse by an uncle. She next recalled a problem that had arisen because neither her husband nor she could remember the terms of their divorce agreement. She felt unreasonably angry with him, as though he should have been the one to take responsibility for their contract. This reminded her of another situation where she had to take responsibility for someone else. The other day her daughter had wanted to leave school early and asked her to write a note requesting permission for her to do so. Mrs. Barglow refused to write the note, telling her that she was better off learning to follow the rules rather than finding ways to be the exception. She eventually realized that her daughter was trying to avoid having to take a difficult exam that afternoon.

The last image in this material—getting off early to avoid a difficult exam—tells us something important: It alludes to the patient's unconscious realization that her request for a change of hour had come at a time when a number of difficult issues were beginning to emerge in the therapy. Indeed, the very act of altering the frame eliminated these issues from the sessions for some time and reduced the pressure, albeit in an inappropriate, or pathological, way. As for the remainder of the patient's encoded imagery, it is clear that Mrs. Barglow was still working over unconsciously the fact of the deviation as a breach of contract, as a cause for mistrust, and as a sanctioned means of escaping a difficult yet necessary confrontation. She also provided a model of rectification—her own refusal to let her daughter change her scheduled appointment.

Deep unconscious perceptions are remarkably consistent from patient to patient in response to the same kinds of deviations. Perhaps it all sounds too much like a broken record, but patients and therapists alike have been tone-deaf and have ignored these encoded messages—and the unconscious appraisals that they reflect. We have so utterly neglected these messages that they seem harsh and extreme. But I promise you—if you learn to decode your own messages in the context of a psychotherapy, you will most certainly discover the same themes and the same kind of ratings in your own deep unconscious experience. And you will discover, too, that these unconscious ratings reflect worries that have real consequences.

In Mrs. Barglow's case, the humane act of changing an hour was unconsciously perceived as a sexual assault. Think about this for a second. If you are depending on a structure for support, a change—for any reason—*is* assaultive and intrusive. There is a seductive aspect about such a change as well, insofar as power and control are used to manipulate another. For Mrs. Barglow, these aspects of what was certainly innocuous on the surface (in the conscious system) actually created in the deep unconscious memory system the reexperience of a terrible early trauma—the near-rape by an uncle. Small wonder that for some months after this incident, Mrs. Barglow experienced considerable difficulties in her sexual relationship with the man she was currently seeing. In her therapy, the connection between these problems and the changed hour went unrecognized, and the issue remained unresolved for the patient.

Similarly, the deep unconscious rating of a psychotherapist who either shortens or lengthens the duration of a session is also quite negative. When sessions are deliberately or inadvertently cut short, patients tend to rationalize the experience and excuse their therapists, all the while producing displaced and disguised stories of people who are depriving, out of control, assaultive, and otherwise insensitive and destructive. On the other hand, the therapist who extends a session—for whatever reason—is experienced unconsciously as seductive, entrapping, overgratifying, and unable to define proper boundaries in his or her relationships with others.

In one specific instance, a male therapist, Dr. Wallace, inadvertently extended the session with a young female patient, Ms. Sprauer, fifteen minutes beyond its actual time. Ms. Sprauer herself was only dimly aware that the hour had lasted longer than usual, but she wondered about it; she wondered if the therapist had been so interested in her material that he just forgot the time.

As her next session began, Ms. Sprauer suddenly recalled an incident when her brother had locked the door to the basement of their house, blocked her exit, and tried to involve her in adolescent sexual experimentation. Though not an issue for Ms. Sprauer consciously, in the deep unconscious memory system, the alteration of the boundaries of the therapy session actually repeated on some level Ms. Sprauer's earlier life trauma. The patient's deep unconscious system proposed a *Dangerous/Beware* rating in this instance.

A similar rating was afforded Dr. Scanell, a male therapist who asked one of his female patients, Ms. Clark, to trade hours with another patient. Wanting desperately to please the therapist, Ms. Clark agreed. Not surprisingly, however, after agreeing, she began to talk in great detail about the way her mother always favored her sister. Dr. Scanell interpreted this material as a reflection of Ms. Clark's feelings of sibling rivalry. Ms. Clark responded to this intervention by becoming vehemently angry. She said that her feelings of rivalry weren't the issue; her mother happened to be a lousy mother who favored one daughter at the expense of the other. This is a very plain unconscious evaluation of Dr. Scanell in light of his exploitative deviation and inability to recognize its effects.

To conclude this discussion, we can look at an instance where a seemingly minor deviation had a major effect on the patient. When Ms. Benjamin's regular hour fell on Memorial Day, her therapist, Ms. Raglin, a social worker, offered to see her anyway. Ms. Benjamin was a lawyer in her late twenties whose main difficulty was an attraction to sadistic and ungiving men. She had recently ended a two-year involvement with a particularly cruel but compelling man, Jean-Luc. In fact, she had made this decision not long after Ms. Raglin had refused Ms. Benjamin's request that she see both her and Jean-Luc in a joint session. Ms. Raglin had maintained the frame in this regard based on Ms. Benjamin's own unconscious directives.

After this frame-securing moment, Ms. Benjamin had begun to delve for the first time in her therapy into memories from her childhood that were vague but suggested traumatic violence. The power of this material had actually unnerved Ms. Raglin, and she was late in starting one of Ms. Benjamin's sessions. At this point, the early memories disappeared. The bulk of Ms. Benjamin's material was now devoted to unconsciously working over the therapist's failure to adhere to the time aspect of the framework.

When Ms. Raglin offered to see Ms. Benjamin on Memorial Day, Ms. Benjamin simply refused. She began the next session by saying that she would have to cancel an hour the following week because of a business commitment. She then went on: "I had a pretty good holiday, but I felt depressed for some reason. My mother kept calling me, like she was after me, bugging me. I thought a lot about the death of my grandfather and the sense of loss I had experienced, and it all made me feel very much abandoned and alone. I don't like being alone as a rule, but it was really worse this holiday weekend. Anyhow, I called Jean-Luc, and met him at a bar for a few drinks, and before I knew it, I was back in bed with him. In the morning, I hated myself for going after him; I don't know why I did it. It was just that the depression about being alone seemed to build up to an unbearable level. I really should stop seeing him; I hope I can do it."

The trigger here is clearly Ms. Raglin's offer to see Ms. Benjamin on the Memorial Day holiday. In this instance, the patient consciously refused, yet nonetheless shows us that her therapist's offer had a powerful unconscious influence on her. Unconsciously, Ms. Benjamin perceived Ms. Raglin as a depressed woman who could not tolerate being alone—being without her patient even for one session. The offer of the session was also unconsciously perceived—as revealed in the image of Ms. Benjamin's mother and in her own behavior with Jean-Luc—as an attempt to pursue and seduce the patient as a way of repairing Ms. Raglin's sense of abandonment and aloneness.

As we can see, this deviant offer led not only to incisive unconscious perceptions, but also to a self-destructive piece of behavior by this patient. Ms. Raglin's depression and loneliness, as well as her way of dealing with it by trying to entrap or merge inappropriately with someone, was taken in psychologically by Ms. Benjamin, and it led to something more than a dream or story—to an actual enactment. It seems likely that Ms. Raglin and Ms. Benjamin were suffering from comparable anxieties and tended to deal with them in similar fashion: by "acting out" self-destructively in a desperate attempt to be with someone—anyone. Whatever the reason, the intensity of Ms. Benjamin's unconscious perceptions of Ms. Raglin's offer was so great that Ms. Benjamin was unable to contain their power; as a result, she actually lived out the implications of her therapist's offer. Once more, a low-rated deviant-frame intervention shows both communicative and real-life consequences.

As we saw in chapter 7, a consistent, professional, truly neutral and anonymous locale for a therapist's office is also part of the ideal, secure frame. At times patients, and perhaps therapists, will request a change in locale—either to a new office, to another office used by the therapist, and sometimes even to the home of the therapist or the patient. In one situation, where a male patient became terrified of leaving his home and stated that he could no longer have sessions in his therapist's office, the therapist elected to hold sessions in the patient's house. The patient was quite grateful; however, the first session under these conditions began with the patient's report of a dream: A poisonous spider had invaded the patient's bedroom and was ready to attack.

Here is another example of a well-meaning alteration in the ideal frame that is viewed unconsciously as dangerous and assaultive and incapacitating. This therapist intervention is seen consciously as a benevolent and considerate act; but the deep unconscious system says *Dangerous/Beware*—this is an invasive, poisonous, and destructive act. The very fact that the patient remained phobic and ill for a long time, and manipulated many other people through his illness, speaks again for the actual consequences of this low-rated frame break.

In situations where a therapist changes his or her office locale, unconscious perceptions of abandonment and death are not uncommon. When the move is from a professional and private office to a home-office, the prevailing images involve indecent exposure, leakage of information to others, the presence of spies, the fear of being alone with the patient—to cite just a few. On the other hand, when the move is from a home-office to a private setting, the imagery is typically quite the reverse, shifting from themes of insecurity and exposure to those of strength, privacy, safety, and trust. In one instance, an adolescent patient reacted to such a move by describing the fact that his parents had at long last given him his own room, so that he no longer had to share a bedroom with his maturing sister. There was a strong sense of safety, privacy, and of a setting in which the patient could mature and grow strong.

The deep unconscious system will, indeed, provide high ratings for therapists who can hold and maintain the frame, but it will forever remain critical of those who do not. This is especially true of issues related to the fee and temporal aspects of the frame, because it is these conditions of treatment—the ground rules and "hold"—which, when properly managed, provide the fundamental safety and security of a deeply constructive therapeutic relationship and experience.

Table 5: The Fee

RATE YOUR THERAPIST

This is how my therapist handled/is handling the fee:

Sound Answers
- He/she proposed a single, reasonable, fixed fee.
- He/she didn't barter or bargain with me.
- He/she holds me entirely responsible for the fee; I can't use a third-party payer.
- He/she won't let me build up a debt.
- He/she won't accept gifts or other forms of compensation beyond the agreed-upon fee.
- He/she has not changed the fee during the therapy.
- He/she holds me responsible for the fee for all scheduled sessions.

Questionable-to-Unsound Answers: Reconsider Your Choice of Therapist
- He/she let me decide what I wanted to pay.
- He/she gave me a fee range.
- He/she told me that he/she was charging more (or less) than his/her customary fee.
- He/she says that I don't have to pay the fee when I go on vacation, take business trips, get sick, attend a wedding or funeral, etc.
- He/she increased (decreased) the fee during therapy.
- He/she accepts third-party payment (from parents, an insurance company, a governmental agency, etc.).
- He/she gives me/accepts small gifts on rare occasions.
- He/she lets me build up a temporary debt when I'm having a hard time financially.
- He/she takes the fee in cash (and keeps no record).
- He/she asks to be paid in advance of the sessions.

Dangerous Answers: Beware of This Therapist

- He/she is willing to falsify a fee to an insurance company for me.
- He/she negotiated a barter arrangement with me, which bypasses taxation.
- He/she gives me expensive gifts and accepts them from me.
- He/she accepts financial tips/stock information from me.
- He/she traded me a low fee for cash payment.

Table 6: The Schedule

This is how my therapist handled/is handling the schedule:

Sound Answers
- He/she arranged a definite schedule for my therapy—day, time, frequency, and length—and these have not changed through the course of my therapy.
- At most, the schedule has changed because of a major change in my work/school schedule or life circumstances or a new and major professional commitment by the therapist.

Questionable-to-Unsound Answers: Reconsider Your Choice of Therapist
- There are minor and occasional shifts in the time and length of sessions; a rare emergency hour.
- There isn't really much of a fixed schedule.
- When I don't come, I don't have to pay, and I can have makeup sessions.
- As therapy was coming to an end, my therapist decided to reduce the frequency of my sessions—a sort of tapering-off strategy.
- He/she has lapses, but rarely: extending or shortening an hour, failing to be there for a scheduled session.

Dangerous Answers: Beware of This Therapist
- He/she repeatedly changes the time and/or day of the sessions.
- He/she often starts late because other patients stay past their scheduled times.
- He/she often lets me stay longer than my scheduled hour, particularly if there's no one else waiting to see him/her.
- He/she has asked me to shift my hour so he/she can see some other patient during my scheduled time.

- He/she has canceled sessions in order to vote, move into a new house, take his/her dog to the vet, etc.
- He/she keeps recommending that I see him/her more often than I want to.
- He/she often walks out with me and hangs around making small talk before the next patient comes in.

·10·

Privacy, Confidentiality, and Relative Anonymity

I n the previous chapter, I spoke about the temporal aspects of a secure frame—the fixed boundaries, so to speak, of a treatment session. The secure frame also includes boundaries for the communication that goes on in a treatment session. That is, a therapeutic relationship is not sustained merely by meeting at a given time and place, sitting in an accustomed chair or lying on a couch, and paying a set fee. It is also sustained by the maintenance of privacy and confidentiality, and by the neutrality and anonymity of the therapist.

A patient who is attempting to resolve his or her emotional problems will inevitably speak of matters that are personal, sensitive, disturbing, and often terrifying. It is natural to expect that a psychotherapist will provide a setting in which privacy and confidentiality are assured. Less apparent, perhaps, is the fact that total privacy implies a one-to-one relationship. This means that privacy is modified not only by the direct presence of a third party in the treatment session, but also by the practice of reporting to a third party about the transactions of the session. Any kind of third-party involvement in a therapy results in a deep unconscious sense of exposure, vulnerability, and mistrust.

Even less apparent to the conscious system is the relationship that exists between privacy and the anonymity of the therapist. By anonymity I mean that the patient has, to the greatest extent possible, no knowledge of the therapist's personal life, opinions, and reactions. Of course, much is inevitably known about any psychotherapist—his or her choice of office, decor, manner of dress, speech, carriage, and so forth. These attributes are a matter of self-*presentation*. Self-*revelation*, on the other hand, is a different order of communication. It is the absence of self-revelation that separates the therapeutic relationship from other kinds of social relationships.

Relative anonymity is ensured by the therapist's neutrality. By neutrality I mean the therapist's use of appropriate silence, sound interpretations, and frame-securing interventions (see chapter 11). By restricting himself or herself to neutral interventions, the therapist establishes a safe environment for the patient. If a patient knows that the therapist will not impose judgment on or recoil from or elicit particular kinds of material, it becomes possible to share even the vilest and basest secrets and fantasies. It is the absence of responses that stem from the therapist's own personal needs, along with the presence of warmth and empathy appropriate to the patient's therapeutic needs, that ensure the patient's trust and make it possible to speak the unspeakable: to confess, to attack verbally, to fantasize aloud, to attempt to seduce—in short, to express the deepest and most terrible aspects of the personality to another person, whose entire commitment is to respond therapeutically.

Just as the therapist's anonymity and neutrality go together, privacy and confidentiality go together as well. Confidentiality implies that the therapist will take no notes and make no recordings of the treatment experience. The session is ideally an evanescent and passing exchange between two human beings. This, too, assures the patient that it is safe to speak, that there will be no leakage, that no one will exploit the conscious and unconscious truths of the moment, and that the therapist has no need to misuse the painful revelations of a psychotherapeutic experience.

In all, privacy, confidentiality, and therapist anonymity and neutrality create a therapeutic space designed to hold the patient well and to promote deep insight and inner change. A therapist who adheres to these ground rules conveys warmth and concern within limits appropriate to a therapeutic relationship.

We have discussed the matter of privacy in other contexts in this book—for example, with respect to third-party payment, the inclusion of a spouse or family member in a treatment session, the presence of secretaries and assistants in the therapist's office, the presence of other patients in a shared waiting room, social or professional acquaintance with other patients of the therapist, and so forth. The issue is so important that I will raise it once more in its own right. Modifications of total privacy are so common today that they are taken as accepted practice by the vast majority of both patients and therapists. I've known individuals in therapy who are elated when the therapist takes a lengthy note; they think it means they've just said something interesting and worth writing down. Many patients are fascinated by the diagnosis required by their insurance companies or funding agencies before reimbursement for therapy will be approved. Some will actually go to a library, look up their diagnostic code number in a manual of disorders, and read the criteria listed—just as though they were discovering classified information about their own psyches. Others feel quite gratified when a therapist asks permission to use one of their dreams or sessions for a journal article. Third-party involvement is really the rule rather than the exception. I must emphasize, therefore, that in a private therapy what happens ideally occurs only between the two people involved—and only for the moment. Sometimes a patient's words, feelings, or behaviors will draw a comment by the therapist; beyond that, they pass into memory, or into oblivion.

The conscious system is extraordinarily matter-of-fact on this issue, but encoded communications from patients consistently speak against all forms of third-party involvement as an intrusion.

To begin at one extreme, there is Mrs. Perkins, a depressed widow in psychotherapy with Dr. Rath, a male psychologist in supervision with me as a way of learning how to do psychotherapy.

Dr. Rath was puzzled by a session he'd had with this patient. Mrs. Perkins had come into the hour quite anxious—almost in a paranoid state: She felt that people were staring at her, particularly men, and she was feeling suspicious of everyone. The night before, she had been taking a shower and heard noises; she was convinced that a robber had come into the house and that her life was in danger. She called in a neighbor, an attorney, who searched her apartment and found no one. She nonetheless remained convinced that there was an intruder in her space.

Often a therapist will pause to examine a story that a patient tells, not knowing that the source of its imagery was his or her own intervention—usually one related to the ground rules or frame of the therapy. In every case, however, the best way to proceed is to use the images as a guide to the unknown trigger. So my first question to Dr. Rath was: "Is there some third-party involvement here? An insurance company? Have you seen any of her friends or relatives?" Dr. Rath said no, there was no third-party involvement of any sort. The images were so strong, however, that I pursued the issue further. "Where are these images coming from, then?" I asked. Encoded images are not figments of a patient's imagination; they are always disguised perceptions. Somehow the privacy of this woman's therapy had been intruded on. "I can't imagine what I've done that would trigger these images," Dr. Rath replied. "I really think this suspiciousness is part of Mrs. Perkins's overall problem. Unless . . ." Here Dr. Rath hesitated, and I knew that I was about to get the answer I was looking for. "Unless—no, there's no way she can know about it." "About what?" I asked. "About the tape recorder I have hidden in the drawer of my desk," he said. "I decided to record her last couple of sessions because I was having trouble understanding her material. But there's no way she could know that."

I agree. Consciously, Mrs. Perkins may have had no awareness at all of the quiet winding of Dr. Rath's tape recorder. But it is clear that in her deep unconscious mind she correctly perceived what her therapist was doing and understood its implications.

While her conscious system seemed oblivious, her deep unconscious system gave a *Dangerous/Beware* rating to her therapist's
surreptitious act. (If Dr. Rath had told his patient about the re-
cording equipment and taped their sessions openly, the rating
would still be *Dangerous/Beware*.) The unconscious perceptions on
which Mrs. Perkins's symptoms were based readily explained their
existence and form. They were a telling consequence of her therapist's frame deviation. Disturbances of this kind are commonplace
under such conditions. Yes, they certainly reflect trends in the
patient, but the usually unrecognized contribution of the therapist
is crucial to their development.

The same principles crop up when therapists take notes in their
sessions. In actuality, there is little or no value to note taking,
unless the therapist is engaged in supervision. And supervision,
although a necessary step in learning how to do psychotherapy,
is nonetheless a violation of privacy with all of its attendant consequences for both parties. Apart from these circumstances, the
therapist's analytic work and efforts at understanding should be
carried out while listening to the patient.

A pertinent *Unsound/Reconsider Your Choice* rating was given unconsciously to Ms. Troy, a female social worker, by Mr. Silver, a
young man in psychotherapy because of difficulties in becoming
involved with women. Ms. Troy was an avid note taker, and Mr.
Silver was silent on the matter, except for one session during which
he commented half-jokingly on the therapist's getting writer's
cramp because she was so busy with her notes. Soon after, in the
same session, he suddenly remembered a dream: He is a prisoner
in a Nazi concentration camp, present at a meeting that is being
tape-recorded. The proceedings are certain to be published, and
the head of the concentration camp will see the material and tor-
ture the prisoners who participated.

It is clear that Mr. Silver's sense of disturbance came from the
deep unconscious rating he gave to his therapist's practice of taking
notes. Even when a therapist limits himself or herself to taking
brief notes, a sense of entrapment, broadcast, and punishment will

arise in the deep unconscious system. Though consciously, patients sometimes feel that note taking shows concern and interest, the deep unconscious reading is far different and rates this practice as *Questionable* to *Dangerous/Beware*. In general, note taking is another way of minimizing a patient's unconscious communication and the possibility for genuine insight in favor of some other, far more defensive mode of relief. As a rule, only those patients who feel better when their deep unconscious images are barred even from disguised expression will feel a degree of relief when psychotherapy is in any sense made public.

The completion of insurance forms, the presence of a secretary, or the involvement of a family member or other third party in a patient's therapy will all obtain comparable low ratings and generate similar images of intruders, fears of intimacy, and criminality. In fact, the therapist who sees a relative of the patient is experienced in the deep unconscious system as lost to the patient—in effect, dead. The conscious system experiences no such feeling, but the deep unconscious sense of loss is profound. Often a patient suffers terribly under these conditions, unaware of a major source of his or her grief.

Consider Ms. Ferry, a young woman in her twenties, who sought psychotherapy with Dr. Dennison because of an extremely conflicted relationship with her mother. Both patient and therapist agreed that Dr. Dennison would obtain a better grasp of the situation if he had a session with Ms. Ferry's mother. Perhaps he could intervene in some way that might lessen the patient's difficulties. These are not uncommon conscious rationalizations for interviews of this kind, but their main function in the therapeutic interaction is to rationalize a violation of the privacy of the patient's psychotherapy—a violation that is powerfully motivated by pathological needs in both patient and therapist.

During the session after Dr. Dennison had seen his patient's mother, Ms. Ferry thanked him and said that she felt a great sense of relief to have her own impressions of her mother either corroborated or questioned by an impartial observer. As the session went on, however, the patient's thoughts shifted to a funeral that she had attended earlier in the week. The father of one of her friends had died. While she was at the funeral, her mother had broken into her apartment and snooped around, not only checking up on her, but actually taking some of her groceries when she left. Worse, she had gone to her daughter's landlord and told him about something that Ms. Ferry had wanted to keep private. Ms. Ferry immediately called her mother and told her that she didn't want her in her space—she felt violated and betrayed. She wished there were some kind of school that would teach her how to be a good mother.

The deep unconscious view of Dr. Dennison's deviation—his session with Ms. Ferry's mother—is clearly stated here in displaced and disguised images. Unconsciously, Ms. Ferry experienced death and loss—in a sense, of both therapist and mother; the interview had invaded the patient's private therapeutic space and involved revelations that the patient wished to keep to herself. The last image represents unconscious advice to the therapist to get further training—in substance, to learn how to be a better therapist.

Another example: After a therapist had seen the father of a young adolescent boy, the young man spoke of a strange relationship in which the father of one of his friends borrowed condoms from his son. The patient remarked on the lack of boundaries in the relationship, and spoke of how the friend's father often barged into his son's room without knocking. In the patient's own life, a much younger brother had been born and placed in his room. He felt that his privacy had been invaded and his need to have his own space violated.

Another male therapist was seeing an adolescent boy for therapy; a year later he began to treat the boy's mother. The mother was consciously pleased to be working with the therapist, because she felt that her son had been doing very well with him. Early in the therapy, however, she spoke about the death of her father, her fears of being alone, unprofessional conduct, and the problems she had had as a child when she had to share a meager amount of food with her several siblings. She also recalled an upsetting dream in which she was having an illicit affair with a married man that was discovered by his children. In associating to the dream, she expressed her longing for a healthy, one-to-one, truly intimate relationship—something she had never achieved in her life. It seems more than evident that this woman's material, her dream, and her associations were connected to the lack of privacy in her psychotherapy—in the deep unconscious system, the son was always present in the mother's sessions.

Because the deep unconscious system is definitive, it rates third-party payers negatively notwithstanding conditions of financial need. This is not to say that some form of psychotherapeutic relief cannot occur in the presence of insurers; it is only to indicate that nature cannot be fooled. A patient simply will not reveal his or her deep unconscious secrets in public. Moreover, money often corrupts; both patients and therapists will sometimes make dishonest arrangements in order to exploit insurers. In general, the greater the degree of blatant dishonesty in making these arrangements and the greater the amount of information released to the insurance company about the patient, the closer the unconscious system comes to rating these violations of privacy and confidentiality as *Dangerous/Beware*. At best, effective therapy under these conditions must again and again explore, analyze, and interpret the patient's unconscious perceptions of the ramifications of a third-party payer to the psychotherapy, thereby generating insight into the consequences of this alien presence.

To cite a typical example, we can take a look at the psychotherapy of Mr. Anderson, a tax accountant, with his female therapist, Dr. Bassey. After two months of psychotherapy for depression and psychosomatic physical symptoms, the patient asked his therapist for a summary bill that he could submit to his insurance company—including the dates of his visits, the therapist's diagnosis, and her fees. Dr. Bassey agreed to do this, and had the bill ready for Mr. Anderson at the beginning of the following hour.

Mr. Anderson said that he was grateful—psychotherapy was taking a big bite out of his salary, and insurance would be a real help. He then went back to several comments made by his therapist toward the end of the previous session. He said that he didn't understand what she had meant. Moreover, he felt confused about therapy in general and didn't feel that he knew where they were headed. On the other hand, he said, he'd had a profitable week: He'd done some moonlighting for one of his firm's clients. Although he had violated the contract he had with his company at great risk, the money was really good—and so was his sense of being able to to get away with it. This latter pleasure was all mixed up for him with feeling exploitative and dishonest—enough so that he decided he wouldn't take that kind of chance again. He didn't like the anxiety. For example, there had been a recent bomb scare at work, and the company had hired someone to stand guard. Mr. Anderson felt relieved by the idea that someone was watching, but he also had a wild thought—that the guard had really been hired as a spy and would find out about his illicit moonlighting.

With great wisdom, Mr. Anderson's deep unconscious system produced a series of disguised images that communicated the unconsciously perceived dishonesty of his therapist's behavior: involving a third-party payer in the therapy and giving out information about the patient. Notice that at the conscious level, there is no real criminality; yet, in the deep unconscious system, there is always a sense that the loss of privacy and confidentiality is a criminal act. Mr. Anderson's images indicate as well a feeling of satisfaction in having a third party function as a safeguard against disturbing material that he might otherwise communicate. On the other hand, this advantage is offset by the spying qualities of third-party payers, which arouse suspicion and create a need for concealment. Indeed, later in this and in other sessions, Mr. Anderson became silent for long periods of time. Even though he was consciously unable to fathom the source of this withdrawal, we are in a position to realize its root in the very deviation he had requested.

Modifications in privacy tend to shade into breaches of confidentiality. Again, although the deep unconscious system expects
total confidentiality for a psychotherapeutic experience, revelation
to third parties is taken almost for granted consciously. Child therapists discuss their patients' material with parents; marital therapists explore the difficulties of one spouse with the other; most
therapists will release information to insurance companies, attorneys, governmental agencies, law enforcement offices, parole of-
ficers, etc.

Not surprisingly, the deep unconscious system sees this leakage
as a form of exposure (usually experienced as highly sexual and
aggressive), a betrayal of trust, an insensitive breach of faith, and
as an expression of the therapist's allegiance to an outside party
being greater than to the patient. The release of information tends
to create, on the unconscious level, a basic sense of mistrust of the
therapist within the patient, and unconsciously justifies a need to
maintain secrets and to create a variety of resistances that oppose
the progress of the psychotherapy.

Low ratings for breaches of privacy and confidentiality abound.
Mrs. Kaufman was being seen by a psychoanalyst in so-called
supportive therapy, when he advised her that it would be best to
shift to couple therapy and include her husband in her sessions.
This very much pleased the patient, but her next thought was about
the affair her husband was having with her best friend. She felt
betrayed and depressed. The irony was that she had always expected him to become involved with another man, because he
seemed to have strong homosexual needs. But there was no sense
worrying about it anyhow; he had long since abandoned her and
was never available when she needed him.

Mr. Adler, who was seeing Mr. Lamm in psychotherapy, accepted Mr. Lamm's two closest male friends into treatment as well.
Soon after, Mr. Lamm began to have involuntary fantasies of
homosexual orgies with two or three other men, images that were
very disturbing to him. He also dreamed that he had two penises,
and he began to worry about castration.

Another therapist, Ms. Binder, agreed to see a woman with

whom her patient, Mr. Edwards, was having an affair. Mr. Edwards thanked the therapist, then immediately alluded to a mistake and to promiscuous women.

Similar low ratings and negative images appear when therapists modify the relative anonymity of a psychotherapy. In these cases, images pertain to the therapist's need to expose himself or herself, the abusive misuse of the patient as a way of working over the therapist's own pathological needs, the loss of interpersonal boundaries, and a sense of having been seduced or violated. This is another area where the conscious system takes deviation for granted. Anonymity may be violated either within or outside of therapy, and the information may be personal or professional. Many patients actually insist on superfluous professional information regarding their therapists, rationalizing a need to be an informed consumer as justification. As I said earlier, none of this information is meaningful to a prospective patient—except for the fact that the therapist has allowed for self-revelation. The only pertinent therapist factor in the therapeutic experience is how he or she conducts the psychotherapy—intervenes, behaves, manages the frame, and the like.

Outside of psychotherapy, a patient may learn from mutual friends or colleagues a small or large amount of information pertaining to the therapist's professional and social life. Within the treatment encounter, the therapist may make comparable self-revelations either voluntarily or at the request of the patient. By "self-revelation" I also mean the therapist's offer of personal opinion, directives, and associations of his or her own. All such communications violate the relative anonymity of the therapist and, although they may appear to be reassuring on the surface, are consistently perceived by the deep unconscious system as enormously destructive. Thus the silent long-range effects of this group of deviations can be considerable, operating as an invisible toxic virus influencing the course of the psychotherapy, and influencing the present and future life of the patient.

In taking a look at some clinical examples, let's begin with the other side of the coin, a situation in which a therapist held fast against pressures from his patient to become self-revealing. The situation occurred in a first session offered by Dr. Whitney to Ms. Allen, a woman in her mid-twenties who was suffering from anxiety attacks. The referral had been professional and "clean"—without contaminating influence. Midway into the session, the patient suddenly asked the therapist to spell out his professional background—his graduate school, professional training, whether it was psychoanalytic, and so forth. Dr. Whitney responded by simply advising his patient to continue to say what came to mind.

After expressing a bit of conscious annoyance, Ms. Allen spoke of a man she knew at work who was married and to whom she was quite attracted. She had made some rather strong efforts to develop a personal relationship with him and to initiate an affair. "He had the good sense to keep me at a distance," she said.

"He was very nice about it, but firm. I was really angry with him at first, but in the long run, I respected him for it. I mean, I really don't know why I came on to him; I must have been really depressed when Roger [her former boyfriend] left me. So anyway, I was furious with the guy, but now he's my best friend."

To offer a brief word of explanation, we see here that Dr. Whitney's maintenance of his relative anonymity generated an extremely positive unconscious perception and a *Sound* rating in the deep unconscious mind of Ms. Allen. In this instance, the mixture of initial resentment and later appreciation is well characterized. In the same way, in the actual therapy situation, this patient was able to put aside both her curiosity and frustration over not having her wish satisfied, and to establish a psychotherapy with Dr. Whitney that proved to be most helpful.

It is important to recognize the patient's participation in this regard of the establishment of a secure frame. Many patients, unknowingly plagued with deep unconscious needs for a deviant relationship with their therapists, would have pressed harder for professional, and sometimes even personal, self-revelations. Those with extreme needs for altered ground rules would have sought out another therapist, someone with whom the deviant-frame contract could be made. All this would take place without any realization that the rejected therapist had obtained the highest ratings from the deep unconscious system.

Let's turn now to several illustrations of low-rated modifications in a therapist's anonymity. A male patient, a mental health professional, chose as his therapist a female psychologist from the office in which he worked. He knew a great deal about the therapist both professionally and personally, and had met her husband on several occasions. Although he was pleased with his therapist consciously, his encoded stories included one about a fellow worker who had tried to choke him, a memory of sharing a bed with his sister, another of eavesdropping on his sister so that he knew all of her secrets about sex and boyfriends and could blackmail her, and a dream about being in bed with his mother.

A female patient in therapy with a male psychiatrist received a copy of the therapist's autobiography from him. She was fascinated with the revelations in the book, which included vivid descriptions of the therapist's sexual difficulties. That night she had a dream in which the psychiatrist was examining her genitally with a rusty, contaminated tongue depressor.

Another patient, a young married man, was in therapy with a male therapist who maintained a home-office. When the patient arrived for therapy, the therapist's wife answered the door, and children could be heard through the walls. The therapist often shared personal information with the patient, in an effort, he said, to show the patient that his problems were not unique. Although the patient had no particular conscious reaction to any of this, he soon developed a near-delusion that a male dentist friend was trying to seduce him homosexually. In time, he had a disastrous affair with his therapist's secretary. Low-rated therapeutic practices all too often generate self-destructive behaviors with real consequences for the patient and others.

A female patient told her therapist about her marital difficulties, and the therapist's response was to describe his own. The patient's next association was to a friend who had had a nervous breakdown and was desperately ranting to virtually anyone who would listen to him.

Mr. Shea was in psychotherapy with Dr. Mead, a male psychologist. He spoke in one session early in the therapy of his longing, as a city dweller, for a house in the country. The therapist responded with the information that he owned such a house, and described it in some detail. Mr. Shea suddenly remembered a dream: He is in a small, dirty men's room where a drunk, who is urinating in front of him, falls down in a faint. What seems innocuous to the conscious system is often quite offensive to the deep unconscious mind, where low ratings are given to even the least break in anonymity. The revelation of where a therapist resides is no exception to the rule.

A last example will show that sometimes consequences of sacrificed anonymity are quite dire. Mrs. Fish entered psychotherapy with Dr. Page, a female psychiatrist, because of a severe depression. Mrs. Fish was married and childless and she fought with her husband almost constantly. The referral could be described as a self-referral: The psychiatrist attended the same church as the patient and they had been on several church committees together. Sometimes, if they were sitting near each other in church, they embraced each other during the Kiss of Peace.

Quite early in the first session, images emerged that were to plague both patient and therapist throughout this short-lived treatment. They involved direct fantasies of being personally involved with the therapist—going to the theater with her, making love to her, being very much in her life. Part of Mrs. Fish's fundamental problem was rooted in her childhood; both of her parents had been blatantly seductive. However, it was the lack of interpersonal boundaries in the therapy that triggered these blatantly homosexual fantasies. Significant modifications in the anonymity of the psychiatrist had provoked a reaction that proved intractable to therapeutic intervention. On the other hand, these therapeutic efforts did not address the break in anonymity.

Consciously, Mrs. Fish did not connect her distressing fantasies to her prior and continued outside contact with the therapist. And for her part, Dr. Page had been trained to think of such fantasies as what is called "an erotized transference"—a set of inappropriate feelings and images surrounding the therapist that stem entirely from the past life and inner conflicts of the patient. As a result, Dr. Page suggested that Mrs. Fish's fantasies came from the over-stimulation she had experienced as a child. Although this intervention made sense to Mrs. Fish, it had little emotional impact and did not affect the intensity and frequency of the images.

In her deep unconscious system, however, Mrs. Fish understood that the fantasies were unconscious perceptions of the seductiveness of the therapist, and of herself. A vivid memory from childhood showed an additional unconscious appreciation for the situation: Her mother had insisted that her daughter bathe with her, only to become enraged and attack the child mercilessly when the child touched her breast. Only in her deep unconscious mind could Mrs. Fish appreciate that her therapist's so-called interpretations were blaming her for what the therapist had stimulated. There's something of a domino effect here: A break in anonymity is supported by a particular way of intervening that permits further breaks in anonymity, and so on. Were it not for Mrs. Fish's unconscious sense of guilt and unrecognized need for punishment, the treatment situation would have been intolerable.

There are a host of ground rules that are not explicitly stated and are seldom recognized as aspects of the ideal frame; yet they are an implicit part of sound therapy. I will conclude our discussion of how to rate the therapist's handling of the framework of treatment with two such issues: the use of medication and physical contact between patient and therapist.

Regarding medication, we must distinguish between its utility and its influence on a psychotherapy. There is an enormous over-use of psychotropic medications, drugs that tend to undermine the constructive and autonomous functioning of the individual who takes them. Though some therapists believe that medication fosters psychotherapeutic work, this is true only in extreme cases, where the emotional disturbance is so severe as to preclude a patient's meaningful participation. Medication is often ineffective in bringing relief to emotional disturbance and is fraught with side effects—both physical and psychological. Furthermore, in looking for relief through medication, relief through insight is sacrificed. Strange indeed is the therapist who treats drug dependence and other abuses of chemicals with still another chemical. Equally contradictory is the reliance on medication with a patient for whom healthy, independent functioning is the goal. All this considered, the therapist who prescribes a psychotropic drug to a patient will receive a *Sound* rating only in the presence of clear and strong indications for pharmaceutical treatment, and only for as long as such treatment is absolutely necessary. All other use of medication will obtain *Questionable*–to–*Dangerous/Beware* ratings from the deep unconscious system, whatever the conscious acceptance.

To offer one example of the issues involved, let's look at the first session between Ms. Blair, a woman in her early forties suffering from depression, and Dr. Clinton, a male psychiatrist. The patient had been referred to Dr. Clinton by a clinic because she could afford a private psychotherapy fee. Although her depressions were frequent, Ms. Blair had been able to continue to function as a freelance writer and had shown no physical or psychological signs of an extreme depressive syndrome. Nonetheless, after hearing her out for about twenty minutes of the first hour, Dr. Clinton indicated that he felt that her difficulties called for antidepressant medication, and immediately wrote out and handed her a prescription for her to fill.

"My problem is that I'm often so inept," she said in response, as she continued to free-associate in this first hour. "I lost my apartment because I bungled an assignment. My father is retired now. I used to take a lot of cocaine, even though I knew it was destructive for me—and dangerous. Once, I took a drug I didn't know anything about, and I collapsed with stomach pain. It was when I was seeing this man. Sexual relationships never work out with me. This guy had a drinking problem and it was like he was defective in some way. He couldn't handle very much stress. I knew on our first date it wasn't going to work out, but it took me two years to break up with him. If I hadn't been taking that cocaine stuff, I might have handled the whole relationship a lot differently. I'm going to need a lot of help from you in order to shape up. The way I act now, I don't feel I'm worth two cents plain."

Rather typically, the low rating given to Dr. Clinton by Ms. Blair's deep unconscious system is conveyed in images about herself. All too often, the self-castigations of patients unconsciously belong to their psychotherapists; self-allusions are a handy way of disguising perceptions of the treating person.

The *Unsound/Reconsider Your Choice* rating of this particular prescription is seen in the patient's unconscious sense of loss of both her therapeutic space (her apartment) and an opportunity to function well. Unconsciously, she equated the medication with an illicit drug, cocaine, and viewed it as a poison that would cause toxic side effects. Immediately, in her deep unconscious system, Ms. Blair realized that this therapy was not going to work out—but she also realized that she would stay with this therapist for a long time before acknowledging that fact. Had she decoded her own displaced and disguised messages, she could have acted far more quickly and far more effectively.

Indeed, Ms. Blair's own unconscious assessment suggests that unneeded medication deserves either an *Unsound/Reconsider Your Choice* rating or should be treated as a *Dangerous/Beware* item—a sign that a therapist feels incapable of working meaningfully with the patient's problems, and that it may be best to move on. Whatever relief the medication may bring—and in Ms. Blair's case, it was actually very little—the price is far too high to justify its use. Medication does at times have a place in psychotherapy; and when the use of medication is completely justifiable, the deep unconscious system does not issue a low rating. But under most circumstances, medication exacts an unnecessarily high price.

For many people, even the conscious system recognizes sexual contact between patient and therapist as a *Dangerous/Beware* item. Merely affectionate physical contact receives a more mixed reception: readily accepted by some, frowned on by others. In the deep unconscious system of virtually every patient, however, all forms of physical contact between therapist and patient receive a devastatingly low rating.

Although many patients would be repulsed by sexual overtures from their psychotherapists—and justifiably so—it is a clear sign of the power of sick or unconscious pathological needs that not a small number of patients accept such overtures. Generally, the rationalization for sexual contact with a therapist is the idea that the therapist is helping the patient to resolve sexual conflicts; sometimes both parties believe that they've fallen in love. Despite most patients' doubts and self-recriminations, relationships of this kind tend to continue for long periods of time, and the consequences are considerable. Although some of the patients involved in such liaisons are suffering from severe psychological disturbances, others are plagued by guilt and unwittingly make use of their errant therapists as psychological executioners.

One female patient became sexually involved with her male psychotherapist because of guilt over a suicide attempt made by her daughter. She responded to the first sexual contact symptomatically—with the near-delusional belief that a robber and rapist had invaded her bedroom. Another female patient was seduced by her therapist in the name of helping her to achieve sexual maturity. She, too, had a limited psychotic reaction, resolving her conflicts about the involvement through a delusion that Christ had entered her body and purified her mind and soul.

It is clear in these two illustrations that the therapists in question took advantage of their patients' problems and exacerbated them. And society has become more aware over the last generation that the sexual seduction of a patient constitutes an abuse of power and a breach of faith. Less apparent is the abuse involved in nonsexual physical contact between patient and therapist. I once interviewed a man whose therapist had engaged him in a wrestling match in front of an encounter group. The therapist's stated purpose was to bring out the patient's hostility and aggression. In fact, the patient lost control and nearly murdered the therapist in this provoked fight, whereupon the therapist actually felt vindicated and pronounced the exercise a great success! Shortly after this incident, the patient began to experience the near-delusional belief that everyone in the encounter group was now convinced that he was an overt homosexual. Notice that this patient had the same kind of limited psychotic reaction as the female patients who became lovers with their therapists. It took the patient many months to recover from his beliefs and fears that people were seeing him as homosexually inclined.

Finally, there is the case of Mrs. Grana, who became sexually involved with her therapist, Dr. Cleese, over a period of months, as he persuaded her that he was in love with her and was planning to leave his wife to marry her. (He never left his wife.) Mrs. Grana, a victim of incest, felt flattered and reassured by her therapist's gradual and patient seduction of her; she claimed that her poor self-image had been bolstered by his attentions. As it turned out, Dr. Cleese was impotent with her during most of their encounters, which is not atypical of therapist/patient relationships; still, she felt consciously enhanced by her ability to attract Dr. Cleese's sexual interest.

In this particular case, the patient's deep unconscious response was almost undisguised. Early in the relationship, Mrs. Grana had a dream. In it, Dr. Cleese was naked, sitting next to her on his analytic couch; she noticed that his penis was incredibly small and immature. As he attempted to engage her, she felt repulsed and pushed him away, telling him that his behavior was inappropriate.

In another dream, Mrs. Grana was in bed with a man who turned out to be a devil with horns and fangs. He bit at her neck, drew blood, and provoked an excruciatingly painful wound. Mrs. Grana cried out for help, but no one was there to answer. In still another dream, a man was chasing her with a knife, trying to kill her. In another, she was being tortured. She told her torturer that he was crazy, but there was no letup on the torment.

Little need be said about the patient's unconscious perceptions of this psychotherapist. All therapists who make physical contact with or attempt to seduce their patients precipitate images of this nature. Even a therapist who simply kisses a patient at the end of a session, or holds a patient's hand when he or she is in distress, obtains powerfully low ratings from the deep unconscious system. One female patient whose male therapist would hold her hand from time to time dreamed of a man holding her head under water, trying to drown her. Physical contact of any kind deserves a *Dangerous/Beware* rating, and repetitive or clearly sexual or aggressive contact is particularly dangerous.

Given the power of wishes for deviation in the deep unconscious memory system, it is inevitable that there are frame alterations that we have not specifically addressed in this chapter. I have tried to identify the most common frame breaks in present use, and to point to the most appropriate ratings of such situations if they occur.

Creating a composite score for your psychotherapist in this crucial area of framework management must be left to you, the reader and rater. This overall rating should be developed against a background of understanding that in today's world, deviant psychotherapy is the rule and secure-frame treatment the great exception. Until this changes, all that can be hoped for is to find a therapist whose departures from the ideal frame are relatively infrequent and not especially glaring or extreme. Too many deviations with respect to too many aspects of the frame—for example, departures from the ideal with respect to fee, time arrangements, privacy, confidentiality, and the like—produce a chaotic therapeutic experience, sometimes on the conscious level, but always within the deep unconscious system.

The decision whether to proceed with a particular psychotherapist is an individual one, and it can be rendered especially sensitive if you take the time to decode your own dreams, preoccupations, fantasies, and inner stories as they unfold after the first hour with your new psychotherapist. The combination of drawing from the ratings of others as presented in this book and from your own personal, unconscious ratings places you in the best possible position to decide how to proceed. Repeated *Unsound/Reconsider Your Choice* ratings from both sources immediately suggest the need to proceed with caution or to consider another psychotherapist. And all *Dangerous/Beware* ratings should be taken quite seriously; at the very least, if the decision is made to continue with the psychotherapist involved, efforts should be made to explore the conscious and unconscious meanings of the disturbing deviations, both with the psychotherapist and on your own. At the same time, engaging in a bit of self-rating regarding your own needs for deviant-frame therapy can be quite illuminating.

Rating your psychotherapist is a complex business. Doing so can be simplified only up to a point; beyond that, you must be prepared to deal with many uncertainties. Still, it is possible, despite conscious resistance, to be quite clear on low-rated items and to come to terms with their existence—either by changing therapists or by exploring and resolving the deviations at hand. Therapists who are able to respond favorably to your questions about deviant ground rules deserve acceptable ratings. Those who respond defensively to your concerns, and who stubbornly maintain the deviant ground rule—especially without exploration and interpretation, and without some acknowledgment of the validity of your complaints—remain in the *Unsound/Reconsider Your Choice* or *Dangerous/Beware* category. The time has come, for you as an individual patient and for the field of psychotherapy at large, to acknowledge and appreciate the extensive ramifications and consequences of how the ground rules of psychotherapy are created and maintained. Doing so can only promote a higher level of mental health—not only for patients but for therapists as well.

Table 7: Privacy, Confidentiality, and Anonymity

This is how my therapist handles the issues of privacy, confidentiality, and anonymity:

Sound Answers
- He/she is not deliberately self-revealing.
- Total privacy and complete confidentiality have prevailed throughout the therapy.
- When I ask my therapist about himself/herself, the response is an attitude of listening and exploration.
- He/she has not prescribed medication.
- He/she does not take notes and does not record the sessions.

Questionable-to-Unsound Answers: Reconsider Your Choice of Therapist
- He/she, on rare occasions, has offered a personal opinion or alluded to his/her professional status.
- He/she is obligated to send specific reports to my employer.
- He/she has to provide nonspecific information to the agency that pays for my therapy.
- He/she occasionally offers opinions or information about himself/herself if I'm persistent enough.
- He/she prescribed medication when I was in a state of extreme emotional dysfunction.
- He/she does not usually make physical contact with me, but has done so on rare occasions, for example, when I was experiencing a sudden traumatic loss.
- He/she sometimes takes notes when I'm talking.

Dangerous Answers: Beware of This Therapist
- He/she is more like a friend than a therapist—telling me about his/her own life, introducing me to his/her spouse, offering me the use of his/her books/home/car, etc.

- He/she talks about my material in his/her books/lectures/classes.
- His/her secretary clearly knows a lot about what I've said in my sessions.
- He/she videotapes our sessions for use with his/her psychiatric residents.
- He/she spends so much time talking about himself/herself that I have to fight for my own therapeutic space.
- All I have to do is say I've been feeling depressed, and he/she will ask if I want medication.

·11·

The Treating Psychotherapist

We have already discussed in detail the therapist's handling of the ground rules and framework of treatment. Having taken the initial session as the context for this discussion, I should stress that ground-rule issues come and go from the beginning to the end of a psychotherapeutic experience—and long after as well. It is time now to rate the substance of how a therapist handles the remaining aspects of an ongoing psychotherapy.

To reduce this area to its simplest terms, you might say that, in general, a therapist is either talking to the patient or remaining silent. You might ask: Is it really possible to rate my psychotherapist's silence? I don't even know enough to rate my therapist's comments, advice, and interpretations. Besides, if I'm constantly listening to what my therapist says in order to assign a rating, won't I short-circuit the spontaneity and value of the relationship? How would you even categorize the wide range of remarks made by therapists in the course of a psychotherapy?

As you have come to expect, the questions being asked here are conscious-system questions. You're picturing a deliberate assessment process conducted according to a set of learned criteria. But the fact is that your deep unconscious system is always rating your therapist's manner of intervening—whether or not you ever become aware of its perceptions and impressions. The deep unconscious system recognizes silence that is appropriate and silence that is a disavowal of encoded messages. The question, again, is one of learning to decode your disguised images as you react to the various immediate efforts of your therapist. Attending to these encoded images is part of a viable therapeutic experience and need not interfere with the natural flow of your associations in a therapy session.

With this in mind, then, let us turn now to how the deep unconscious system rates the silences and verbal intervention of psychotherapists. What I mean by this is the therapist's behaviors or comments, general attitude and demeanor, and overall approach to handling the therapy. Because the territory is so vast, we will concentrate on central issues and develop a set of ratings that should serve as a general guide. Here, too, the ratings can be supplemented through the analysis of your own dreams and stories, using your therapist's particular interventions as the guiding trigger and key to the analyzing or decoding effort.

Sigmund Freud characterized the appropriate stance of a psychotherapist or psychoanalyst as one of *neutrality*, a term that has received many definitions throughout the history of psychoanalysis. Here we will define neutrality in a very specific way, namely, as an inherent property of an intervention that: (1) maintains or secures the ideal conditions and ground rules of treatment at the behest of the patient's encoded communications; (2) maintains silence when silence is called for by the patient's material; or (3) incisively and correctively identifies and helps the patient to understand the unconscious meanings of his or her emotional symptoms as communicated in the associations of a given hour. Years of clinical study have shown that a proper intervention given at the right time is typically followed by an encoded response from the patient. This response usually contains images of well-functioning individuals, which can be decoded to reveal unconscious perceptions of the effectiveness of the therapist's effort. In addition, a proper intervention is often followed by a fresh set of encoded communications that shed new light on the unconscious basis of the patient's emotional problems.

Before considering the vast realm of a therapist's active interventions, let's take a look at a therapist's use of silence—that is, silent listening.

Everyone is familiar with the caricature of the silent analyst who says nothing to his or her patient for weeks or months. How should this or any extended period of silence be rated? Actually, silence can take two distinct forms: A therapist may be silent because he or she correctly perceives that no intervention is called for; and a therapist may be silent in error—that is, he or she may fail to speak when an intervention is warranted. Short of offering a course on psychotherapy—and it would have to be a course that is extraordinarily sensitive and perceptive about these issues—this much can be said: Appropriate silence leads to encoded images of a positive kind, whereas inappropriate silence evokes negative images.

Although I will illustrate these two forms of silence here, much of your assessment must depend on your own responsive ratings—and on decoding your own dreams and images in order to get to them. The basis for rating a psychotherapist's silence can also be expanded to include how well you, the patient, are doing at the time: If you are suffering acutely, if your symptoms are getting worse and you are anxious and uncomfortable, it is highly likely that your therapist's silence deserves a low rating. Under conditions of distress, patients tend to communicate meaningful material available to interpretation by their therapists, and you should expect some kind of intervention from your therapist. Conversely, if you are feeling safe and symptomatically stable or improved, there is a good chance that the therapist's silence is appropriate, and that your own deep unconscious system is orchestrating a quiet interlude for your psychotherapy.

You should also pay some attention to how you feel consciously about a therapist's silence. If the silence disturbs, angers, or even infuriates you, chances are good that the therapist has failed you by missing an intervention called for in your associations. Yes, there are times when direct anger will prove to be defensive on your part, but in combination with other kinds of ratings—a reading of your own encoded images, the status of your emotional difficulties, and your conscious feelings toward the therapist in general—your direct response to silence can be corroborative.

On the other hand, what if you are feeling irritated with your therapist's silence, but your other means of rating his or her behavior do not indicate a missed intervention? Remember: Conscious assessments are not always on target; it may be that your complaints about your therapist's silence are actually displaced from a frame break that he or she has carried out. In other words, you may be unconsciously irritated by a frame break, and your conscious system feels pressured to complain, but the focus of the complaint has been disguised. Instead of complaining about the frame break, you have focused on the therapist's silence.

Short of gaining a full understanding of the type of silences and interventions confirmed by the deep unconscious system, we can establish a general rule of thumb. If you respond to an extended period of silence by your therapist—for much of a session, for an entire hour, even for several sessions—with images of quiet, safe places; silent, attentive people; images of being protected and cared for; and other positively toned dreams and stories—then it is quite likely that the therapist's silence is the right intervention at the moment, and that your therapist's silence deserves a high rating. There are many interludes in psychotherapy when patients need to lie fallow—to quietly work over what they have already learned before venturing into new issues and anxieties, and to pause before the next assault on the unconscious basis of their problems. Unquestionably, many therapists have difficulty being quiet during such interludes; in fact, such periods of time are generally not recognized for the respite they offer; but even the most well-intentioned comment offered during such a time is experienced unconsciously as intrusive and a sign of the therapist's anxiety. In general, both patients and therapists greatly underestimate the curative power of appropriate silence.

On the other hand, inappropriate silence (i.e., silence at a time when intervention is called for) generally elicits images of not being heard; of people who are blind and insensitive; of people who fail to respond at times of need; and comparable images of neglect, oversight, and avoidance. Indeed, the consistency and accuracy with which the deep unconscious system is able to monitor the exact implications of a therapist's silence is remarkable by conscious standards. Armed with this knowledge, it is always possible to identify the very moment at which a therapist's silence should be changed into an intervention. As soon as the moment occurs, the patient produces an image of someone who has failed to attend to another's need for such a response.

A dramatic example of an unconscious rating of a therapist's silence can be seen in the psychotherapy of Ms. Felice, whose therapist, Dr. Oakes, was relatively active and direct, with little sensitivity to unconscious communication. Recently, Dr. Oakes had begun to recognize a need to reduce his activity level in his sessions with Ms. Felice, and to be more selective in the comments he made. As a result, when Ms. Felice's associations offered no material for interpretation at the moment, Dr. Oakes became uncharacteristically silent and adopted a listening posture. Ms. Felice continued to free-associate. Then, toward the end of the hour, she began to talk about her boss—how helpful he had been lately, which was a notable change from his usual grumpy, carping attitude. She then spoke in some detail of her relationship with her present boyfriend. "I usually don't like staying at his apartment," she said. "He's always hovering about and talking too much. But last weekend, things were really different. For some reason, after I'd been out shopping all day and was feeling exhausted, Dennis had enough sense to go into his study and keep himself busy. I sank into a living-room armchair for an hour of absolute peace and quiet. He finally seems to be giving me some space every now and then."

Clearly, the patient had unconsciously perceived Dr. Oakes's shift from provocative and unnecessary interventions to appropriate silence. Two sessions later, when Ms. Felice's material required interpretation, and Dr. Oakes intervened properly, the patient spoke about a man at work who tended to be quiet at corporate meetings, but knew just when to speak up and what to say. It can truly be said that the deep unconscious system never sleeps; it very much informs both our dreams and waking life.

In contrast, consider the imagery that occurred in the treatment of Mrs. Wayne by Dr. Satinover, a female therapist. Dr. Satinover would intervene from time to time, much of her commentary in touch with unconscious meanings, but she tended to become impatient when there was no need for intervention. At such times she often made supportive comments. At one point in the therapy, she had made a series of supportive comments during two consecutive sessions. In response, Mrs. Wayne spoke of how much pleasure she got from sitting in her den at home with the door closed, the lights out, and peaceful silence about her. "Of late," she added, "my husband has taken to barging in without knocking. Worse, he just talks me to death when I really need him to be quiet. I don't really want to say something to him because he seems so needy, but I really wish he would stop doing that."

Notice the similarity of this image to the one used in the prior example. Here it is used to convey an unconscious perception of unneeded interventions from a therapist who otherwise is mostly capable of maintaining appropriate silence.

To examine still another example of unconscious ratings of therapist silence, we can look briefly at a session in which a homosexual young man returned to therapy after his therapist's vacation with vivid descriptions of a "sexual binge." There were many images that indicated that the patient was unconsciously reacting in large part to an extra session that the therapist had offered him just before he went away. In the face of this severe disturbance and highly meaningful material, the therapist—who felt quite overwhelmed—remained silent throughout the hour.

Toward the end of the session, the patient spoke about his father. He tended to be neglectful, the young man said—unavailable when the patient needed him, and constantly promising things, but failing to deliver. Just the other day, he'd promised to lend the patient money for some much-needed cooking utensils for his new apartment. But when the son came to get the money, the father didn't even remember making the offer and balked at the request.

The principles we have developed earlier apply here: Stories of disillusionment and disappointment toward the end of sessions where a therapist is silent tend to represent *Questionable*-to-*Dangerous/Beware* ratings of the psychotherapist in the patient's deep unconscious system. This is especially so, as I said earlier, when the patient is in distress—as reflected here in a young man's unaccustomed promiscuity. Almost always, at times of emotional need, patients will communicate material that calls for intervention.

We come now to the things therapists say—their active interventions. As a general system of classification, interventions take the form of:

1. Questions
2. Clarifications—attempts to make material clearer
3. Confrontations—directing a patient's attention to something he or she has said or done
4. Interpretations—broadly defined as making something conscious to a patient who has been unaware of that particular feeling, meaning, or implication
5. Reconstructions—attempts by the therapist to define something that happened, usually in the early life of the patient, which is no longer remembered
6. Noninterpretive interventions—direct support, personal opinions, directives to the patient, personal reactions, self-revelations, and other dramatic departures from efforts directed toward understanding

Among these classes of interventions, the most poorly defined is that of interpretation. Virtually anything a therapist tells a patient that the patient was not immediately aware of is considered to be interpretive. And in many instances, the patient has no way of gauging whether the therapist is correct; the validity of the therapist's formulation is taken for granted.

For example, a male patient described two dates with two different women; both dates had gone badly. The therapist suggested that the patient was in a rage toward women. Technically, this is not an interpretation; the basis of the therapist's formulation was an assumption on the therapist's part. The patient had not said anything about feeling rage; in fact, the patient hadn't felt rage; but intellectually, he thought that the therapist might well be right. Maybe he was suppressing his anger. Such interpretations are, unfortunately, commonplace, but they are hollow.

As for rating a psychotherapist's active interventions, the deep unconscious system follows but a few clear and precise principles, and these can be readily stated as general rules. To do this, we need to review some additional perspectives that will orient us on this topic.

Certain interventions are clearly problematic and will receive *Questionable*–to–*Dangerous/Beware* ratings not only from the deep unconscious system, but also from the patient's conscious system. In general, these are interventions that contradict the idea of a calm, concerned psychotherapist interested in helping the patient to understand the unconscious basis of his or her behaviors and communications. You have good reason to question any therapist who responds to your communications with anger, frustration, irritation, or elation. And patients are generally uncomfortable as well with a therapist who is overly polite, obsequious, harsh, stubborn, insistent, dogmatic, or opinionated.

Sound interventions are based entirely on the communications from the patient in the hour at hand. This is an important point. If a therapist is interpreting encoded messages, he or she does not need to reach backward into past sessions for amplification. The ideal therapist recognizes the patient's need for an intervention, formulates it in light of the material just presented, and proposes it in a thoughtful, tactful, timely, and empathic manner. Such interventions are essentially interpretive—explanatory—in nature.

Consciously, for reasons of defense, as well as because of an inner dread of unconscious meaning, patients will accept a wide range of interventions that depart from the ideal interpretation. But as we have come to expect, this is not the case in the deep unconscious system: There, only frame-securing and insightfully interpretive interventions are accepted, validated, and used as a basis for constructive inner change. You'll recall my earlier example of Mr. Fredericks, who asked his therapist, Dr. Clark, to change the hour of his next session, and then complained about the boss having created a staggered work schedule at his office. The patient clearly thought the boss was wrong. "Either things should go back to the way they were or everyone should be given a set time to come to work each day. We need that kind of certainty."

At this point, the therapist intervened. She suggested that the patient's communications indirectly indicated his own proposal for her response to his request for a schedule change. Though disguised, the images clearly indicated that the patient was requesting consistency and stability; in other words, he was unconsciously directing the therapist to keep the schedule certain in the psychotherapy.

You may recall that this patient, following the therapist's intervention, went on to talk about a young man with whom he lived when he was in his twenties. The patient always knew where this fellow stood, could always rely on him, and always felt safe in his presence.

Here the patient was consciously requesting an alteration in the ground rules, while unconsciously, through encoded images, he was indicating strongly the need to maintain the secure frame. The therapist's response was both interpretive and frame-securing, and was based almost entirely on the patient's encoded communications. The patient validated the interpretation by responding with a highly positive image that revealed a favorable unconscious perception of the therapist in response to her handling of both the request and the patient's material. It is this type of intervention, and this type alone, that is truly neutral in the sense understood by the deep unconscious system of all patients.

Departures from this ideal characterize virtually every form of psychotherapy in existence today. Those interventions that are only mildly hurtful and that are fundamentally well-meaning leave room for some type of uninsightful relief of symptoms, though some price will be paid for the absence of genuine insight. But as the interventions depart more and more from the ideal of neutrality, as they become more and more hurtful and attacking of the patient, and as they become more defensive for the therapist, the main hope for symptom relief is through paradoxical cure. I have mentioned this phenomenon before. A paradoxical cure is constituted by the development of new and different defenses or the replacement of a very bothersome symptom with one that is either denied or of lesser concern.

When the departures from the ideal interpretation are extreme and involve attacking, assaultive, seductive, and otherwise blatantly hurtful interventions from a therapist, even the likelihood for paradoxical forms of relief diminishes. Instead, it is most likely that the patient will feel worse emotionally and experience an increase in emotional dysfunction or, at best, show little change of any kind at all. If you, as a patient, notice a lack of symptomatic improvement over a span of a month or two of psychotherapy, or if you experience an intensification of emotional symptoms, you should make a careful inventory of the ways in which the therapist has been intervening, with special emphasis on his or her interpretive approach. This does not mean, of course, that failure to improve in psychotherapy should automatically lead you to suspect that your therapist is inadequate. What I'm saying is that you should examine the specifics of your psychotherapeutic experience and identify the ways in which your therapist's interventions have departed from the ideal and obtained *Questionable*–to–*Dangerous/ Beware* ratings. As I discuss in chapter 12, a decision about whether to stay with or leave a particular psychotherapist should be made on the basis of the broadest possible range of knowledge—the largest number of ratings feasible under the circumstances.

Noninterpretive interventions include a group that is only mildly to moderately in error and traumatic—simple questions, efforts at clarification, mild confrontations, and pseudoefforts at interpretation and generating insight. These comments are generally focused entirely on the patient, and tend to hold the patient completely accountable for any disturbance within the treatment experience itself and within the patient's emotional life. Seldom is the therapist held accountable for provoking reactions within the patient or for any of the difficulties the patient might experience. Certain kinds of patients will stay with a noninterpretive therapist for years. For example, depressed patients will gain paradoxical relief in such a therapy by enduring verbal punishment for unconscious guilt. Paranoid patients will experience relief because the attacking and abusive nature of confrontation tends to confirm their unconscious suspicions as valid.

Strong confrontations, directives, manipulations, advice giving, personal opinions, seductive innuendos or direct remarks, and the entire gamut of personal reactions by a psychotherapist tend to be far more destructive than the more neutral set of interventions just cited. The ratings of these comments range from *Questionable* to *Dangerous/Beware*. And these negative ratings are especially severe in the face of repetitive use or when there are signs of a malevolent streak in the psychotherapist.

The patient's unconscious perceptions of an error in intervention are powerful and consistent. Interventions that have failed to capture the essential meanings of a patient's communications tend to split the patient in two: Consciously, if such work is well-tempered, the patient believes in the therapist's efforts, while unconsciously, there is criticism and hurt. After each errant intervention, the patient's material abounds in themes of not being understood, of being hurt or attacked, and of error and ignorance. In contrast, sound interventions evoke themes of wise people, of being helped and understood, and similar constructive images.

In any form of psychotherapy, the patient's deep unconscious system is focused on the immediate interaction with the psychotherapist—the setting, the ground rules, the therapist's interventions, and the rest. It is this moment-to-moment interaction that is the central stimulus and organizer for the patient's communications in therapy, and especially their unconscious meanings. The unconscious structure of the patient's emotional dysfunction, and of any interpersonal difficulty the patient is experiencing in his or her everyday life, also becomes organized around the therapeutic experience. Once a patient enters therapy, his or her investment in the therapist's communications is so intense that often an emotional disturbance is a displaced and disguised expression or reenactment of issues primary to the psychotherapeutic interaction.

A secondary unconscious structure does continue to exist with respect to the patient's outside life, but the central organizer of unconscious meanings lies in the therapist's management of the ground rules of treatment and his or her silences and comments to the patient. For many readers, this assessment will sound strange because it is so different from a patient's conscious experience. Consciously, your everyday life seems more central, and therapy may or may not be regarded as important. This is simply not the case in the deep unconscious system. The symptoms with which a patient enters therapy are, in the main, responses to traumas and frame breaks in their daily lives—issues that are quickly refocused in the therapy once it begins.

Because things are the way they are—again, nature is nature—the communications from the deep unconscious system are consistently generated as encoded responses to the interventions of the psychotherapist. Thus the deep unconscious system will confirm or validate only those interpretations from the therapist that take this actuality into account. There is, then, only one form of interpretation that the deep unconscious system accepts and responds to favorably. Such an intervention always identifies the stimulus for the patient's disguised and encoded (unconscious) narratives and images as a particular intervention that has been made recently by the psychotherapist. Having identified this trigger, the therapist next spells out the patient's encoded or unconscious perceptions of the meanings of that intervention. Finally, the therapist shows the patient how this unconscious structure has formed the basis for the patient's symptom or interpersonal disturbance. This is the only kind of intervention, sometimes accompanied by a link to childhood frame-securing effort, that is rated highly by the deep unconscious system. And the more an intervention reveals about the therapist's personal life and opinions, the more it manipulates the patient—the lower the rating.

Having reviewed these principles, let's now look at some typical interventions and how they are rated by the deep unconscious system. Remember, most of a patient's encoded communications are organized around the therapist's management of the frame. It is instructive, therefore, to look at a flawed therapeutic relationship, where the patient's communications clearly reflect the stimulus of the therapist's prior intervention. Ms. Baxter was a young woman who sought psychotherapy for difficulties in her relationships with men; she selected a male therapist, Dr. McCarron, whom she had met at a weight-training center. We already know from previous chapters that the deep unconscious system will react quite negatively to a patient's social acquaintance with his or her therapist. In this particular case, Dr. McCarron knew better, but had accepted Ms. Baxter anyway. Through the first six months of therapy, the two discussed consciously whether treatment could be successful, given not only this prior social contact, but the fact that the therapist and patient continued to see each other from time to time at the center. No clear answer was found on this surface level.

Following one such outside meeting, Dr. McCarron felt anxious and unhappy about their contact apart from therapy, and said a great deal about it in the next session he had with Ms. Baxter. Ms. Baxter responded by saying that she felt both confused and pressured, which was certainly an immediate unconscious expression of her perception of the therapist in light of his intervention.

At the beginning of the following hour, the patient was silent. She explained that she had little to say. She had left work early because her boss had done her job, leaving her with nothing to do. It was a new job, and the patient felt convinced it wasn't going to work out. "Why are you so quiet?" she asked the therapist. "Why don't you ask me some questions? You were really rough on me last session. You looked friendly talking to other people when I saw you at the center last week, but you're so awful to me."

Dr. McCarron responded with an interpretation that went like this: "You've brought up our last session, and you seem to be saying that I have not only been too aggressive, but that I've begun to do your 'job'—fill up this therapy hour with my own doubts and confusion. As a result, you don't want to talk to me, and you're beginning to question whether treatment will work out. Your doubts about the therapy are also connected to seeing me at the weight-training center."

Ms. Baxter paused for a moment and then said that she really didn't want to hear more about the center unless the therapist was suggesting that they discontinue the treatment because of their contact there. She then described a fantasy she had never mentioned to the therapist or to anyone else—of being a stripper and undressing all over the world, and having men expose themselves to her. "I've always felt like I want to show off for men," she said, "but when I see how horny men are," she said, "I don't feel so bad about myself. Maybe that sounds like a strange sort of relief. There's this guy at the health center who seems different, though. He seems to be some kind of executive, and smart. Also sensitive to the way people feel."

This is, admittedly, a complicated vignette, but it tells us a great deal about rating the interventions of a psychotherapist. As mentioned, the meeting between the therapist and patient in a social setting is a dangerous basis on which to form a therapeutic relationship. Ms. Baxter's encoded images confirm the low rating this kind of referral warrants; her outside contact with Dr. McCarron was viewed as a form of sexualized and mutual exposure. This contaminant generated an image of a horny psychotherapist—an image, paradoxically, that reassured the patient. This last aspect again illustrates the strange and ultimately destructive way that low-rated interventions of a psychotherapist bring ill-gotten relief to patients. Dr. McCarron was capable of interpreting this unconscious dimension of their outside contact. If he had not been able to decode Ms. Baxter's unconscious messages, the therapy would have continued to duplicate the very problems that Ms. Baxter had sought therapy in order to resolve. She would have gained paradoxical relief by establishing a therapeutic relationship that involved mutual exposure and a lack of appropriate boundaries.

Notice that the therapist's first intervention was explanatory, but was not based on the material of the hour, nor on the associations of the patient. These are necessary requisites for a high-rated intervention; all therapist comments that depart from this ideal receive *Questionable–*to*–Dangerous/Beware* ratings. Indeed, the more a therapist departs from formulating and using the patient's own material, and the more the therapist includes his or her own associations and/or reactions, the lower the rating of the deep unconscious system. In this illustration, the low rating is reflected in the patient's belief that her new job—decode as her psychotherapy—would not work out. As Dr. McCarron pointed out, the patient was also indicating that she had unconsciously perceived his unneeded intervention as an attempt to do the patient's work— free-associating, rather than listening as he should have.

Dr. McCarron's second intervention had the fundamental structure of a correct interpretation. It alluded to two of his own interventions—his inappropriate comment in the previous hour and his contact with the patient at the weight-training center. It then identified the patient's responsive encoded perceptions and used them to help the patient understand the unconscious basis for her silence in the hour, her doubts about the success of the therapy, and her overall concerns about how therapy was going.

The patient responded with a set of images that validated the therapist's interpretation. The first set involved positively functioning individuals (the bright and sensitive businessman at the weight-training center), and the second set provided new encoded information that amply extended and confirmed what Dr. McCarron had said (the patient's new image of mutual exhibition and horniness). In these last encoded images the patient revealed for the first time that, unconsciously, she had chosen her psychotherapist because he was already someone to whom she had exhibited herself, and who had exhibited himself to her in return. Recognizing this unconscious and sexual meaning, and the means by which it reassured the patient, was important. Both therapist and patient gained a new understanding not only of the unconscious basis of the patient's choice of therapist but of her fundamental emotional problems. The latter were constituted around problems in childhood with an exhibitionistic father and an extremely angry mother, and around problems with men as an adult. Ms. Baxter stayed in therapy with Dr. McCarron for several more months, during which she worked over these issues and effected a suitable termination to her treatment.

I will provide another, much more condensed example of a sound interpretation. Mrs. Teller was in therapy with Dr. Perez, a male pyschiatrist, for severe manic and depressive episodes. Though divorced, Mr. Teller wrote the check with which his ex-wife paid Dr. Perez's fee; initially, the check was accepted without comment.

In one session, after handing the therapist her ex-husband's check, Mrs. Teller spoke at length of an episode that week in which she had stolen merchandise from a store. She had forged her ex-husband's name on an old check of his that she had found in her dresser drawer. It was a dishonest thing to do, she said, and she had no idea why she had done it; but she knew that behaviors like this had to stop.

Dr. Perez intervened and pointed out that he himself had just accepted a check from Mrs. Teller's ex-husband. The images that followed indicated that Mrs. Teller saw this unconsciously as a kind of stealing and as participation in a criminal act, such as forgery. The admonishment that such behaviors had to end made clear that Dr. Perez was being directed to stop accepting payment from Mrs. Teller in this form. To continue to accept would be implicitly to support the dishonesty Mrs. Teller was now engaged in and suffering with.

The patient paused a moment and then revealed for the first time that she was thinking of finding employment. She recalled a television story in which a criminal went straight with the help of a devoted social worker. She thought, too, of a man she had begun to see socially—he was as honest as the day is long.

Within a month, Mrs. Teller established two independent sources of income and began to pay for her own therapy. Her stealing stopped and she made restitution of the money she had gotten by forging the check.

Here, then, we see again the use and validation of an ideal interpretation. The intervention begins with a frame-related trigger—a deviant stimulus within the therapy. It then shifts to a decoding of the patient's unconscious perceptions of the meanings of the therapist's deviation, and accepts the patient's encoded directive to set the situation straight—the offered model of rectification. Finally, the understanding that has been developed is used to identify the ways in which the therapist's deviation has been unconsciously supporting the patient's symptoms. The result is an interpretation that is both validated and responded to with dramatic clinical improvement.

This is the kind of therapeutic work that is rated most highly by the deep unconscious system. We can turn now to a host of interventions that receive lower ratings, all of them in common practice in today's world of psychotherapy. Establishing the ratings of this work from the deep unconscious system will give you, as a patient, a unique opportunity to compare both your rating systems—the conscious and the unconscious. With this new information in hand, you can see where you stand and proceed accordingly. (How to respond to a relatively low-rated psychotherapist will be discussed in the final chapter.)

We begin with *questions* from the therapist. For most patients, consciously at least, questions seem innocuous enough if they appear to be designed to clarify some material, feeling, or issue, and if they are unassaultive and do not reflect some prejudice or difficulty in the psychotherapist. Questions are probably used by virtually every psychotherapist in practice in the world today. Nonetheless, they receive *Questionable–to–Dangerous/Beware* ratings from the deep unconscious system.

Why should this be the case? Questions are directed at the surface of the patient's associations, at their manifest and direct meanings. They reflect the therapist's investment in manifest content and suggest an insensitivity to encoded or deep unconscious meaning. Quite correctly, the deep unconscious system recognizes that the therapist who asks questions is implicitly directing the patient to shut off encoded imagery, and to produce associations with a great deal of intellectualization. Although the avoidance of unconscious expressions can bring a measure of relief, it does so at the price of losing access to the unconscious dimension—to both its expression (which can be helpful at times in and of itself) and its interpretation.

Though the effect is unrecognized by both patient and therapist, the questioning therapist generally provokes images of people who are afraid of meaning and who distract, pester, and bother others. A good example of this is provided by Ms. Holme, a psychotherapist treating Ms. Yancy for depression and a tendency to be attracted to men who abused and demeaned her. In one session, following an hour with many questions from the therapist, the patient described taking off from work for several days to go away with an abusive boyfriend. Her company's offices were located in a dangerous neighborhood and he wanted her to change her job, but she really didn't like the pressure from him.

Ms. Holme asked the patient why she had not looked for a new job, and Ms. Yancy offered a variety of superficial excuses and rationalizations. Other questions and clichéd rationalizations followed. Ms. Yancy then spoke of being afraid to travel on the subway; she was always worried that she'd miss her station or be pushed onto the track while waiting on the platform. This brought up the memory of a recent robbery at work. She spoke, too, of being frightened by horror movies, which gave her nightmares.

Ms. Holme asked her to talk about these nightmares. All the patient could remember, however, was a dream of going home to see her old boyfriends, and her mother not liking them. The therapist asked why this was so, and Ms. Yancy launched into minute and empty details about her various relationships with boys her mother didn't like. As the session neared its end, the patient complained that her present boyfriend was always annoying her with constant pressures and constant chatter. He did it to irritate her, she said, and she just complied with his demands and hid her anger. The hour concluded with the therapist asking the patient why she would get involved in such a relationship, and all the patient could say is that she did so over and over again, and wondered why. Ms. Yancy ruminated about this question until the session was over.

We see again that the therapist who questions the patient can easily become part of a sadomasochistic couple. Certainly, the questioning therapist is unconsciously perceived as abusive and demanding. In this instance—which is not atypical—the therapist unconsciously and unwittingly engaged the patient in an abusive relationship much like the relationships for which the patient had sought psychotherapy in the first place. The deep unconscious memory system, in which our pathological past and its related needs reside, directs most patients unconsciously to find a psychotherapist who will repeat the past rather than depart from it. Ms. Yancy, for example, had a very sadistic father. The result is the kind of unfortunate source of reassurance that keeps patients bound to such psychotherapists, despite the likelihood that the patient's problems will continue—which was certainly the case with Ms. Yancy, who continued to be attracted to very abusive men.

Let's take a look at Ms. Yancy's communications with an eye toward their unconscious meanings. Early in the hour we have just seen, the patient complained about pressure from her angry boyfriend. Ms. Holme responded with a superficial question about Ms. Yancy's job location. The patient thereupon encoded an unconscious perception of the violence of the therapist's intervention: being pushed onto the tracks while waiting on a subway platform. She also referred unconsciously to the therapist's fear of encoded meaning: being afraid of underground travel, missing the right station. The same fear is represented in the dread of horror movies. The therapist responded to this communication, again, by asking a question—this one seemingly designed to probe for unconscious meaning, but actually shutting down such meaning.

Not surprisingly, the hour ended with the patient complaining about her boyfriend's constant pressures—an encoded perception and complaint directed at the therapist. The patient then explained, through her displaced and disguised image, that she simply complies and hides her anger; this suggests again an unconscious need to maintain relationships with hurtful and sadistic individuals. Questions are often the instrument of unconsciously hurtful psychotherapy.

Much the same can be said of *clarifications*. Here, too, the focus is on the surface or manifest contents of a patient's material, and the wish to avoid encoded meaning is evident to the deep unconscious system.

Mrs. Green was in psychotherapy with Dr. Bujold, a female psychologist, for problems with depression. Mrs. Green's mother had died during abdominal surgery when the patient was quite young. At one point in the psychotherapy, Mrs. Green became exceedingly anxious and called her therapist at home. Although the call seemed to calm the patient, and no emergency actually existed, Dr. Bujold offered to schedule the patient for an additional session. The patient said that she was grateful for the opportunity but didn't think it was necessary.

In the session that followed, the patient spoke a great deal about a recent dental procedure that had required the use of an anesthetic. There were vague allusions to feeling trapped and to terrors of being put under. The therapist asked the patient to clarify exactly how she felt—the kinds of fantasies she was experiencing, and anything else that could illuminate her anxieties in the dentist's chair. Mrs. Green responded at length, detailing aspects of the situation, but not really clarifying what had happened any further. She concluded the hour, which lacked resolution, by telling the therapist that she felt her dentist was anxious about performing the service she required, and she wondered if she should continue to use his services.

Most of the time, a therapist will ask a question precisely when the patient's material could lend itself to genuine interpretation of unconscious issues. That is, when a patient's material contains encoded messages about ground-rule issues and the patient's unconscious responses, therapists tend to move away from the unconscious meaning by intervening about a superficial issue. This particular vignette illustrates what I mean.

Mrs. Green's comments about her dental procedure were encoded responses to Dr. Bujold's offer of an extra session. Though Mrs. Green had not questioned this intervention consciously—indeed, she had seen it as kind and caring—her deep unconscious system saw the offer as dangerous and entrapping. These qualities are well portrayed in the images of the dental procedure and the administration of the anesthetic. When the therapist failed to interpret this material in terms of its evident stimulus and unconscious perceptions, and instead attempted to clarify the patient's surface or manifest images, a great deal of empty description followed. The hour concluded with a telling unconscious perception: the psychotherapy was rated unconsciously in light of the therapist's "clarifying" intervention: Dr. Bujold seems anxious about her own services; perhaps continuation with this therapist is unwise. The rating is justifiably low, and the perception of the deep unconscious system quite accurate. Seeing a psychotherapist who fears deep unconscious meaning as much as—or more than—a patient does can also be a source of reassurance—though at a price.

Confrontations and *pseudointerpretations* usually go hand in hand. A pseudointerpretation is a superficial effort to interpret a patient's material—one that leaves out the ongoing therapeutic interaction. Both types of intervention are low-rated in the deep unconscious system. The confronting therapist willfully addresses the surface of the patient's associations. He or she typically generates images of people who are assaultive, pressuring, angry, disruptive, and uninsightful. This is understandable; a confrontation is both sadistic and an attempt to avoid active unconscious meaning. Pseudointerpretations tend to generate images of people who try to look smart but are actually quite ignorant; of well-meaning but wrong explanations; and of people who are especially uninsightful and self-defensive. This last image arises because pseudointerpretations virtually always hold the patient accountable for some type of resistance or emotional problem, exonerating the psychotherapist from any responsibility for the difficulty. All such interventions receive *Questionable*–to–*Dangerous/Beware* ratings, depending on just how assaultive and defensive the comment happens to be.

Examples of unconscious responses to confrontations are legion. One young man in therapy with a male therapist went on a rampage when his therapist decided to have a session with the patient's mother. The therapist ignored his own part in the incident and confronted the young man's behavior again and again. The patient did, in fact, pause in the session to reflect on what he had done. He finally ascribed it to an involvement with destructive friends and a lack of self-control. In the following hour, the young man spent much of his time describing an angry confrontation with his father, who had failed to recognize, the patient said, that at the very moment he was asking his son to be less angry, he himself was in a state of rage.

In this encoded image, the patient incisively captured the double-bind message from the confronting therapist: He was consciously asking the patient to recognize the patient's anger and be controlled, while the therapist himself was unconsciously angry and out of control. The deep unconscious system recognizes the contradiction and the craziness conveyed in this kind of double message, and rates such interventions as hypocritical and dangerous. But here, too, we can identify the paradoxical reassurance that an angry patient might well feel to discover that his therapist is every bit as angry as he or she. The price here is likely to be the continuation of expressions of anger in the patient, now justified by his unconscious perceptions of the therapist. Sometimes, however, the pattern changes and the patient unconsciously decides that one of the two people in psychotherapy should be in control; he or she becomes a model to the therapist—and suddenly gets well (at least on one level).

Another common confrontation in psychotherapy involves so-called resistance shown by a patient. Absences, lateness, silence, wanting to leave therapy—all these are understood as ways of fighting the therapy. In general, however, as communications from patients, resistances tend to be encoded responses to interventions from therapists.

Confrontation of resistances generally resembles the old one-two punch: a confrontation followed by a pseudointerpretation. A young woman in psychotherapy with a male therapist for multiple obsessive fears came late to one session and was silent a good deal of the time. The therapist confronted her with these behaviors and suggested—that is, offered the pseudointerpretation—that the patient was angry with him. The patient agreed offhandedly, and then went on to say that she felt like two different people when she was around her parents. They were always nagging her and giving her a hard time, she explained, and her response was just to collapse and accept their criticism. But somewhere inside of herself, she knew that she was infuriated and wanted to kill them. At the very least, she said, she'd like to show them how focused they are on what's wrong with their children, while never seeing themselves. They think they know so much, but they actually know very little.

In this instance, it was a telephone conversation between the therapist and the patient's father that had evoked unconscious anger and resistance in the patient. This source of the patient's resistances went unnoticed by the therapist, who chose instead to make an angry confrontation. The patient's unconscious response is clearly spelled out in her displaced and encoded allusions to her parents.

The comment about the parents thinking they know so much when they know so little is a typical disguised response to a pseudointerpretation. And when I say pseudointerpretation, I do not mean that the therapist's reference to the patient's anger was misplaced and wrong. The patient's lateness and silence most certainly did reflect her anger toward the therapist; in fact, the patient's encoded images tell us as much—she said, essentially, that she had complied with the therapist's decision to speak with her father, but inside, she was furious and wanted to destroy the therapy. The point is that the therapist's confrontation completely ignored his own role in precipitating this anger and held the patient entirely accountable for a situation to which both parties had contributed. Comments of this kind serve as a kind of psychoanalytical cliché, creating an illusion of meaning where meaning is functionally lacking; they also involve efforts to mask the truth with a pseudotruth. In this particular case, where would the patient go with this "interpretation"? At best, she might be encouraged to "explore" her apparent need to thwart the therapeutic process. This is to completely bypass the unconscious structure of her emotional problems. The deep unconscious system virtually always recognizes a false issue that proceeds from a kernel of truth.

Mrs. Appleby was in psychotherapy with Dr. Gates because of sexual frigidity and problems in her marriage. When her husband lost his job, Mrs. Appleby asked for and received a reduction in her fee. In the session that followed, she spoke of a single woman she knew who slept with quite a number of men and had recently discovered she was pregnant. The therapist offered the pseudo-interpretation that the patient had an unconscious wish to bear his baby. In psychoanalysis, this kind of interpretation is called a *transference interpretation*: It proposes to show the patient that he or she harbors an unconscious wish directed toward the therapist—a wish that is inappropriate to their relationship. As a rule, these wishes are then traced to the patient's childhood. In this case, the therapist eventually proposed to the patient that her wish for his baby stemmed from similar wishes she had toward her father when she was a small child.

Mrs. Appleby said that she had had no thoughts of this consciously—a response viewed by the therapist as a resistance, because he readily assumed that his transference interpretation was correct. The patient went on to describe a married friend who was coming on to her. He had lent her husband some money in this time of financial need, and seemed to feel now that her gratitude and sense of obligation gave him sexual license. Mrs. Appleby was really incensed by his attitude.

The therapist in this situation took the patient's material as confirmation—because it elaborated on the theme of inappropriate seduction. However, by decoding the patient's material in light of the therapist's prior intervention, we can see that the picture is actually otherwise. Through this encoded image, the patient is actually communicating to the therapist that his reduction in fee—in substance, his lending the patient and her husband money—is a seductive act that is unconsciously seen as a wish on his part to seduce and impregnate the patient.

By decoding this material as an unconscious response to a framework-deviation intervention by the therapist, our picture of what the patient is communicating is exactly the opposite of the formulation made by her own therapist. Where this therapist saw an unconscious wish in the patient, we discover an unconscious perception of the therapist. Where the intervention of the therapist accuses the patient and holds her entirely accountable for this imagery, our own formulation would begin with the therapist's responsibility and help the patient to understand the sources in herself of her own, however accurate, reading of the sexual implications of the therapist's deviation. This kind of intervention would recognize the truth in the patient's perception—indeed, all deviations have a sexual quality on the unconscious level—while helping the patient to recognize the influence of this sexual quality in her own, internally generated selective perceptions of the situation.

Despite their widespread acceptance by both patients and therapists, pseudointerpretations obtain uniformly low ratings from the deep unconscious system. Any patient who decodes his or her imagery in response to these kinds of attempts at explanation from psychotherapists and psychoanalysts will readily come to see that fact. Although pseudointerpretations are well-meaning—and this aspect is also recognized by the deep unconscious system—their false aspects are unconsciously perceived and have their effects on the patient and on the psychotherapy. In some ways pseudointerpretations are the most benign of errant interventions, but they still exact a price that should be recognized and handled—modified—whenever possible.

We come now to the last class of interventions that we will consider—*noninterpretive interventions*. These, too, are common in the world of psychotherapy, and in general tend to be quite well accepted on the conscious level by psychotherapy patients. Often a patient will ask a therapist for advice, will show conscious appreciation for direct support, will happily accept manipulation and directives, and will even welcome self-revelations from the therapist. All the while, the deep unconscious system reacts with violently negative ratings and with encoded perceptions of individuals who are grandiose, destructive, manipulative, prone to expose themselves psychologically and physically, exploitative of others, and a host of other powerfully negative images.

A female therapist reassured a young female patient that her pending visit to her hometown and family would certainly go well now that she'd had some psychotherapy under her belt. The patient responded by telling the therapist that she hated going home to her mother because her mother never had any confidence in her and was always telling her what to do. In the deep unconscious system, surface support by a therapist is experienced as a lack of confidence in the patient.

Another female patient, when told by her female therapist to find a way of meeting a man between now and the next session, returned to the therapist with the information that she had picked up a woman who, though bossy, was somehow attractive to her.

Still another female patient, when informed by her male therapist of his own marital problems, came to the following session with a dream of a midget exposing his grotesque genitals to her.

A male patient, when advised how to behave in a difficult situation by his male therapist, immediately revealed that he had been having masturbatory fantasies of submitting to powerful men.

The low ratings of these types of interventions are so pervasive and commonplace, we may be inclined to wonder why they have been neglected for all these years. The answer has been stated before: Decoding material from patients in light of the interventions from their therapists is utilized by no more than a handful of psychotherapists. Of course, there is an occasional patient who is consciously offended by interventions and manipulations of this kind, but such people are the exception. And given the realization that paradoxical types of relief from emotional suffering can be obtained through such interventions, it has been all but impossible to recognize and respond to their detrimental aspects.

Mr. Kagan was a young man in psychotherapy with Dr. Zorn because of his reluctance to date women. The patient was seen once weekly; his mother was also seen by the therapist once a month. After several months of treatment, Mr. Kagan revealed many active homosexual fantasies. He revealed, too, that he often slept in bed with his mother; his father would leave the bedroom and sleep in his son's bed. This particular image appeared in a session immediately following a meeting between the therapist and Mr. Kagan's mother; however, Dr. Zorn chose to respond by directly suggesting to the patient that he desist from this behavior. In response, Mr. Kagan stated that it might be hard to stop without upsetting his mother. She had already told him that she liked having him in bed and wanted him there; going against her request might be a problem. On the other hand, she seemed to want to make him too dependent on her, so maybe he should rebel in some way. The therapist simply reiterated his advice to the patient.

In the following hour, Mr. Kagan revealed that he had once again gone into bed with his mother. He had had a dream that his father wanted to block his way into the bedroom, but then suddenly collapsed and died. He associated to the fact that his father liked to tell him what to do, but that was more because of his own weakness than from any constructive intent.

Very often, when a therapist uses noninterpretive interventions, he is viewed in the deep unconscious system as unavailable or dead by the patient. Strikingly, though the therapist in this case intervened actively and extensively, the patient's unconscious image was one of absence and loss.

Beyond that image, it is clear that Mr. Kagan had responded unconsciously to his therapist's decision to see his mother with an unconscious perception that the therapist was in some way sexually involved with her. Here again, the therapist was unconsciously replicating the patient's problem. His advice, then, was unconsciously perceived as hypocritical—the therapist was in bed with the mother even as he was advising his patient against such behavior; the patient also perceived the advice unconsciously as manipulative, homosexual, and as an attempt to force the patient's dependence on the therapist. Unconsciously, the therapist was seen as attempting to bar the patient's access to the mother; but the effort failed and the therapist was now dead—ineffective or unavailable.

In another situation, a young woman in psychotherapy with a female therapist in a clinic became anxious when her therapist announced that she was leaving the clinic in a month. The therapist responded almost immediately that the patient needn't worry, she would do very well with her next therapist. In response, the patient spoke of despising people who needed reassurance and who behaved as others wished in order to please them. She remarked, too, on how hypersensitive her boyfriend was whenever she spoke up—he really couldn't tolerate any criticism.

Notice once more the poor rating that a therapist's efforts to reassure a patient receive from the deep unconscious system. Despite conscious acceptance, the deep unconscious system does not appreciate a therapist's need to manipulate his or her patients. Here this is being done, according to the deep unconscious system, to avoid the patient's anger or some other disturbing reaction to the therapist's departure.

Finally, let's look at a well-meaning supportive intervention from a male therapist, Dr. Polster, to his female patient, Mrs. Vaughn. The patient was in treatment for depression and difficulty in establishing a lasting relationship with a man. The material we will look at emerged after the therapist had rescheduled the patient's sessions because of his own personal need. The patient had responded by saying that she felt abandoned by her friends, forced to do everything for herself, and doomed because no one was ever there for her.

Dr. Polster had reacted to these associations by reassuring the patient that she could accomplish a lot more than she imagined, and by telling her that she was in therapy in order to develop the means for having a more effective life. The patient went on to say that nothing ever seemed to change. She felt stuck. Even now, she was involved with a married man who hadn't called her in several weeks. He just walked away whenever it suited him and spent time with his family and wasn't there when she needed him. Trying to talk to him about it was useless; he just shut her out. He was always telling her that things were going to work out for them, but she knew it wasn't true. She would almost rather he'd be up front about it, admit that he didn't love her, and they could go on from there.

These are all familiar themes by now. The changed hour—an alteration of the frame—evoked disguised and unconscious images of abandonment and depression. Instead of interpreting the source of these communications as related to the change in the hour, the therapist tried to reassure the patient directly. In response, Mrs. Vaughn indicated that she and the therapist were stuck; nothing was changing. Even the conscious effort at reassurance was unconsciously perceived as an abandonment. By talking about the situation with her married boyfriend, the patient was unconsciously indicating the uselessness of false reassurance and asking the therapist for a more straightforward and honest relationship. Notice that the patient also alluded to her fear of speaking up— perceiving the likelihood of the therapist's responding, consciously or unconsciously, with anger, resentment, and further abandonment.

As I have said, beyond all of the technicalities of the interventions discussed in this chapter, there lie comments from therapists that are blatantly angry or seductive. The deep unconscious system reacts violently to such measures, though consciously, patients are surprisingly amenable to such abuse. All of this is a reminder that the conscious system is extremely unreliable in rating your psychotherapist. The presence of a deep unconscious rating is indeed a great gift; as this book has already shown, much will change when we all use these ratings in assessing our psychotherapies and our psychotherapists.

Table 8: The Therapist's Interventions

RATE YOUR THERAPIST

This is how my therapist intervenes:

Sound Answers
- He/she doesn't say anything most of the time; I do most of the talking.
- When he/she intervenes, it's almost always to explain the unconscious basis of my problem in light of my unconscious perception of something the therapist said or did.

Questionable-to-Unsound Answers: Reconsider Your Choice of Therapist
- He/she is sometimes silent for long periods of time, even though I have dreams that suggest the silence is inappropriate (dreams about people who don't understand, are insensitive, neglecting, etc.).
- He/she asks questions, repeats what I've said to clarify it, and confronts me sometimes on contradictions in what I've said.
- He/she generally tells me what something I've said means unconsciously—but says that I've brought certain ways of seeing the world from childhood that I need to make conscious and resolve.
- He/she occasionally picks up on something I've said and asks me to say more about it.
- He/she occasionally offers an empathic response, such as, "That must have been very painful for you," or "It sounds like you were pretty angry."
- He/she has occasional lapses in neutrality—sometimes gets quite angry with me/says something flirtatious/seems bored/falls asleep.

Dangerous Answers: Beware of This Therapist

- He/she is often silent for several sessions running, even though I've told him/her outright that I'm uncomfortable with it. In fact, I wind up spending a lot of those sessions talking about people who don't care about me or are afraid of a real relationship.
- He/she is constantly directing me to talk about particular issues, such as, "You haven't said anything about your mother for a while; how's that relationship going?" or "I'm interested in the fact that you were smiling when you mentioned being hurt. Why do you think you did that?"
- He/she is always telling me what I should be doing with my life, such as, "What are you afraid of? If I were you, I'd go for it."
- When I said that I resented his/her accepting phone calls during my sessions/keeping me waiting/taking notes, he/she said that other patients don't see things that way, and that I have a problem.
- He/she seems positively hostile to me—alternately sarcastic and indifferent.
- He/she is seductive with me and seems hurt when I don't respond.

·12·

Termination and Beyond

Termination, that ominous word, refers to the end of psychotherapy. The impetus toward deviation and immediate relief regardless of cost that we have seen in other dimensions of psychotherapy is all the greater in the termination phase because of the way in which the end of psychotherapy mobilizes our fundamental and universal anxieties about mortality. With death-anxiety pressuring both patient and therapist—indeed, both are experiencing an ending and a significant loss—powerful wishes to deny death come into play: the wish to break rules and to create moments of fusion and maniclike celebration.

Breaks in the frame are quite common in the termination phase. And it is easy to rationalize them consciously—as a way of equalizing the relationship, bringing the treatment to an end on a cordial note, allowing the patient to know the therapist better, reducing the tension of termination, and so on. But the chief aim of such breaks is to preclude a deep experience of loss and its affiliation with death, and to defend against any significant measure of death-related imagery. To a degree, these defenses may be successful; but they virtually preclude any possibility of analyzing, resolving, and reducing the power of the patient's (and therapist's) death-anxiety issues—problems central to emotional dysfunction and to life itself.

Deprived of this opportunity for resolution, death anxiety will unconsciously contribute to much of the future behavior of the terminating patient. In particular, it will leave the patient vulnerable to behaviors, life choices, and relationships designed primarily, though on the unconscious level, to maintain an extreme form of denial of death and its ramifications. Although a measure of this kind of denial of death is certainly healthy and adaptive, the patient who is deprived of a suitable separation experience in terminating his or her psychotherapy will require denial mechanisms far beyond a level of constructive utility.

A male patient who ended his psychotherapy by becoming friends with his psychotherapist needed for many years afterward to maintain strong ties to at least two women at any given moment. This tendency was unconsciously developed in order to prevent possible loss—in the unconscious part of the mind, as long as two of something are available, even if one is lost, the other is still present. The various "solutions" provided to patients by psychotherapists have considerable unconscious power during and after psychotherapy. And, indeed, the unconscious "solution" negotiated by the psychotherapist to the ending of a psychotherapy is among the most fateful determinants of the future life of the patient.

We will begin our ratings by considering who—patient or therapist—introduces the end of the treatment. This is a complicated question, though the ideal preferred by the deep unconscious system can be stated simply: It is best, as a rule, for the therapist to allow the patient to introduce termination. Ideally, this is done unconsciously, through encoded messages, which the therapist interprets to the patient. Such communications generally emerge when the difficulties for which the patient entered treatment, and all other notable emotional problems, have been reduced to the point of comfort and effective functioning by the patient. In other words, the ideal termination occurs when the patient has resolved his or her emotional difficulties on the basis of a secure therapeutic frame and relationship, and through validated insights.

Because termination issues are so intense, and because unconsciously patients are reluctant to end a relationship with a truly effective psychotherapist, the first allusions to the need to bring therapy to a close often occur, as already noted, in disguised or derivative—unconscious—form. Without realizing he or she is doing so, the patient will begin to tell stories and have dreams about endings, loss, and death-related experiences—including important losses suffered in early childhood and the like. The stimulus for these images is the inherent realization that the work of therapy is more or less completed, and that the therapist is—ideally—now prepared to terminate with the patient. Through a series of appropriate interpretations, the therapist then helps the patient to be aware of the recommendation of his or her deep unconscious system—in effect, the patient's own inner sense that the time has come to end treatment provides the guiding light.

Of course, there are many therapies where the patient's encoded messages are neither understood nor decoded. In these situations, the termination of the therapy may be introduced by either party to treatment. This should occur only when the patient's emotional disturbance appears both to be more or less resolved and somehow more soundly understood. It is best in such a therapy for the patient spontaneously to recognize his or her sense of improvement and to introduce the wish to bring therapy to a close. Failing that, the therapist should assess the diminution of symptoms, and whether the basis of this reduction is secure; if so, he or she should suggest that the patient work toward completing the therapy.

Ideally, once the realization that termination is at hand is consciously recognized by the patient, the therapist should allow the patient to select a specific date for the last psychotherapy session. Here the patient can rely on his or her own conscious sensibilities, since they will be operating under strong unconscious influence. That is, the patient should decide whether he or she needs a week, a month, or several months to complete the termination experience. (We are assuming the proper resolution of the patient's emotional problems.) Some patients sense a need for a somewhat extended termination experience, recognizing on some level their great vulnerability in this area—a vulnerability that is likely to have been caused by early and difficult death-related experiences. However, a termination phase that is longer than three to six months would receive a *Questionable* rating; the announced final phase of treatment should be accomplished in less time.

Much hinges on the definition of a "proper resolution" of a patient's emotional issue. How can you recognize a "moment of sound cure," so to speak? In essence, this type of relief may occur in both short- and long-term therapies. It generally follows one or more periods of genuinely new insight—ideally generated by the type of interactional interpretations discussed in chapter 11. At the very least, "cure" should follow a kind of understanding that truly clarifies the patient's emotional state in decidedly new ways. Sound, secure-frame "holding" will also often contribute to this type of solid symptom resolution. In addition, this type of cure is supported by encoded images—dreams and stories—of appropriate endings, completed tasks or jobs, and allusions to constructive ways of moving on to new stages of life.

You should be wary of any thought of termination that appears without prior insight, at times of resistance to the therapy, and without an extended test of the durability of the symptom relief. In addition, you are well advised to question your thoughts of ending therapy if displaced and encoded images emerge that speak of premature flight, needs to cover up or hide, escape without genuine resolution, and similar themes that point to defense in the presence of unfinished therapeutic work.

In all, it is best to check out your decision to terminate your therapy, first, on the surface level: (1) Are you feeling better and not suffering in some way that you haven't been paying attention to? (2) Were there clear and strong moments of fresh insight? If you can answer Yes to these questions, then check out your dreams and narratives. Do the encoded themes speak of sound solutions and against unfinished business and escape? A sound decision to end a psychotherapy will be well supported by assessments made by both the conscious and deep unconscious systems of the patient.

When the patient has established a specific and apparently valid termination date, it should be accepted and acknowledged in context by a very simple comment from the psychotherapist. With the ending of treatment now fixed, the therapeutic work will focus on the unconscious meanings of this termination experience for the patient—an issue that is certain to further illuminate the unconscious basis of the emotional difficulties for which he or she sought treatment. But once the date is fixed, it should not be changed. Although it is true, of course, that emergencies may arise, we will have to reserve *Questionable*-to-*Dangerous/Beware* ratings for therapists who propose modifications in the termination date—or approve of modifications proposed by the patient. This is not a matter of rigidity and inflexibility; adhering to a set termination date is a sign that the patient's emotional difficulties have indeed been suitably resolved. Shifts in the end point cast an uncertain light on the entire psychotherapy and on the state of the patient's emotional health.

In the ideal situation, the established frequency of visits is maintained to the very end of treatment. The deep unconscious system strongly objects to either increasing the number of sessions or to the more common practice of gradually decreasing the frequency of sessions until termination is effected.

Similarly, the deep unconscious system has a strong and clear picture as to how the posttermination phase—the period after psychotherapy—should be handled: There should be no further contact of any kind between patient and therapist. In particular, the deep unconscious system offers *Questionable*-to-*Dangerous/Beware* ratings for psychotherapists who offer follow-up visits, or who otherwise make contact with their patients—professionally or socially (the latter is particularly dangerous)—once treatment has been completed. On the other hand, if some months or years later, the patient should experience a fresh emotional disturbance, we would expect the psychotherapist to make time available for a new period of psychotherapy—if the patient so chooses.

There are, of course, countless low-rated variations on this ideal psychotherapy termination. As stated, many therapists choose to introduce termination themselves, and to either set a specific date or leave the date open. There are also therapists who will see no need to terminate a therapy, even though the patient's emotional dysfunctions have been pretty much resolved. On the other hand, sometimes a therapist will propose a termination when the patient is still experiencing emotional difficulties.

Beyond these possibilities, there is the unexpected termination necessitated by the professional or life circumstances of the therapist—*forced terminations*, as they are called. Although these are common in clinic settings where trainees and other staff come and go at an alarming rate of change, they also arise in private practice when a therapist elects to leave a particular geographic area, to retire from practice, or to otherwise change his or her life in a manner that precludes continuing to see patients. This last type of termination is especially traumatic for both patient and therapist, and is often handled in ways that deserve *Questionable*–to–*Dangerous/Beware* ratings. The tendency to modify the ground rules of treatment and to intervene noninterpretively is often at its greatest height under such circumstances.

Another traumatic type of termination comes about when a patient decides that a therapist is not being effective, and/or that he or she is actually destructive, seductive, or otherwise behaving in a way detrimental to the best and therapeutic interests of the patient. Therapists use the term *premature termination* to characterize such endings, because they occur before the patient's emotional difficulties have been resolved.

There appear to be two types of premature termination—one based mainly on the patient's inappropriate anxieties, and the other based mainly on the patient's valid conscious and unconscious perceptions of difficulties in the therapist. The two are easily distinguished if the patient takes the time to rate his or her psychotherapist. In the first situation, the therapist has received high ratings in that he or she has secured an ideal set of conditions for the psychotherapy—or something very close to this ideal. In addition, the therapist has been responding to the material from the patient with the kind of interpretive interventions described in the previous chapter—comments that take into account the triggers of the therapist's interventions as well as the unconscious responses of the patient. In the second situation, the therapist has consistently obtained low ratings or has received one or more *Dangerous/Beware* ratings in significant areas. That is, the wish to terminate prematurely from psychotherapy will usually involve a therapist whose management of the ground rules and framework of treatment is loose at best, and destructive at worst; it will also involve a therapist who tends to intervene noninterpretively with advice, manipulation, and self-revelations.

Still, even with a low-rated therapist, something curative may begin to materialize. It is when the price paid for the cure is too high, or when the cure does not begin to appear, that patients tend to become concerned—eventually. Although it is good advice to consider early termination with any repeatedly low-rated psychotherapist, termination before relief has been obtained should be considered whenever a psychotherapy is extended beyond a year or two without significant symptom reduction. Indeed, in the usual course of a psychotherapy a patient can expect some relief in the first weeks of treatment (much of it as a result of the strength gained through his or her experience of a therapist able to secure a strong set of ground rules). Additional relief should materialize during the following six months of treatment (here, mainly because the framework continues to remain secure and some interpretive work has been carried out); the remaining improvement should occur within the following year or two.

Any psychotherapy that extends beyond two to three years deserves serious reconsideration; in all likelihood, you will discover that you have been in treatment with a relatively low-rated psychotherapist. But even in situations where the ratings are somewhat high, it is likely that something is amiss if the therapy goes on too long. There is a need to reassess the situation—to carry out a fresh set of ratings, and to make a careful search for unnoticed factors that could be impairing the process of cure. Although disturbing and traumatic life circumstances might well play a role, you will find in general that problems within the psychotherapy and in the way the therapist is handling the treatment will account for the greatest number of the underlying sources of the stalemate. Psychotherapy should "take" and be effective within a year or two as a general rule, and in fewer than five years with patients who are notably disturbed and who have, in general, been especially traumatized in their early lives.

Yet, given these broad guidelines, each individual patient must make his or her own assessment and evaluation. Inappropriate and unconsciously determined resistances do exist—and they may well take the form of wishing to terminate treatment before it has been completed. And yet, in most instances, neurotic wishes of this kind are based on a dread of the secure frame and of valid unconscious meaning—anxieties that can now be properly recognized. In most situations, the issue is quite different: The wish to terminate prematurely has arisen from failings in the psychotherapist and his or her work.

When a decision is made to terminate treatment prematurely, it is always advisable to explore your choice with your psychotherapist. Unfortunately, it is difficult to be optimistic and to expect that the errant therapist will be able to change his or her attitudes and technique sufficiently to alter the course of the psychotherapy. Of course, if the therapist becomes angry and attacking in response to your proposal, it becomes clear that the decision to terminate is a wise one.

The problem becomes more difficult to sort out when the therapist responds to your wanting to end therapy with a listening and analytic attitude, and attempts to explore and to get at the unconscious reasons for your decision. Carefully rating your psychotherapist at such times becomes important: If the wish to leave is appropriately traced to secure-frame anxieties and to the dread of unconscious meaning, there may be reason to stay on—and, indeed, the insights gained from this work should help you to do so. On the other hand, if the wish to leave is traced to alterations in the ground rules and to failures in the therapist to properly interpret unconscious meanings, it may make sense to continue the psychotherapy if these problematic areas are properly explored and interpreted.

Of course, if a deviation cannot be corrected—for example, if you have come to your therapist through a referral from another of his or her patients—then you might work, hopefully with insight, toward a suitable termination that would enable you to seek psychotherapy under less contaminated circumstances. What I am saying here applies, of course, to a therapist who is capable of understanding unconscious communication. An attempt to get at the unconscious basis of your wish to terminate with a therapist capable only of pseudointerpretation and noninterpretive intervention will not be helpful to you. Such a therapist is unlikely to understand the unconscious issues involved.

In this regard, we should briefly consider the question of whether to seek a consultation with another therapist while still in treatment with the present one, or to wait until the current therapy has been terminated before seeing someone else. Some therapists, at times of extended patient resistance and stalemate, will suggest a consultant to the patient. In the deep unconscious system, this is not a welcome approach and it receives a *Questionable*–to–*Dangerous/Beware* rating. The therapist who is having difficulty treating a particular patient should seek supervisory consultation on his or her own, without informing the patient that this is taking place. Such a step, although it will indeed have a subtle and disturbing influence on the psychotherapy, is geared toward a constructive solution to the difficulties in the treatment and will, if successful, prove helpful to the patient—as well as to the therapist.

In general, then, it is best for the patient to terminate one treatment before beginning another. Seeing two therapists during the same time period will have consequences and create problems, particularly because it will not allow a full termination experience to occur with the first therapist. Second therapists who are contacted under these conditions are rated most highly if they indicate that it is best for the patient to explore the issues leading to thoughts of termination with the present psychotherapist and to complete that therapy before making an appointment with a new therapist. Therapists who simply agree to see patients under these conditions must be given a *Questionable* rating. Still, the final decision on whether to start therapy with the new treating person should be based on the full range of ratings received by the new therapist with respect to the first telephone contact, the office setting, and the handling of the first hour.

The possible variations and issues related to the termination of psychotherapy are almost infinite. We might therefore consider the main points dictated to us by the deep unconscious system. To illustrate: Mr. Tyler was a married man in his thirties who sought psychotherapy from Dr. Zachary because of bouts of depression, uncertainties about his marriage, and a tendency to become involved with other women despite his wish to be faithful to his wife. The referral was professional, the setting frame secure, and the work interpretively oriented. Within the first six months of this once-weekly therapy, the patient's job situation, which had been confused and emotionally disturbing, settled down; his commitment to and relationship with his wife and children had greatly improved; and his involvement with other women had diminished but did not stop.

Seven months into treatment, Mr. Tyler began one session by telling his therapist that when he had left his session the week before, the patient he discovered in the waiting room—a young woman—was actually his cousin. Mr. Tyler was convinced that the therapist knew of this relationship, and that he had deliberately exposed him to one of his relatives. Memories of being humiliated by a doctor who had exposed his naked body to his sister when Mr. Tyler was a child seemed to offer encoded support for the patient's unconscious view of the situation. There was in this memory one qualifying recollection, namely, that the incident hadn't been the fault of the doctor—Mr. Tyler's sister had walked into the doctor's examining room by mistake. Nonetheless, all things considered, the patient was consciously convinced that his therapist had betrayed him.

In truth, Dr. Zachary had not deliberately betrayed Mr. Tyler. The cousin was related to Mr. Tyler on his mother's side of the family. Since there was no name in common, there was no way the therapist could have known the young woman was Mr. Tyler's cousin. Nonetheless, tension once again increased between Mr. Tyler and his wife, and his involvement with other women also increased. There followed an extended period of therapy during which these issues and the patient's unconscious anger toward his therapist were repeatedly analyzed in light of this particular stimulus. Adhering only to the communications from the patient, the therapist did not impose the truth of the situation on the patient; instead, he consistently and patiently analyzed Mr. Tyler's own associations and indicated the patient's own unconscious view of the situation to the extent that it was revealed by his material.

This kind of work continued for some eight months, during which Mr. Tyler actually stabilized his life, made a firm and clear commitment to his wife and family, and almost eliminated all contact with other women. He was no longer depressed, and in his work Mr. Tyler experienced a creative thrust that led to a significant promotion and a notable increase in income as well. In the last few months of this period, there had been no conscious or unconscious allusion in the patient's material to the intrusion by the cousin; instead, other, lesser matters had concerned him and had been the basis for the therapist's occasional interpretations. (The frame otherwise remained secure; and though the therapist continued to see the cousin for part of this time, her hour had been arranged at a different time and there had been no further contact between the two of them—in fact, the patient almost never saw this cousin because of family differences.)

Then, in one particular session, Mr. Tyler mentioned the cousin in passing, and reported a dream of a woman robber with a knife invading his bedroom despite the presence of a bodyguard. The therapist was able, eventually, to analyze the dream in light of the meeting with the cousin in the waiting room. With much additional material and therapeutic work, Mr. Tyler gradually came to the realization that it was likely that the therapist knew nothing of his relationship with his cousin. During this time, he recalled an entirely forgotten incident from his childhood: a sibling had been born and died at the age of one year. The unconscious meanings of the cousin incident, including its connection to the intrusive birth of a sibling who then died, proved to be interpretable.

Ultimately, the experience was connected to death anxieties that had led this patient to unconsciously dread a commitment to a single person, his wife, and proved to be a factor in his need for other women. As all this was being explored and worked over in the psychotherapy, Mr. Tyler severed his connections with each of the women he had seen outside of his marriage and settled down to a rather happy family life.

It was at this point that dreams of changing jobs, of the death of his father some five years earlier, and other separation experiences began to emerge. Mr. Tyler's associations connected these dreams to his psychotherapy and led Dr. Zachary to interpret the dreams as unconscious promptings to terminate the therapy. In turn, Mr. Tyler began to realize that he had been thinking about ending treatment; everything in his life was now in place, and he was experiencing nothing more than the usual anxieties and concerns of everyday living. Quite spontaneously, he decided to terminate his treatment at the end of the following month—some six weeks ahead. The therapist simply agreed to this decision, and they continued their therapeutic work, frame in place, to the end.

Much of the material during these closing sessions was flat, and the therapist was silent. However, in one hour, the issues related to the death of Mr. Tyler's brother and to the death of his father were connected to a newly remembered miscarriage his mother had experienced at home. This complex of material was connected to the termination experience and to the related death anxieties Mr. Tyler was going through in these last weeks of treatment.

The last session allowed for a few finishing touches, a single interpretation by the therapist, and a final handshake and good-bye. In the ten years since that termination took place, the therapist has not heard from Mr. Tyler at all. There is strong reason to believe that this is a sign of a successful termination, since it was quite clear that the patient had deep respect for this therapist and prob-ably would have contacted him if his life had taken a turn for the worse.

Such are the steps in an ideal termination experience. It is ef-fected after a gradual diminution of emotional dysfunction based on a secure therapeutic frame and genuinely insightful interpre-tations. In this case, an inadvertent frame deviation became a central stimulus for the patient's unconscious communications, and for the working over of the unconscious basis of the patient's emotional problems—in particular, Mr. Tyler's need for women other than his wife. Note, too, that the termination theme appeared first in encoded form; the ending was then set directly by the patient—and was accepted in a simple manner by the therapist. Interpretation and secure-frame conditions continued to be the mode of therapy to the very end. And the treatment concluded with a simple good-bye, a comment from the therapist that he wished the patient the very best of luck, and a final handshake—nothing more. After that, there was silence and absence, with each party to therapy going on with his or her life without further contact between them. As tough as this may seem, it is the stuff of which healthy lives are made.

Let's look now at some samples of low-rated therapist inter-ventions related to termination.

Ms. Bell, a woman in her late twenties who suffered because she managed repeatedly to get herself fired from jobs and had never had an intimate relationship with a man, sought treatment from Mr. Wesley in a clinic. In the first session, the patient, like another we considered earlier, extracted an agreement from her therapist to exclude her social life from the therapy, and to focus on the job-related difficulties. The treatment, which lasted three months, was entirely focused on the details of the patient's work situation, and included actual enactments where the therapist played a provocative boss and the patient reacted with rage and frustration. Mr. Wesley offered Ms. Bell repeated reassuring interventions about her normality, and again and again he presented himself as a model for the patient since he had had similar difficulties in keeping a job until recently. There were also many self-revelations, including intimate details of the relationship between Mr. Wesley and his wife.

Intellectually, the therapist suggested that Ms. Bell's difficulty with her bosses stemmed from her anger at her father, who had been tyrannical toward her in her childhood. Meanwhile, Ms. Bell's material was filled with images of people who talked a lot and said nothing. Despite this unconscious reading of her therapist, Ms. Bell began to function better on her job. On the other hand, she continued to have considerable difficulties in her relationships with men—her only comment in this area was a repeated remark to her therapist that she could never envision herself as his friend. To this, Mr. Wesley said that of course there could be no personal relationship, since the patient hardly knew him, and that even though he would like to be her friend, it was pretty much out of the question.

For several months, session after session seemed to come from the same template—an enactment of the boss-employee relationship, some intellectualized comments by the therapist, and his restatement of the belief that Ms. Bell's problem stemmed from her childhood relationship with her father. In time, Ms. Bell began to feel that the sessions had become repetitious and boring. She actually concealed these feelings from her therapist, and simply announced one day that the present session was her last. She brought and gave to the therapist a gift related to one of the interests he had spoken about in their sessions, and when Mr. Wesley reacted with indifference, Ms. Bell felt offended and relieved that the treatment was over. In her thoughts in the days that followed, she realized that she had experienced sexual feelings toward her therapist, but had never felt safe in expressing them. She began to believe it had been a terrible mistake to have avoided the entire sexual area. In fact, her main issues with her father had occurred in adolescence. He had found reason to become furious with his daughter when she began to date.

In this treatment, there were many ways in which Mr. Wesley would have obtained low ratings on both his frame management and style of intervening. The very basic contract, which excluded social and sexual material, would have obtained a *Dangerous/Beware* rating. This alone might have warned this patient that the psychotherapy could not be truly effective.

In this instance, termination was effected abruptly and directly by the patient. Even though there was extensive justification for ending this therapy, Ms. Bell compromised the benefits offered by termination by making her decision so suddenly and by concealing from her therapist many of the factors that influenced her choice. Still, Ms. Bell's actions must be seen in light of the way in which Mr. Wesley created an entirely unsafe environment and relationship—especially unsafe for the communication of sexual feelings and images.

Notice, too, that this therapist simply accepted his patient's termination decision without exploration—itself a low-rated response. On the other hand, genuine analysis of the unconscious basis of the decision was virtually impossible—even conscious factors had been concealed from the therapist. Of course, Dr. Wesley might have gone in any number of low-rated directions. He might have confronted Ms. Bell on her resistance. He might have insisted that treatment continue. He might even have supported her decision by pointing out how well things seemed to be going at work!

In fact, there is little a therapist can do in the face of a patient's decision to terminate a therapy prematurely, other than listen to the patient's continued associations and to attempt to discover the triggers that have contributed to the decision—that is, the frame breaks, pseudointerpretations, and noninterpretive interventions that have created this need. In general, as I said, the therapist who has made errant interventions of this kind is unlikely to prove capable of understanding the patient's encoded references to them anyhow—or of suddenly modifying his or her way of working, or of responding in a way that would obtain a fresh and relatively high rating.

Still another variation on these issues was seen in the treatment of Ms. Gabe with Dr. Felzer, a male psychologist. Ms. Gabe, who was in her early thirties, sought treatment because of depression and a tendency to become involved in violent arguments with her brother. Referral was professional, but the frame was loose—the therapist shared his waiting room with other therapists, tended to be self-revealing and noninterpretive in his interventions, and tried to be directly supportive of his patient. When financial pressures loomed large, there was also a reduction in Ms. Gabe's fee.

Soon after the fee had been decreased, Ms. Gabe decided to terminate her treatment. Her brother had left the area for a while, and although she still felt depressed and confused, she did not wish to continue therapy. Her dream of a huge feast and of being over-stuffed seemed to connect this decision to a low rating of her therapist's reduction in the fee—a form of overfeeding. This particular image went uninterpreted. Instead, the therapist indicated that the decision was premature, but that there was little he could do to stop her from leaving.

In general, any extraneous comment about terminating made by a therapist, no matter how well-meaning an evaluation, must receive a *Questionable* rating. This follows from the principle that the therapist's responsibility is to interpret the patient's material in light of a termination decision, and should not add his or her opinions to the mix. Certainly, if the therapist is concerned with the risk of suicide, homicide, or psychosis, extraordinary measures may need to be taken in response to a wish to terminate treatment. But these situations are rare, and the therapist's deviant efforts, although necessary, will nonetheless be rated as *Questionable* to *Dangerous/Beware* by the deep unconscious system. In general, this type of clearly inappropriate termination decision by a patient would probably require that the therapist hospitalize the patient or arrange for a close relative to oversee the care of the patient. In addition, it would be necessary to press the patient to continue treatment—either with the present therapist or with someone else. Not infrequently, when such a disturbance occurs in the course of a therapy, the therapist involved will obtain low ratings on his or her therapeutic work; because of this, it is often best to change therapists at such times.

Returning now to the situation with Ms. Gabe, a week after she had terminated treatment, Dr. Felzer called to ask how she was doing and to suggest that she return to treatment. There was something appealing about his pressure, but Ms. Gabe held fast in her decision not to return. She felt that perhaps her therapist was attracted to her, and she found this flattering. Still, she had repetitive dreams about being pursued and about her house being invaded by thieves and other intruders.

The calls continued for several weeks, after which the therapist desisted. Soon after, Ms. Gabe became involved with a married man with whom she had an exciting sexual relationship despite the knowledge that their relationship could go nowhere. Over time, she would fight with him, break up, only to have him call so that they became reinvolved. It requires little in the way of decoding to recognize that this is, on the unconscious level, a clear reenactment—a version—of what had happened between Ms. Gabe and Dr. Felzer. The therapist's failure to accept the patient's termination, and his need to pursue her after treatment and to enter her private life through the telephone calls, had led unconsciously to a personal involvement that was extremely disturbing and destructive to the patient. Here again, we have an example of the price that patients have unwittingly paid for the low-rated interventions and failings of their psychotherapists.

Table 9: Terminating the Therapy

This is how my therapist handled/is handling termination issues:

Sound Answers
- I introduced directly the possibility of ending therapy.
- My therapist interpreted my unconscious allusions to termination.
- I felt a sense of new insight and deep understanding, and my symptoms had largely been resolved, so it seemed like the right time to terminate.
- I set a specific date for termination, and it remained unchanged.
- All the ground rules were maintained to the very last session—frequency, time, etc.
- Once therapy was over, I had no more contact with my therapist.
- The therapist maintained his/her analytic attitude to the very end.

Questionable-to-Unsound Answers: Reconsider Your Choice of Therapist
- My therapist introduced the possibility of ending the therapy because my symptoms seemed to be alleviated.
- My therapist says we have to terminate because he/she is moving to another state/giving up clinical practice/taking another job.
- My therapist proposed we terminate therapy even though my symptoms are not entirely resolved.
- I think termination is indicated, but my therapist thinks we ought to continue, despite the fact that I feel much better.
- As the termination date got closer, my therapist said we didn't need to see each other as often.
- Toward the end of therapy, my therapist began to tell me more about himself/herself and treat me like a colleague.
- I set a termination date, but we decided to move it up/back.

- My therapist arranged for a series of follow-up visits just to make sure I'm really okay.

Dangerous Answers: Beware of This Therapist
- We decided to end the therapy even though my symptoms hadn't changed very much.
- My therapist continued the therapy long after my symptoms were gone.
- My therapist told me very abruptly that we would have to terminate and never explained why.
- I decided somewhat impulsively to stop going to therapy, and my therapist simply accepted my decision without exploration.
- I decided to stop going to therapy, but my therapist insisted that I still needed help/wrote to my parole officer, saying that I shouldn't quit yet/told me that I'd be sorry.
- My therapist stopped seeing me so that we could date each other.
- When we knew therapy was ending, sessions got very informal—we'd see each other over breakfast or walk in the park, trade favorite books, etc.
- As termination got closer, my therapist stopped interpreting and began to give me advice on how to handle my life once therapy was over.
- After we stopped seeing each other as therapist and patient, we became friends.
- We made arrangements to be in touch with each other professionally after therapy was over.

Epilogue

We have come now to the termination of this book. Heeding my own words of advice, I will be appropriately brief.

It is best to rate your psychotherapist from the first moment to the last. There can be no hard-and-fast rules; personal judgment will always come into play. As the ratings accumulate, keep a tally. High ratings support the work the therapist is doing, but they need to be understood in the context of the course of the therapy and how the treatment is going. Low ratings are cause for concern, but here, too, a perspective must be maintained. Often, as I have indicated, there may be paradoxical relief, and if so, keep a wary eye for the price you may be paying. Consider the total picture of your life and combine that with the ratings of your psychotherapist, and use all available information for your assessment.

The likelihood of finding yourself with a therapist who has received a series of low ratings by deep unconscious standards is considerable, given today's accepted psychotherapeutic practices. For your part, without carefully rating your psychotherapist, you are likely to be drawn to the most hurtful therapist available whose efforts you are able consciously to rationalize and accept. Still, low ratings and self-harmful needs should not be matters for despair. For one thing, you can always terminate your treatment and, hopefully, find another, higher-rated psychotherapist. For another, it is from the knowledge of low ratings that a fresh and constructive solution can rise up. Further, having been alerted to your own vulnerabilities and to the viewpoint of your deep unconscious system and how it operates, you are now in a position to carry out a measure of self-analytic work that will help to keep your psychotherapy and its outcome on a more even keel and positive note—or to find a new psychotherapy that will have these qualities. Absorb the knowledge of these ratings from the deep unconscious system slowly and wisely, and the path you choose is likely to be a favorable one. This is a payoff more than worth the trouble of rating your psychotherapist.

Index